"Stephen Dobyns, a great American poet, gives a lucid explanation of his craft. This book is valuable for poets, filmmakers, novelists, playwrights, and anyone interested in the clear expression of original thought."

—Fred Wiseman, filmmaker

"Stephen Dobyns' new book on poetic craft defines, with an impressive breadth of reference, what is required for poets to give their subjects significant form, a nuanced aesthetic embodiment that is true to the poet's deepest concerns and open to a process of discovery, resistant to any idea that might limit a full exploration of the chosen materials. This book should be of genuine interest not only to apprentice poets but to anyone who wants to understand the choices involved in making a poem substantial and persuasive."

—Carl Dennis, winner of the Pulitzer Prize in Poetry and author of *Poetry as Persuasion*

"Robert Frost said that a poem 'must begin in delight and end in wisdom.' Here is the rare book about the process of poetry that does both, and brilliantly. Luminous erudition coupled with a palpable love for subject, *Next Word, Better Word* is sure to be an education and an inspiration for student poets, seasoned poets, and—dare I say—there's plenty here for prose writers, too. Dobyns not only takes us deeply into the matter of the poet's craft, but into the poet himself: how the knowledge necessary to write a good poem intersects with the enlightenment born of experience."

—Binnie Kirshenbaum, writing chair, School of the Arts Writing Program, Columbia University and author of *The Scenic Route*

"Serious but playful; stylish and true; honest yet magical—this is a comprehensive and beautifully written book about the thorny, joyous art of making poems. It is the best contemporary guide to poetry I have read."

—David Morley, national teaching fellow, University of Warwick and author of *Enchantment*

"Stephen Dobyns states in his introduction that 'writing a poem is one of the ways to love the world,' and the rest of the book demonstrates, in exquisite, careful detail, exactly how. Full of invaluable insights and basic information for aspiring poets, Dobyns' collection also has much to say to his peers—and he peoples his essays with some of the art's most engaging practitioners, from the well-known, such as Baudelaire and Rilke, to those who will be new to many, such as the Russian Acmeists, and most valuably, he gives us their poetry as well their thoughts and lives. It's a book to study, to return to, to annotate with marginalia, but it's also a book to curl up with and simply enjoy."

—Cole Swensen, professor, Iowa Writers' Workshop
and author of *Goest*

"Stephen Dobyns unpacks the essential kit of the trade, all the taken-for-granted tools which poets think with and work with to find out what their poems want to say: line breaks, how syllables behave, the hide-and-seek of metaphor, how a poem hangs on the page like a bird in flight. He enters into dialogue with a galaxy of poets, to help us listen better to poems, to read better, and also maybe write better this most central of arts."

—Ruth Padel, author of *Darwin: A Life in Poems*
and *The Poem and the Journey*

next word,

better word

the craft of writing poetry

stephen dobyns

NEXT WORD, BETTER WORD
Copyright © Stephen Dobyns, 2011.
All rights reserved.

First published in 2011 by PALGRAVE MACMILLAN® in the U.S.—a
division of St. Martin's Press LLC, 175 Fifth Avenue, New York, NY 10010.

Where this book is distributed in the UK, Europe, and the rest of
the world, this is by Palgrave Macmillan, a division of Macmillan
Publishers Limited, registered in England, company number
785998, of Houndmills, Basingstoke, Hampshire RG21 6XS.

Palgrave Macmillan is the global academic imprint of the above companies
and has companies and representatives throughout the world.

Palgrave® and Macmillan® are registered trademarks in the United
States, the United Kingdom, Europe, and other countries.

ISBN: 978–0–230–62180–0 (paperback)
ISBN: 978–0–230–62182–4 (hardcover)

Library of Congress Cataloging-in-Publication Data
Dobyns, Stephen, 1941–
    Next word, better word : the craft of writing poetry / Stephen Dobyns.
        p.   cm.
    ISBN 978–0–230–62182–4 (hardback)—ISBN 978–0–230–62180–0 ()
    1. Poetry—Authorship.   2. Creation (Literary, artistic, etc.)
3. Poetics.   I. Title.
PN1059.A9D63   2011
808.1—dc22

                                                                    2010045299

A catalogue record of the book is available from the British Library.

Design by Letra Libre

First edition: April 2011

10 9 8 7 6 5 4 3 2 1

Printed in the United States of America.

contents

introduction

When I was 18, I met a married couple who remained my best friends for many years. They lived on a farm outside of Lansing, Michigan, and had moved there sometime before from Greenwich Village, where they had been active in little theater and knew a large number of poets and novelists. The man was 16 years older than I, the woman eight. At the age of 18, the name Greenwich Village was, for me, always italicized and underlined. I had been there a few times in the previous two years, visiting bookstores and bars and staring at young, long-haired, and braless women who wore peasant dresses and a lot of Mexican jewelry. I couldn't imagine a nicer place to live.

My friends were not farmers; rather, they used their hundred acres for dog-walking, and a local man leased their fields to grow wheat. What my friends did instead was read and have interesting conversations. Bookcases filled half the house. The woman was an incredibly fast reader, and each year she would reread her set of Wilkie Collins. In fact, it seemed to me that they had read almost everything. The man also wrote poetry in a style that later reminded me of Edith Sitwell, and he made innumerable lists that he kept very private.

One thing that I liked about my friends was that they took me seriously, were never patronizing, and did not display their knowledge like a flag. This in fact was how they treated everyone. The man volunteered tutoring local high school boys who had gotten into trouble. In a small book-lined study thick with cigarette smoke, they would talk passionately about Plato, Shakespeare, and sometimes Edith Sitwell. The woman volunteered with VISTA programs in Lansing. She had inherited some money, not a lot, but they could live on it.

What they did was read, listen to music, look at great art, tutor, talk civilly to people, and write.

Of course I romanticized them—after all, I was 18—but I also felt sure they had the sort of life I would like for myself. Actually, they legitimized that sort of life for me. For several years, I had been writing dreadful poems and stories, and I also read a lot: a mix of Philip K. Dick, Camus, and Sartre, which did nothing for my psychological stability. But they suggested many books for me to read, some of which I found peculiar, like William Beckford's *Vathek*, Frank Wedekind's "Lulu" plays, and M. P. Shiel's *The Purple Cloud*. And I read Yeats and the Yellow Book poets, and turned more in the direction of poetry. After all, it was short. But despite this seeming advantage, I also thought poetry was something from which I could always learn more. It was a country whose boundaries were never fixed, that always seemed to expand. My friends encouraged me in this.

Like many ideas I had when young, this one turned out to be more complicated than anticipated. The main problem with turning the world into language is that it's, well, impossible. The word is always less than the thing it is meant to represent. No matter how complicated, exact, true, and beautiful the language may become, it is always a diminishment of the reality described. In journalism this doesn't matter; the reporter knows that he or she is reporting the substance of an event, not the event itself. But good poetry deals with emotions, and its purpose is not just to give the reader a sense of those emotions, but also to let the reader experience them as directly as possible. This is trickier than I had first thought.

It also seemed back then that poetry was something I could pick up and use for my pleasure, in the same way I might pick up a cigarette or a glass of whiskey. But with any pastime that becomes a passion, it's not your plaything; rather, you become *its* plaything. This is a humbling discovery. It makes my ego not a tool, but a bothersome accessory, something that often gets between the poem and me. But I only learned this later.

With other occupations or callings—philosophy professor, garage mechanic, nurse, or nun—the participants have a shared sense of endeavor. But the poet remains separate. There may be poets' and writers' groups, clubs, associations, and unions, but the very privacy and particularity of writing is so deeply seated in the individual and uses so many different aspects of his or her personality that it makes strangers even of one's closest friends, even if those friends are poets themselves. Mostly this doesn't matter, but sometimes it grows difficult, and it is probably one of the reasons why artists are particularly susceptible to substance abuse. As with those hard-drinking Russians and Scandinavians, at times there is just too much darkness. Dorothy Parker once rented a small office in which to write, and she grew so lonely that she hung a sign on the door that read "Men."

There is a moment, however, when one first completes a poem that appears so perfect, so completely encompassing of one's fleeting ideas and emotions on a particular subject, and expressed in language so unique and beautiful that one is electrified in an event that seems to combine enlightenment and orgasm. It doesn't last. Still, I think any poet or poetry student continues to hope that in the brief moment between the reading and the response of the individual or the class or audience, that people will all rise up of one accord, slap their foreheads, and say, "You have changed my life!" Over the years, this expectation diminishes, but it never goes away entirely. It reminds me of the last line of *The Incredible Shrinking Man:* "For God there is no zero!" The smallest tidbit always remains.

I like to say that the first thing I must deal with in the process of revision is my own propensity for self-deception. I need to see what is there without interfering with it. This too is a matter of humility. I must strip away not only my ego but also my opinions and prejudices, my psychological constraints, my roller-coaster emotions. It makes a long list, and unfortunately it's impossible, a Sisyphean task. But over time, I've gotten better at it. Indeed, I have conquered the foothills of self-deception, though the Alps still rise before me.

Nadezhda Mandelstam (the wife of the poet Osip Mandelstam) in *Hope Abandoned* wrote that a poet needs to have "a sense of his own sinfulness."[1] I would emend this to say that the poet needs a sense of his or her own totality, the sins and virtues, the faults and qualities altogether, rather than to have only a sense of one's censored or improved or even dreadful self. To chip away at self-deception means to seek a sense of one's totality.

It is difficult to keep learning about my craft when often I would rather go to the beach. Compromises must be made. Yeats and Rilke said that the poet must choose either the life or the work. Rilke, I think, came closer to this than any other successful poet, and at times, in the ferocity of his endeavor and exclusion of the world, he seems like a monster. When he was dying of leukemia at the age of 51, he refused to take medicine to reduce the pain for fear that it would cloud his thoughts and perceptions. Fortunately, Whitman,

Apollinaire, Neruda, and many other poets led gregarious and active lives, although each also wrote of their isolation, of the feeling of being a witness, an outsider, even though they were also great participants. Any poet constantly makes compromises with the business of living.

I think when I first started writing in my teens and became increasingly committed to it in my early twenties, I wrote to be a contributing member of some great community made up of people like my two friends in Lansing. And I did it to be noticed, to be loved and authenticated. I did it to be important. I did it to give myself a voice. I did it to be published. I did it to have a job. I did it to earn a merit raise. I did it to push back the night. I did it to sing. Oh, I wrote for all sorts of reasons. Then those reasons began to drop away, and now I do it mostly for itself. I do it because I love it; I do it because I have no choice. But the act of letting the poem go, of sending it out to be published, is now something I must make myself do. And I do it to maintain my tenuous connection to the world, as though to stop would send me spinning into the dark like an astronaut cut loose from his safety cord, who spins away from the ship. I like to think the world needs poets, but whatever the case, poets need to maintain their connection to the world. The alternative isn't death, but solipsism, the enemy of any writer. This connection, however, might be to only one person, one reader with whom the poet feels an affinity. Nowadays I write for quite a few people who are no longer living.

Many years ago I was teaching a college course in the gothic novel, and a student demanded with some petulance why he should have to read *Melmoth the Wanderer* when he could read Shakespeare. I explained that *Melmoth* was Baudelaire's favorite novel and greatly influenced his poetry, that Melmoth was a romantic icon. (See Chapter 10 for more about Baudelaire and *Melmoth.*) Later, I realized this was not exactly the issue. The student was like a man saying, "Why should I eat hot dogs when I can eat steak?" The subject isn't about what is better, but of enjoyment and educating the palate. In terms of reading, the writer must be a gourmand. This isn't the reading of a scholar, though poets may also be scholarly, but the reading of someone flooding himself or herself with images of the world, mythical figures, and metaphors. I read to steal, some writer said, meaning, in part, that he read to challenge his own ideas and permit him entry to others.

And a few years ago a fellow in *Poetry* magazine wrote that he couldn't imagine why so many people wrote poetry when their poems wouldn't last a nanosecond past their deaths. He was making an argument about mediocrity, although what made up his criteria for judging I don't know. I expect the primary fault of these seemingly ephemeral poets was that they didn't happen to be him. But he made the same mistake as the student in my gothic novels class. It wasn't the examples that were at issue; rather, he had no appreciation of the category. It wasn't a matter of taxonomy or antipathy; it was a lack of understanding of the medium and what a poet does. Certainly, many poets have a passionate desire to publish, but that comes second to their passionate desire to write. The relationship is not causal. The pleasure I received, and still receive, when the poem first feels finished is total, and only afterward do I imagine readers smacking their foreheads. This pleasure doesn't depend on the quality of the poem, necessarily. Even the worst poets experience it. The fellow in Camus's *The Plague* who rewrites the opening sentence of his novel again and again may be a fool, but he, too, is consumed by a passion. A true poet doesn't have to be a good poet, and that person will keep writing even if isolated on Mars. Writing a poem is one of the ways to love the world, which is something the fellow in *Poetry* didn't understand. Surely, if I didn't love the world, I wouldn't bother to write.

Nadezhda Mandelstam, describing the Russian literary world at the beginning of the twentieth century, wrote: "Tiny groups of young artists or writers, with their extravagant manifestoes and ridiculous hullabaloo . . . are probably the best, if not the only way, of setting out in new directions. . . . To see a far-off speck of light and walk toward it alone is far harder without companions and friends. The existence of a thousand minute groups is amply justified if in only one of them somebody finds himself and the words he needs."[2]

In human society, art has several definite purposes, and it has served them in every culture going back as far as traces of humankind can be found. Poetry, by showing us that other human beings can feel exactly as we do, educates our sense of empathy and teaches us to live in a society. Art is very opposite of the sociopathic. An artist always bears witness to the world, and that act of witness has the potential of endlessly increasing the reader's, viewer's, or listener's own sense of the world. Tolstoy's *War and Peace* not only gives me the keenest perception of Napoleon's invasion of Russia and the savaging of Moscow, but it also shows me people's interactions and intensity of feeling down to the smallest levels. How is it possible not to read this novel and find oneself within its pages?

What makes human beings different from any other creature is their sense of possibility. We can speculate about things that don't exist, from the wildest and most surreal imaginings to new cures for awful diseases. This, as well as art and metaphor, dream and humor, is a product of the right brain. The left brain can analyze, but it cannot imagine. It can move logically along a sequence, as in a syllogism, but it cannot hypothesize. A metaphor—and all art is metaphor—presents us all at once with a complete totality of meaning that we dwell upon and continue to learn from as we consider its implications.

Here is one: "Mouse grows proud, invites the cat to tea." And another: "Dips his words in honey; you still taste the salt." And a third: "He loves you until you're out of sight." Another: "Tomorrow rubs its hands; yesterday wrings them." And a longer one: "Cherry blossoms blow across the courtyard; he too once had smiles in excess." A last one: "No trace of the perfect world you saw as a child. Art is its shadow."

Aphorisms we call these, though the word—like a paper bag containing an elephant—can hardly hold its complexity. The word derives from the Greek word for "definition," but no aphorism declares its meaning as directly and logically as a syllogism; rather it offers its meaning through another word, image, picture, or whatever, and most often it is made up of sense data. The word "metaphor" comes from the Greek for "transfer" or "to carry across"; that is, one thing is used to mean another. We have to think about the metaphor; we have to imagine its possibilities. Then there is a paradox: we understand it all at once, yet it continues to give back meaning. More importantly, for what I am saying, it is the product of the right brain and can only be understood with the use of the right brain. The left brain is tediously literal. Separate the connection between the two halves—which can happen with drugs or through an accident—and an aphorism like "Parades his malice with morality's bass drum" becomes nonsense.

And the most practical function of the arts? They expand our sense of possibility, which is the source of all discovery. Remove them from schools and you limit or even cripple the future engineers, scientists, all sorts of people, even politicians. And, of course, the arts are meant to give pleasure.

In 1996, I published a book of essays mostly on poetry titled *Best Words, Best Order*. In 2003, three further essays were added, and a second edition was published. Those fifteen essays began as lectures delivered in the master of fine arts program at Goddard College and in its second incarnation at Warren Wilson College. They were the result of conversations with other writers, conversations that set my mind off in pursuit of all sorts of ideas as I tried to define to myself how poetry worked. There were too many writers to name them all, but they included Ellen Bryant Voigt, Louise Glück, Robert Hass, Michael Ryan, Larry Levis, Raymond Carver, Tobias Wolff, Peter Cooley, Francine Prose, Lisel Mueller, Heather McHugh, Joan Aleshire, John Skoyles, Steve Orlen, Brooks Haxton, James Longenbach, Carl Dennis, Tony Hoagland, Thomas Lux, and Peter Turchi. If not my teachers, they were catalysts who energized my own explorations. Some of the writers who influenced these ideas are dead, some I haven't seen for many years, but in my mind I talk to them still. I continue to learn from them, just as I continue to learn from the friends who lived on a farm outside of Lansing, though they have been gone a long time. These are conversations I never expect to be finished.

So perhaps it was inevitable that I would eventually compile another book of essays. But while *Best Words, Best Order* was made up of essays jostled into some sort of sequence, the present book tries to be more methodical, and it tries to speak to both writers and people who read simply for the pleasure itself.

Although made up of new information, *Next Word, Better Word* doesn't replace the earlier book; rather, it complements and continues it. Inevitably, there are instances of overlap; but only basic information is repeated. One can't discuss meter without defining the iamb. In addition, while I have read many new books in the past fifteen years, many of the old books still hold their power. Yeats and Rilke remain undiminished as exemplars. Susanne Langer, whose books on aesthetics solidified and corrected many of my ideas on the arts and their relation to society, continues to teach me. But most of the substance of these pages is new, even though it is material I couldn't have arrived at without the previous book. If it were possible at the end of one's life to have a segment of time outside of time to rearrange and revise all that one has written into one tidy package, that might be preferable. Instead, the essays, along with my creative work, describe a journey that has been my main occupation for many years.

This book begins with three chapters discussing the nature of subject matter. There is an Asian saying, "If you have a song, sing it." My approach is more laborious. What is "if," what is it to "have," what is a "song," and "sing" and "it"? They are the same questions and the same pleasure I took in asking questions as a child—what is sunlight? how does the moon change its shape?—but the queries have grown smaller and more complicated. For instance, the fourth chapter discusses the syllable. Just how small can you get? The next chapters discuss how lines are broken, how poems are begun, how they are developed and ended, and how they are revised. Then there is a more general chapter on poetry as moral inquiry and another on how a poem or piece of fiction is set against our ideal sense of the world, much in the way that in the *Dialogues* of Plato a chair may be set against the Platonic ideal of a chair. Then, lastly, a chapter on the development of language and metaphor that attempts to describe our ancestry and identify our concerns.

The poems I have chosen to exemplify these ideas tend to be accessible and short. This is both a quality and a disadvantage. The quality should be obvious: they easily fill the requirements of exemplars. However, many great poems exist that are long or obscure or both. Although they too might work as exemplars, they would take an inordinate amount of space to explicate and make a compelling argument. Their exclusion, however, should not be taken as a judgment.

No master of fine arts program will turn a person into a writer, but it offers shortcuts. For one thing, it makes available practical knowledge that might otherwise take a long time to learn. But what someone does with that knowledge is another story. Goethe, as quoted by Walter Jackson Bate, said that Shakespeare "'gives us golden apples in silver dishes.'" By careful study we may acquire the silver dishes while discovering we have "only potatoes to put in them."[3] Ideally, the information within this book might help someone with those silver dishes, as well as indicating how poems might be read.

For many writers, the world isn't real until they have put it into language. They have to translate it into a medium that, they think, promises to make sense of it. Then they look at what they have made—a thing that has become an object as much as a vase is an object—and even if they decide it is accurate, they see it is still incomplete. After all, language is a diminishment. And so, being hopeful creatures, they attack it again. This takes me back to the beginning, the youthful perception that poetry was a country whose boundaries were never fixed. No matter how much I pursue those boundaries, they continue to expand and elude me, offering me a series of essential lessons. This book is the result of those lessons.

one

approaching subject matter

the path of writing poetry begins with a love for the way sounds bang off one another, the hesitations and rush of rhythms, the unwinding of syntax, and the juxtapositions of meanings. But to keep moving down the poet's path, one must ask: What will bear the burden of all that noise? How does a writer first discover, and then approach his or her subject matter?

Perhaps a person believes that he or she has a story to tell, a love affair to describe, an argument to make. Perhaps someone turns to writing because he or she feels there is no other outlet for the mass of emotion and idea bubbling up inside. Pablo Neruda's first published work was an essay entitled "Enthusiasm and Perseverance" (*Entusiasmo y perseverancia*), which appeared in his hometown newspaper when he was thirteen. Neruda felt like an outsider in his family. His mother, a schoolteacher, died two months after he was born. His father, who worked for the railroad, had a low opinion of writing and literature, while the city in which they lived, Temuco in southern Chile, was still a rough frontier town. Neruda's primary confidant became a sheet of paper.

Or the young poet might have undergone a long period of convalescence, as with the Spanish poets Rafael Alberti and Vicente Aleixandre, who suffered from tuberculosis as children and spent the time reading and thinking. Or the sense of being an outsider might arise from great shyness (Hayden Carruth), or mental imbalance (Theodore Roethke), or he might be a stutterer like Philip Larkin, or a have sense of isolation like Emily Dickinson, or the young writer might belong to an ethnic minority, be gay or lesbian, an atheist in a town of believers or a believer in a town of atheists: anything leading to the acute sense that one is different and the feeling that his or her natural voice has been stifled. But it might be none of those reasons. James Dickey once said in a radio interview that he began to write poetry while serving in a U.S. army night fighter squadron during World War II. He had been writing love letters to a number of women back home, and then one day he took another look at the language of his letter, saw that it was good, and decided to write poetry.

The term "subject matter" is an abstraction. An idea is not subject matter, but it might become subject matter. A memory, a love affair—nothing by itself is subject matter, but may develop into it. In fact, anything can become subject matter. Poets like Baudelaire and Gottfried Benn showed that even the ugliest material may become subject matter. But nothing is subject matter by itself.

The subject matter of a poem is not simply its content, in the way a piece of journalism may be said to have a content, announced by its headline. A poem's subject matter is also the manner of its telling—its language and how that language is presented. In the best poems, matter and manner carry equal amounts of information. In fact, the more a poet uses his or her language only as the medium of expression at the service of content—using it journalistically, as it were—then not only does the poet diminish the possibilities of the poem, but he or she also discards many of its primary tools. One might also say the writer is not writing a poem but something else, or is simply writing a bad poem, especially if we define one condition of poetry as an equal combination of manner and matter.

This doesn't mean the language of every poem needs to be rich and noisy. The form and content of many of Frank O'Hara's poems are completely united under the umbrella of his particular aesthetic, which was to create a poem that had the appearance of a quick sketch that seemed spontaneous, off the cuff, and realistic. But it would be a mistake to think his poems were easy to write or easy to imitate.

One doesn't read a good poem for the sum of its content, its kernel of truth, but for the whole experience of which meaning forms only a part. The reading is not a means to an end—some epithanic moment—it is itself an end. The emotion that gave rise to the poem's articulation emerges out of the whole, is integrated into the entire experience. Its meaning is not an answer, like two plus two equals four. A poem is not an essay; it cannot satisfactorily be paraphrased; it is always more than the sum of its parts.

One of the demands of poetry, especially of Romantic poetry and its off-shoots, is that it must have an appearance of spontaneity which creates the impression that the poem was flung off fully formed in a moment of inspiration. Any sign of scaffolding (such as obsessive reworking or refinement) might jeopardize its credibility. As Yeats wrote in "Adam's Curse": "A line will take us hours maybe; / Yet if it does not seem a moment's thought, / Our stitching and unstitching has been naught."[1]

In addition, Romantic poetry demands a high degree of verisimilitude. "In order to excite rational sympathy, [the poet] must express himself as other men express themselves," Wordsworth wrote in the *Preface to the* Lyrical Ballads.[2] I use the examples of Yeats and Wordsworth to stress that ostensible reality doesn't mean writing in nonmetered verse.

For the young poet these requirements of apparent spontaneity and verisimilitude can be a trap; they may create the impression that any utterance can be a poem if the writer calls it a poem; they may make it seem that the language of poetry is indeed no more than a vehicle. Of course, the more the poet reads, the more he or she will see that form is a hugely complicated business, but at the beginning the poem's apparent spontaneity and verisimilitude may seem ample evidence that all one needs is a story to tell and a burning desire to tell it.

The writer who set me thinking that form and content could carry equal amounts of information was the philosopher and aesthetician Susanne Langer. Certainly I knew that form carried information about subject matter, and I understood that the poem was always more than the sum of its parts. And I knew that it did not simply use metaphor but was itself metaphor. But I wasn't quite clear about how these elements fit together. In her book *Problems of Art* (1957), Langer wrote:

> The import of a work of art—its essential, or artistic import—can never be stated in discursive language. A work of art is an expressive form, and therefore a symbol, but not a symbol which points beyond itself so that one's thought passes on to the concept symbolized. The idea remains bound up in the form that makes it conceivable.[3]

Reading this, I found four crucial points. First, the import of a work of art cannot be stated or paraphrased in the language of analytical reasoning. Second, a work of art is a symbol of an expressive form. Or, as she says elsewhere, it is the "symbolic presentation of subjective reality."[4] Third, the symbol doesn't point beyond itself in the way that the symbol of the cross points beyond itself; rather, it is complete in itself. Fourth, the idea is bound up in the form, and only with the form is it possible to conceive the import of the symbol.

Here is William Blake's "London" that appeared in *Songs of Experience* (1794).

I wander thro' each charter'd street,
Near where the charter'd Thames does flow,
And mark in every face I meet
Marks of weakness, marks of woe.

In every cry of every Man,
In every Infant's cry of fear,
In every voice, in every ban,
The mind-forg'd manacles I hear.

How the Chimney-sweeper's cry
Every black'ning Church appalls;
And the hapless Soldier's sigh
Runs in blood down Palace walls.

But most thro' midnight streets I hear
How the youthful Harlot's curse
Blasts the new born Infant's tear,
And blights with plagues the Marriage hearse.[5]

Blake saw himself as presenting an objective portrayal of what he had seen, and he gave us one of the earliest political poems in English. But even though one might paraphrase the poem's general ideas, so much would be excluded that it could hardly be called a paraphrase at all. And although Blake is aiming at objectivity, the poem is also a perceptible form expressive of human emotion. It is subjective, not objective.

The nature of the poem's expressiveness is mostly experienced in the sounds and rhythm of the poem. Does the symbol point beyond itself? Well, yes, Blake is describing London, but the language is not simply a vehicle for the idea; we remain within the symbol to experience the totality of the poem. And the idea remains bound up in the form that makes it conceivable. Nuance in a poem is mostly managed by elements of a poem's form. "London" is written in eight-syllable lines, iambic tetrameter; yet nine of the poem's sixteen lines use metrical substitutions or have headless lines, that is, they are missing an initial unaccented syllable. And there are four spondees, feet consisting of two stressed syllables, in lines 8, 12, 13, and 15. (For these and other technical terms, see the Glossary, page 263.)

The poem's first two lines feel leisurely; the speaker is wandering, not walking. In both lines the four stressed syllables are of long duration, which create a relaxed tone, and the initial consonants are soft: *w, th, ch, n, ch, th,* and *fl.* But as the speaker takes notice of the people around him, he begins to use syllables of shorter duration, harder sounds and repetition—*mark, meet, marks, weakness, marks.* This change to harder sounds and a stronger rhythm indicates a change in the speaker's emotional state—the beginning of anger, indignation, and sorrow.

These emotions continue to build in the second stanza. If one imagines four degrees of stress instead of two, with one being the strongest and four being the weakest, then one sees that most of the unstressed and stressed syllables in the first two lines of stanza 1 are quite close together, say, 3–1, 3–1, 3–2, 3–1 and 3–2, 3–2, 3–1, 3–2. This is called the Trager-Smith method of noting metrical stress, which doesn't mean they invented it. They simply named it. You can find stresses working the same way in Chaucer. In any case, the relationship between the stressed and unstressed syllables at the beginning of the poem represents the speaker's calm. But the twelve feet of the first three lines of stanza 2 are all a vigorous 4–1, 4–1, a vigor that is heightened by repetition and parallelism.

One could point to other formal elements in the first two stanzas—alliteration and internal rhyme—to say nothing about the formal elements in the last two quatrains. All express emotional nuance as well as creating tension and energy. In addition, the poem's four sentences use syntax to delay the most important elements of meaning until the fourth line of each stanza to create an impression of the speaker's gradual sense of discovery. Added to this, each line in each stanza increases in intensity through its eight syllables, in terms of both meaning and sound, making the last word in each line the strongest and most important. The only exception might be the word "blast" that begins line 15.

The poem's last line—"And blights with plagues the Marriage hearse"—uses the same sort of long-duration syllables as the poem's first two lines but with opposite effect; while the first two lines were leisurely, the slow pace of the last line is due to stunned horror. What happens in the thirteen lines in between represents the speaker's education.

The sounds and rhythms of Blake's poem are entirely purposeful, as well as giving pleasure. As Langer said (above), "The idea remains bound up in the form that makes it conceivable."

But it is not necessary that a poem be formal in order to have its form and content carry equal amounts of information, as can be seen in Walt Whitman's "Poets to Come" (1860).

> Poets to come! orators, singers, musicians to come!
> Not to-day is to justify me and answer what I am for,
> But you, a new brood, native, athletic, continental, greater than before
>   known,
> Arouse! for you must justify me.
>
> I myself but write one or two indicative words for the future, I but advance
>   a moment only to wheel and hurry back in the darkness.
>
> I am a man who, sauntering along without fully stopping, turns a casual
>   look upon you and then averts his face,
> Leaving it to you to prove and define it,
> Expecting the main things from you.[6]

Written seventy years after Blake's "London," Whitman's poem uses lines ranging from eight to thirty syllables. We find no end rhyme, and the three stanzas have different lengths. Generally speaking, Blake's poem is easier to describe—four closed quatrains rhymed A-B, A-B and written in iambic tetrameter—but even though "Poets to Come" is without meter, it still uses stressed and unstressed syllables. It can't avoid it; it's a condition of the English language. And one can still imagine four different degrees of stress. Whitman takes advantage of this; his stressed syllables are heavily stressed, and perhaps more importantly, his unstressed syllables come mostly from an assortment of little words: *to, is, and, am, me, a, for, or, the,* and *from,* as well as the unstressed syllables in his two-syllable words—*singer, answer, native, greater,* and so on. This 1–4 ratio of unstressed to stressed syllables dominates every line but one.

The lack of meter contributes to the poem's sense of spontaneity and verisimilitude, but the heavy stress creates a rhetorical effect that makes the poem seem deeply felt. We are hearing a man addressing people who, oddly, do not yet exist. What I do today doesn't justify me, he says; it's up to you to justify me. That's his thesis statement. Then he presents evidence to support it with three metaphors each beginning a line with the word "I." The second metaphor expands upon the first, and the third expands upon the first and second.

Additionally, the third metaphor occurs in the poem's longest line and the line softens the 1–4 ratio of stressed to unstressed syllables. The evidence of Whitman's three metaphors is not the evidence of discursive thought (which I summarize in Chapter 8 as "if this, then that, with these consequences"). It is nondiscursive. The parallel structure of the three sentences, the accumulation of the metaphors, and the softening of stress in the third stanza persuade us that we are hearing something important. And Whitman, in these three metaphors, uses a series of internal partial rhymes that weren't in the first stanza. In the first metaphor he has: *but, write, dick,* and *fute.* In the second: *but, ment, back,* and *dark.* In the third: *saunt, out, stop, look, up,* and *vert.*

Whitman's rhythms were influenced by the preachers he had listened to in New York as a young man. The imperative address, the commands, the use of parallel structures were all affected by these experiences. The rhythmic, twenty-syllable third line is brought to an abrupt stop by the word "arouse" that begins line 4. Indeed, "arouse" wouldn't be so effective if it weren't such a contrast to the previous line and if it didn't contain the element of surprise caused by the line break. Whitman then backs away and reverses the great authority of the first stanza with the display of modesty in the first metaphor, which is then continued in the second metaphor, although the second half of the second metaphor is far more energetic than the first: "only to wheel and hurry back into the darkness."

The third metaphor, and longest line, creates in its rhythm the casual movement of sauntering. Most simply the line reads: I look at you and turn away. What the rest of the line attempts to do is enact that statement using rhythm and long-duration syllables: "I am a man who, sauntering along without fully stopping, turns a casual look upon you and then averts his face . . ."

Then, just as he created a surprise with "arouse," so he creates a surprise with the poem's last two lines. The change in syntax and rhythm, the use of shorter-duration syllables to increase the speed of the line, and the internal rhyme catch us unawares. While the fourth line of the first stanza is basically iambic (the first four syllables are powerful iambs) with an ascending rhythm, the last two lines of stanza 3 are basically trochaic with descending rhythms (the first eight syllables of the penultimate line may be read as trochees; and even though the last line appears anapestic, the trochaic rhythm of the previous line with the second and third syllables of "expecting" continue a sense of the trochaic). At no point can we really say that Whitman is writing an iambic or trochaic line; rather, he may be writing a line in which iambs or trochees are found.

The effect of the metrical difference between the end of the first stanza and the end of the third is to change the demand in the first instance to a request and a hope in the second. We come to understand these changes, these elements of nuance, only by looking closely at the poem's rhythmic and sonic elements. And even if we don't bother to analyze the poem's form, we still feel the effects of that form. It helps to convince us of the sincerity and truth of the poem.

What we also notice in the two poems is tone, which comes to us not only from the meaning of the words but from the nature of the words. The present tense and naturalness of the speech helps to convince us of the speaker's sincerity. Yet the poems move differently—the initial mood of Blake's poem suggests casual inattentiveness. He wanders as Whitman later saunters. But then Blake increases the poem's energy and concludes with a statement of furious moral indignation. Whitman's poem begins with strong commands, which gradually mellow until the poem ends with an appeal. It is not simply the meaning of the words that describe this movement, but also their sounds and rhythms. Indeed, the manner enacts the matter. That enactment lets us experience the poem, which, we imagine, is also what Blake and Whitman experienced. What these poems exemplify is that we can't separate the manner of a poem's telling from what we see as its content. In fact, it is all content, just as it is all form, and any discussion of subject matter has to acknowledge that.

One writes a poem because one is unable to remain silent and from a desire to create something beautiful, but one also writes out of a sense of play, which is a force behind all art. A sense of emotional need and a sense of play can exist side by side without contradiction. We find play in the very artifice of the language—in the arrangement of words, sounds, and rhythms that go into a poem, whether it be comic or somber. The presence of play doesn't mean the poem isn't serious. As I have written elsewhere, the opposite of play is not seriousness but earnestness. Even in a dark poem play can exist, as may be seen in this extract from Sylvia's Plath's "Daddy":

> I have always been scared of you,
> With your Luftwaffe, your gobbledygoo.
> And your neat mustache
> And your Aryan eye, bright eye.
> Panzer-man, panzer-man, O You—[7]

While play is present in the word choice, it also exists in the form—the repeating "oo" rhyme, the off-rhyme and repetition of words. But the effect is not to lighten the poem but rather to make it more chilling. Paraphrase these words in prose and the effect would be lost. The comic element in any poem has a few major purposes. It can make the serious elements even more serious; it can underline the emotional and psychological complexity of an experience; and it can create surprise, which in turn creates energy that drives the poem forward. Here is another mixture of play and surprise in a poem by the Brazilian poet Carlos Drummond de Andrade. The translation is my own.

> don't kill yourself
> Carlos, stay calm, love
> is what you see:
> today a kiss, tomorrow no kiss,
> the next day is Sunday
> and no one knows
> what will happen on Monday.
>
> It's pointless to resist
> or to commit suicide.
> Don't kill yourself, don't kill yourself!
> Keep yourself safe for the wedding,

though no one knows when
or if it will take place.

Oh, Carlos, man of the earth, love
spent the night with you
and now your repressed self
is raising an indescribable clamor,
prayers,
victrolas,
saints blessing themselves,
ads for the best soap,
a clamor for which nobody
knows the whys and wherefores.

In the meantime, you walk
upright and downcast.
You are the palm tree, you are the shout
that nobody heard in the theater
when all the lights went out.
Love in the dark, no, in the light
is always sad, Carlos, my son,
but say nothing to anybody,
nobody knows, nor will know.

Briefly, about the language of a translation: it is the attempt by one or
more people to find an equivalent language in a second language, but it can
never be exactly equivalent. It can hardly come close. It is an approximation, a rough metaphor of the original—sometimes bad, sometimes good.
To work, it must be successful as a poem in English, but we can say little
or nothing about the form. What we have is expressiveness, human sensibility, metaphor, strategies, types of images—a whole range of ability and
methodology.

In Drummond's poem, we find aspects of surprise in the title ("Don't Kill
Yourself") and in the command in the first line—"Carlos, stay calm." We
then wait for a narrative, but the narrative isn't linear and, at best, is inferred
when we conclude the poem. Without a clear narrative we don't know what

is governing Drummond's choices, while the presence of humor makes the whole business uncertain. We don't know how to read the poem's emotional dynamic. The tone and level of seriousness are concealed.

> today a kiss, tomorrow no kiss,
> the next day is Sunday
> and no one knows
> what will happen on Monday.

Lacking a narrative, we look for a governing event that establishes a sense of context.

> Oh, Carlos, man of the earth, love
> spent the night with you
> and now your repressed self
> is raising an indescribable clamor, . . .
> a clamor for which nobody
> knows the whys and wherefores.

Perhaps the narrator, earthy Carlos, has left a woman's bed, doesn't know if he will return, and is upset—a simple, though familiar, situation. And who is this woman? Most likely she is the woman inferred in the second stanza. After all, one can't have a wedding without a bride.

> Keep yourself safe for the wedding,
> though no one knows when
> or if it will take place.

Were the poem paraphrased, it would be commonplace in the extreme. Were it referred to, it would sink into anecdote. The poem, however, enacts the situation, giving it palpability.

> Love in the dark, no, in the light
> is always sad, Carlos, my son,
> but say nothing to anybody,
> nobody knows, nor will know.

One of the poem's conceits is that it takes place in present time. Like Blake and Whitman, the poet speaks as he walks down a city street. The present tense gives the poems a sense of immediacy and verisimilitude. In Drummond this effect may be also heightened by the nonmetered verse, the seeming lack of artifice. In the line "Love in the dark, no, in the light," we see Carlos catching and correcting himself, which creates an illusion of something abruptly occurring before us. He had a good time in the dark; it is only later that love is sad—especially when he thinks his engagement might be over. And at the end there is a little joke—he won't tell anyone, yet obviously the poem tells everyone. But there is no point in telling anyone because he won't be believed—these others, the foolish ones, who continue to have hope, who believe continuing love is possible.

The rush of the poem, its abrupt juxtapositions, single-word lines, its breathlessness, its mix of humor and desperation, the very strategy of its unfolding, the peculiarity of its details ("prayers, / victrolas, / saints blessing themselves, / ads for the best soap"), the oddness of its metaphors ("You are the palm tree, you are the shout / that nobody heard in the theater / when all the lights went out")—these combine to take a simple situation and raise it to a level where here too the idea is bound up in the form, even though the form is an approximation of the original. On a higher level we have a poem about a person being the victim of his own emotional life, of his deepest self, while the tone and humor keep it from being a poem of complaint. Or rather in the split persona of two Carloses, one is complaining, and the other is urging him to endure, which lets the humor create an odd heroism. The Carlos of the poem, the author's persona, isn't bound to the author but functions as the reader's representative. We, too, have been victims of our emotional lives.

Surprise helps to drive the poem forward. Because of the seeming lack of narrative, because of the details and humor, because of the very oddness—we are unable to guess the poem's direction. This delights us. It is like a carnival ride. Yet it is not a comic poem. It is extremely serious—"and now your repressed self / is raising an indescribable clamor, / . . . for which nobody / knows the whys or wherefores." It is simply not earnest.

By the last stanza we put together a rudimentary narrative. It is Friday morning, and Carlos is walking along brooding about what had happened with a particular woman the night before. Maybe she is, or was, his fiancée; maybe they quarreled. The wedding is now in doubt. But even of this we are unsure. What Drummond wants is to create a scene of emotional confusion ending with the speaker's quasi-serious decision that love is sad.

In life we are constantly attentive to the next moment, our elaborate systems of cause and effect, our never-ending watchfulness, our imagining, planning, worrying, evading, and anticipating of what's coming next. The sequential arts—literature, dance, music—are metaphors for that process. We have a sense of how things should be and are attentive to anything out of the ordinary. This attentiveness to stimuli coming out of the future that we haven't anticipated—art makes use of it as play, as seriousness, as medium, as matter.

The use of surprise in a poem, the experience of events coming out of the future that we haven't anticipated, is another example of verisimilitude. In *Feeling and Form,* Susanne Langer discusses how all the arts have a primary illusion and that in poetry it is the illusion of the "experience of 'virtual life.'"

> The semblance of experienced life, the illusion of life, is established with the opening line; the reader is confronted at once with a virtual order of experiences, which have immediately apparent values, without any demonstrable reasons for the good or evil, importance or triviality, even the natural or supernatural characters they seem to have. For illusory events have no core in actuality. . . . They have only such aspects as are given in the telling; they are as terrible, as wonderful, as homely, or as moving as they sound. . . . But nothing can be built up unless the very first words of the poem affect the break with the reader's actual environment. This break is what makes any physical condition that is not intensely distracting irrelevant to the poetic experience. Whatever our integrated organic response may be, it is a response not to little verbal stimuli . . . but a response to a strongly articulated virtual experience, one dominant stimulus.[8]

The poet doesn't build this illusion of virtual life bit by bit; instead, the poem begins with its world already a given, and a factor that makes this successful is the surprise of the first line, that sudden break "with the reader's actual environment." Here are a few lines of "Dog" by Lawrence Ferlinghetti.

The dog trots freely in the street
and sees reality
and the things he sees

are bigger than himself
and the things he sees
are his reality
Drunks in doorways
Moons in trees . . .⁹

The poem, to oversimplify, concerns our subjective vision, that it can either arise naturally out of ourselves or we can let ourselves be dominated by
someone else's subjective vision, for instance by political correctness. Ferlinghetti favors the dog's approach, that the dog can tell us something "about
reality / and how to see it," because the dog isn't burdened by the opinions of
others and still greets the world with a sense of wonder, "looking / like a living
questionmark / into the / great gramophone / of puzzling existence."¹⁰

The movement of the poem, the rhythm, simplicity, and speed, mimic
the dog's movement, and what first seems to border on the comic turns into
a serious poem. This break with the reader's actual environment also offers a
challenge ranging from the mild to the aggressive. We all have a body of definitions that seeks to fix the limits of how we are and how the world should
be. These definitions and limits form the foundation of our complacency, and
we have spent many years weaving these elements together. A good poem will
challenge this. Most simply, our complacency allows us to be comfortable in
the present with little concern about the future or the past. A poem, if only
by presenting us with its underlying question of "How does one live?" can
lead us to consider the entire arc of our lives. This is what happens in Ferlinghetti's "Dog." The apparent lightness and humor lead us to a statement that
questions how we live our lives. If a poem doesn't challenge our composure
and complacency—if it doesn't, even to a small degree, make us feel endan-
gered—then its blandness, its dullness of expression, will lead to the loss of
our attention.

The work of art exists for the one who receives it—reader, viewer, listener,
audience. The poet may see the poem as the enactment, the very embodiment
of self-expression. Perhaps this is necessary. The poem is written out of a sense
of urgency, but that very urgency draws the reader into the poem. Without
it the poem would lose its attraction. But the reader doesn't go to the poem
because of an interest in the writer's life—that would give the poem little more
than anecdotal value—but to find evidence of his or her *own* life. Indeed, the

situation, the symbol of the poem is potentially applicable and belongs to all readers.

Here is "Encounter in the Chestnut Avenue" by Rainer Maria Rilke. The translation is mine.

He felt the entrance's green darkness
wrapped coolly about him like a silk robe
that he was still receiving and resolving;
when, limpid and remote at the distant end,

through green sunlight, as through green window panes,
a translucent and solitary figure
flared up, still far away,
and then, at last—the down driving light
seething over her at every step—

gathered to itself a bright pulsation,
that in the woman ran shyly to the back.
But then at once the shade was deep,
and nearby eyes glanced toward him

from a clear, new, impartial face,
which, as in a portrait, lived intensely
in the moment things again diverge:
first giving forever, and then not at all.

In German this is a rhymed, iambic poem with a mixture of pentameter and tetrameter lines. The situation, we discover, is quite simple. A man turns onto a street overhung with the green boughs of chestnut trees. Then, at the farther end, he sees approaching a white, solitary shape that soon resolves it-self into a woman with blond hair. As she draws nearer, he sees her in increas-ing detail, and then, when they are almost side by side, she glances at him, and in that moment he seems to see her completely and intimately. Then she passes and is gone: "first giving forever, and then not at all."

This is a moment we all have experienced, that fleeting eye contact, that sudden close perception of another human being who then vanishes past us. It is an especially urban moment that teases us with intimacy when most likely we will never see the person again. Baudelaire has a similar poem, "To a Passerby," which Rilke of course knew. In fact, it is the very moment that Whitman describes in "Poets to Come": "I am a man who, sauntering along without fully stopping, turns a casual look upon you and then averts his face, / Leaving it to you to prove and define it, / Expecting the main things from you." The difference, in part, is that the poem changes from first person to second person.

If we read Rilke's letters and other poems from *New Poems* (1907) and *New Poems: The Other Part* (1908), in which "Encounter in the Chestnut Avenue" appeared, we realize that Rilke is creating a metaphor about how poetry functions, that it approaches, draws us from our own existence, declares itself, lives intensely for an instant, and then disappears: "expecting," as Whitman wrote, "the main things from you." This poem in particular is an example of what Langer called "the expression of human consciousness in a single metaphorical image."

The approach of most poems is inductive rather than deductive. We are given a number of pieces of information, and from them we infer a whole. This is because it is necessary, as the Russian Acmeists wrote, that the poem be an event on the page instead of referring to something off the page. In most cases, we have to have a sense of the poem taking place before us for it to be, as Langer says, "a symbolic presentation of subjective reality." It needs to enact something, rather than refer to something.

This is the first of three chapters on subject matter, and what I have tried to do is not so much to define the topic as to indicate the space around it, to describe some of the machinery upon which subject matter is dependent. Five of the six poems I have quoted have concerned people, and a dog, walking down a city street. Their authors are choosing a city street not out of a fondness for walking, but because they wanted a symbol of common human interchange and they needed a vehicle to carry their ideas. The actual peregrination may have occurred or may not have occurred. Unlike memoir, the subject matter of poetry requires not fidelity to events, but fidelity to ideas and emotions. Nor does the event need to have intrinsic value by itself. It is more important that it be shared than that it be unusual, even that it functions as a symbol. In most cases, the event, the narrative, is a pretext that serves to give life to a number of abstractions. Through such details, its inductive method, as well as its subject matter, the poem is able to gain access to the reader's imagination.

joining form and content

We go to art for pleasure, distraction, sustenance, and the apprehension of felt life. We go to expand our moral experience of the world, to come into contact with the beautiful, which may in fact be ugly. We go to find something more perfect than ourselves, to find a graceful, dramatic, and/or unusual relation between the parts, whether colors, sounds, movements, words—the primary mediums of all the arts. We go to experience a particularly harmonious and organic structure, a certain evocativeness or emotional significance, a grouping of metaphors or allusions, and we go to art to engage with the manner of presentation. We go out of curiosity; we go to forget ourselves, become ourselves, move beyond ourselves. We go for knowledge. Most of these elements we need to find to a greater or lesser degree. One or two by themselves aren't enough.

When these elements work together, art has the ability to lead us out of our complacency and ask ourselves the question: How does one live? Art doesn't answer this question, but it pushes us toward it. As Chekhov wrote, art attempts to articulate a question exactly. How well it does this, how forcefully, how compellingly, and how well it unifies these elements and makes us care about them become our criteria for great art. And when a work of art, such as a poem, fails, it fails because some of these elements are missing or have been poorly realized.

George Saintsbury, who probably knew more about prosody than any-body, put it more simply: "To have something to say; to say it under pretty strict limits of form and very strict ones of space; to say it forcibly; to say it beautifully: these are the four great requirements of the poet in general."[1]

Subject matter, as it develops from a nonverbal intuition into the slow joining of form and content, tries to fasten these elements together. "Subject matter" is a teacher's term, and as such it is a simplification. It attempts to cat-egorize, and any time we categorize, we diminish the complexity of the topic. Nothing is wrong with this. We need to do it to discuss a subject, any subject, but we need to know the limitations imposed by simplifying and categorizing. The more we simplify our questions and narrow their scope, the more we increase the probability that our answers are mistaken.

Subject matter begins when something takes our attention, a word that derives from the Latin verb *attendere,* meaning to stretch toward, to give heed to. Before that, we may exist in a state of indifference, or stasis. For the early Greeks this was a person's natural state, and when he or she was disturbed, it happened because of the intervention of a function god—separate gods of anger, fear, joy, desire, courage, ambition, grief, and so on—smaller deities who were directed by the more significant Olympian gods such as Zeus, Hera, or Apollo. When a person was touched by a function god, he or she became animated; that is, filled with breath. The disturbance moved that person from equilibrium through interest—which in Latin meant "to be between"—to a concern, which, again from Latin, for sifting, mixing together, and, by exten-sion, scrutinizing or trying to comprehend.

My emphasis on etymology is an attempt to get past my, or our, being so accustomed to a word that it becomes merely a sign, to try to reach the word's more concrete beginning in metaphor. From a concerned state, we might return to indifference, equilibrium, or remain attentive; or we might move up the ladder of synonyms—concern, anxiety, fear, terror; or con-cern, liking, affection, love; or concern, desire, action, possession. This is the movement of our emotional and intellectual lives. Something takes our attention, whether from curiosity or from being hit over the head. At this point we might lapse back to equilibrium or move forward by attraction (or away through aversion). Clearly, if one is hit over the head, this process is very rapid, but so is the process of falling in love at first sight, or seeing an object—a book or ring—that one wants to possess. Many concerns stay with us over long periods of time, even our entire lives. Our personalities are defined by those concerns.

Subject matter must begin with a concern of a certain stature, by which I mean it must be of more than fleeting importance and an audience must be made to care about it. A concern such as "Should I eat this pear?" is too slight to generate significant subject matter unless it can be turned into a metaphor, as with J. Alfred Prufrock's concern about eating a peach (T. S. Eliot) or William Carlos Williams's poem about eating the plums.

In our lives of fluctuating concerns, an individual concern may not disappear, but may be overshadowed and superseded by others. This is equally true of concerns that lead to subject matter. Looking at the career of W. B. Yeats, we see his early poems concerned with Romantic love and Irish mythology, the poems of his middle age concerned with parenthood, politics and the Irish nationalist movement, the theater, and his studies in magic—and as he approaches old age, that too becomes a concern. Although I oversimplify, we know the poems that arose from such concerns: "No Second Troy," "Easter, 1916," "A Prayer for my Daughter," and "Sailing to Byzantium." In each instance, Yeats's passion to write and one of these ongoing concerns came together in a metaphor. Reading the drafts of "Sailing to Byzantium," we see that happen. Yeats had a vague sense of what he wanted, but for ten or so drafts we see him thrashing around, putting down lines, crossing them out, trying different images. All he had was his concern and an unverbalized *something*, and out of that concern he at last discovered his opening: "That is no country for old men. The young / In one another's arms . . ." When I read the books by Jon Stallworthy, *Between the Lines* and *Vision and Revision*, which lay out Yeats's drafts of a dozen or so poems, I was amazed at Yeats's patience and tenacity as he moved from clumsiness to grace. But in his later poems he had a confidence built upon ways of working that had been successful over many years, and he knew from experience that those unverbalized "somethings" might result in a poem.

Here is "Insignificant Needs" by the Greek poet Yannis Ritsos (translated by Minas Sarras).

The houses jammed one on top of the other,
    or face to face without exchanging glances. The elbows
of the chimneys shove each other in the night. The bakery's light

is a sigh that allows a small passage on the street.
A cat looks behind her. Vanishes. A man
entered his room. On his blanket,
over his iron bed, he found reclining
the crowded desolation of the city. As he was undressing,
he recalled that he hadn't noticed if there was a moon.
The bulks of the houses were shuffling in his memory
like cards in a closed, secretive gambling room
where all the players had lost. And he needed to imagine
that someone must love him, within these numberless houses,
so that he could sleep, so that he could wake up.
But, yes, of course there was a moon—he remembered
its illumination in a ditch with soapy water.[2]

A poem manipulates our memories with its sense data. It doesn't create
the illusion of virtual life by itself; rather, it provides the materials—the sense
data—and we create the illusion. We become participants in the creative process. Ritsos builds his enigmatic, apparent narratives by piling detail upon
detail. We take those details, and out of the great warehouse of our memories,
we make the scene: the nighttime houses jammed together, the light from the
bakery window, the cat looking behind her. Does it matter that Ritsos's city is
Athens and ours is another? Not in the least. The characteristic of "crowded
desolation" is common to all cities. We can imagine it.

Ritsos's poem presents us with a question: What is this, and what does
it mean? The mind engages with the question and remains engaged until the
question is answered, or we decide it's unanswerable, or we reach a place in
between; that is, we reach a sense of meaning that we are unable to paraphrase
but seem to grasp. This is a characteristic of a symbol. It continues to give
back meaning, while a sign, like the glyphs signifying male and female rest-
rooms, quickly reveal their entire significance.

I call Ritsos's poems apparent narratives because we are not drawn to
them by their story interest. They are, in fact, not narratives. Instead they
use narrative elements to set up a lyric moment—"yes, of course there was a
moon." In this case it is a moment of emotional realization and release. We
the readers are the ones who construct this city, which Ritsos complicates by
describing the buildings in terms of the people, but the desolation is the man's

desolation. It is his condition. He looks through this desolation when he looks at the world, until on the very blanket on his bed he finds "the crowded desolation of the city."

And what does he have to set against this sense of desolation? "He needed to imagine that someone must love him . . . so that he could sleep, so that he could wake up." He has this small hope—an insignificant need—and the moon comes to represent that hope. As the man undresses for bed, he tries to remember if he had seen the moon as he walked home. Then the memory comes to him: "But, yes, of course there was a moon—he remembered / its illumination in a ditch with soapy water."

How tawdry and sad Ritsos makes it, but even so it is enough to give the man the hope and sense of connection to keep going. And once we work our way through the poem, we understand that the first three lines represent the man's subjective vision of the city and perhaps he also sees himself as someone who doesn't exchange glances, who shoves with his elbows, who sighs, who vanishes. He is perpetrator and victim, while the heart of the poem is the man's need to imagine that someone must love him, to find something to set against the desolation. The moon's reflection in the soapy water becomes for him the confirmation that such love exists.

Ritsos may have begun the poem with the idea of a man needing to believe that someone must love him or with a sense of the crowded desolation of the city, or it may have begun with a single image: the elbows of the chimneys being like the elbows of people shoving one another in a crowd. Or he may have begun simply with a sound.

But Ritsos's awareness of the tension between the anonymous, indifferent city and the need of an individual to imagine that he is loved did not begin with this poem. It was one of a number of ongoing concerns at the very center of his being, a concern made palpable by his imagination and given emotional energy by his sense of empathy. Personally, I expect the poem began with an image. We can see the process in the first sentence: "The houses jammed one on top of the other, / or face to face without exchanging glances." The first part of the sentence is analytic and discursive; the second part is metaphoric and nondiscursive. Most simply it is a simile: the houses crowded together are like people standing together without exchanging glances. This awareness could have struck Ritsos when he was walking down the street. But once he answers the question of what the houses are *like*, then the poem is under way. And why does the poem go this way rather than another? Because the destructive tension between the city and the individual was one of Ritsos's ongoing concerns and he spent his creative life looking for the images with which to articulate it.

But the subject matter isn't that brief paraphrase of Ritsos's concern; it is the totality of the poem, which, in its combination of form and content, becomes the enactment of his concern. And the reader comes to enact that concern as well by investigating the sense data and narrative details, by trying to understand the metaphors. When we are finished, we feel the man's feeling as our own; we experience his isolation and his need for some small thing—the reflection of the moon in soapy ditch water—to set against that isolation. If we successfully read the poem and care about it, then the poem becomes part of us, a small addition to the filter through which we see the world.

Of course, I have no idea whether Ritsos made the poem in this way, but I do know how poems are often made. Mostly they begin with the sudden apprehension of metaphor or of something that may function as a metaphor, one that links itself to one of the poet's ongoing concerns. The poet often has no sense of this at the beginning; rather, he or she goes through a process, sometimes a long process, of writing to discover why he or she is writing. And the writer's success often depends on his or her patience, the need to listen to the poem instead of growing anxious and impatient and imposing a meaning on the poem. That's a lesson one learns when reading Yeats's drafts.

But even if Ritsos began with the sense that the buildings were like people, he most likely had no awareness of the image of the moon's reflection in soapy ditch water until he was well into the poem. Essentially, he was engaged in working his way through a nondiscursive argument: if X exists (say, the desolation of the cities), then a man needs Y (a sense of love or the moon's reflection in ditch water) in order to survive. The poem enacts that argument, and once it is finished, it becomes an act of witness.

But to have a concern and then to discover a metaphor that can serve as a vehicle isn't enough for the poem to be effective. The writer must also make the reader want to read. Unfortunately, this presupposes that a person will open the book or magazine or electronic screen and read the title and first line of the poem—a rare occurrence at any time. But if a reader *does* appear, the writer should be ready for him.

Every line, every sentence has to have within it a reason to read the next. It is energy that propels the reader down the page, and two major sources of energy are suspense and surprise. We come to care about what is happening.

Without this energy, what is propelling us forward? Mild intellectual interest, perhaps, or charity, or boredom toward all else, or even a faint curiosity like the interest one has glancing over the advertisements stuck to the wall of a subway station while waiting for a train.

Consider John Berryman's "Dream Song #4."

Filling her compact & delicious body
with chicken paprika, she glanced at me
twice.
Fainting with interest, I hungered back
and only the fact of her husband and four other people
kept me from springing on her

or falling at her little feet and crying
"You are the hottest one for years of night
Henry's dazed eyes
have enjoyed, Brilliance." I advanced upon
(despairing) my spumoni.—Sir Bones: is stuffed
de world wif feeding girls.

—Black hair, complexion Latin, jeweled eyes downcast . . . The slob beside
     her feasts. What wonders is
she sitting on, over there?
The restaurant buzzes. She might as well be on Mars.
Where did it all go wrong? There ought to be a law against Henry.
Mr. Bones: there is.[3]

We have three six-line stanzas ranging from a one-syllable line to a sixteen-syllable line. The situation is simple. Henry, the protagonist of the *Dream Songs* and who may be called Berryman's persona, is describing a situation in a restaurant to Mr. Bones, Henry's minstrel show conscience or alter ego. Henry had noticed a woman who appeared to look at him, as she sat with her husband, and he experienced lustful feelings. We are given the stimuli (she glanced at him twice), the reaction (he hungered back), the complication (her husband), the extrapolation (where did it all go wrong), the deduction (there ought to be a law about Henry), and a concluding paradox or reversal (there is). The structure is logical, but while a discursive argument proceeds in a linear manner, a nondiscursive argument defies linearity. Only at the end do we see the poem's progression. Before that the poem's juxtapositions and surprises keep us balanced between the hope it will successfully resolve itself and the worry it will fall apart. Yet the structure of the poem is the same as most of Shakespeare's sonnets: three blocks of language describing a situation and a two-line resolution.

In its telling, Berryman's poem is full of energy. The varieties of syntax, line breaks, the way Berryman delays his subjects, predicates, and direct objects, the word choices and rich variation of sounds—all keep us off kilter, create a constant stream of surprise, and defy our ability to guess the poem's direction. We have no place to rest, which means the tension keeps building until Mr. Bones's statement in the last line, when we experience a sensation of release, an exhalation even in the sound of the words: "there is." The whole business seems hardly in control, which, of course, is illusion.

If we have been reading the *Dream Songs,* we know that Berryman is using a certain form—all the *Dream Songs* are three six-line stanzas, often rhymed. Even in these seemingly unrhymed eighteen lines, the "eyes" rhyme appears twice as an end rhyme, while *twice* and the two *is*'s work as partial rhymes. The "ee" rhyme, beginning with *body,* appears three times; then there are half rhymes—*her, there, Mars; back* and *night*—as well as eight *-ing* rhymes scattered throughout and an *ack* rhyme that is echoed in eleven lines. The whole of the poem is an enactment of sexual excitement, an illusion of vital experience, a scene that moves to the ridiculous, but is then undercut by the line—"Where did it all go wrong?" We understand that first as it applies to the scene, and then in a larger sense, as it applies to Henry. Reading the *Dream Songs,* we see that one of Henry's (and Berryman's) great battles is whether or not, like his father, to commit suicide—a subtext which darkens the poem's conclusion: "There ought to be a law against Henry. / Mr. Bones: there is."

The information in literature, a sequential art, seems to stream toward us from out of the future. This is an illusion because the progression of the work of literature is already fixed; it has been written down. The reader or listener takes in this information and anticipates what is coming next. In this he or she is helped by elements of the form. In literature a major element is the structure of English sentences, the great majority of which precede subject-predicate-object. So we hear the subject and we know that the predicate is coming. (As we should know, in Yeats's line "I have met them at close of day," "I" is the subject, the verb "have met" is the predicate, and "them" is the object.) And we have our sense of logic, of cause and effect, of credibility, our knowledge of the world, and through this and more we sift the information on the page.

As we engage in this illusion and try to guess what is approaching, the poet tries to surprise us with the unexpected. In art these unexpected events are safe, relatively. They are part of the play element, and in a small way they educate us. They keep us quick and light on our feet. They let us imagine the possible. Although their primary function is to make us want to read, they are also part of the game—a ball is being hit over the net.

As in any game, we want to win, which, in reading a poem, is no more than understanding and drawing from the poem such pleasures as a poem provides. But with his twists and turns, his manipulation of tension and surprise, Berryman plays with us. He keeps us on the very line between pleasure and frustration. Will it come off or not? And so, along with the roles of poet, bon vivant, cultural icon, Berryman becomes our primary competitor.

Our engagement with the poem and our interest in winning the game are a ritualization of the very passion to survive in life. That is our primary concern, and whatever else we might do, that concern, survival, comes first. We live not in this moment but in the next, and at any time our senses are busily absorbing data to determine the nature of that moment. We do this without thought until something unexpected happens, and then we see that we were really paying attention all along.

But not only is our attention on the next second; we also spend many waking hours attempting to plot the trajectory of our lives—the next hours, days, years. We consider alternatives. We move between hope and despair. We study other people, analyzing and judging what they are doing, as we measure ourselves against them.

As I said, we go to poetry and the other arts for knowledge, to expand our moral experience of the world, for sustenance, survival, and connection. The degree to which we get this necessary mixture from textbooks, biographies, memoirs, and journalism is limited. We see the apparent effects of a series of uncertain causes. These forms of nonfiction present us with the shadow, while the arts have the ability to present us with the living body. Doesn't one learn more about whaling from *Moby Dick* than from the best piece of nonfiction written on the subject?

In *Feeling and Form*, Susanne Langer writes:

Non-discursive form in art . . . [articulates] knowledge that cannot be rendered discursively because it concerns experiences which are not *formally*
amenable to the discursive projection. Such experiences are the rhythms of
life, organic, emotional and mental, which are not simply periodic but endlessly complex, and sensitive to every sort of influence. All together they
combine the dynamic patterns of feeling. It is this pattern that only nondiscursive symbolic forms can present and that is the point and purpose of
artistic construction.[4]

And in *Problems of Art,* she writes:

. . . every work of art expresses, more or less purely, more or less subtly, not
feelings and emotions which the artist *has,* but feelings and emotions which
the artist *knows;* his *insight* into the nature of sentience, his picture of vital
experience, physical, emotive and fantastic.

Such knowledge is not expressible in ordinary discourse. . . . [T]he forms
of feeling and the forms of discursive expression are logically incommensu-
rate, so that any exact concept of feeling and emotion cannot be projected
into the logical form of literal language. Verbal statement, which is our normal and most reliable means of communication, is almost useless for convey-
ing knowledge about the precise character of the affective life.[5]

The writer's insight into the nature of sentience derives from a mix of
personal experience and what he or she has absorbed secondhand—your
neighbor's gossip is a form of secondhand experience; so too is reading *War
and Peace* as an experience of war or the *New York Post* as an experience
of a crime or an election. Two other qualities also affect the writer's "picture of vital experience, physical, emotive and fantastic." The first, imagination, should be obvious. You can imagine feelings you have not felt. You can
imagine the jealousy and rage of Othello by exaggerating feelings you have
experienced. You can imagine a sexual passion for a giant froglike creature, as
Rachel Ingalls did in *Mrs. Caliban,* by imagining a more conventional sexual
passion and transferring it to the monster.

The other necessary element is that the reader must have some degree of
sympathy, compassion, empathy. The writer can make us care only if the ability to experience that emotion is already within us. Without empathy on the

reader's part, the writer can do nothing, since empathy gives the writer access to the heart of another and, equally, makes him or her care about the reader. But fiction and poetry also educate and increase the reader's sense of empathy. In *Othello* Shakespeare presents a character whom his Elizabethan audience would have seen as a savage, and Shakespeare makes his audience care about that man and realize that their own emotions are not very different from those of the Moor of Venice.

Empathy is also a way the writer gains insight into the nature of sentience. It is a way of experiencing what another person feels, after which it can be worked on by the imagination. Without it, the writer has little chance of success.

Langer's larger point is more complicated. Discursive language cannot communicate the nature of emotion; it can give us the name of an emotion—happy—and the degree of an emotion—very happy—but it can't tell us what the emotion feels like.

The same is true of *lust* and *sexual excitement*—the words are hardly more than labels. Berryman's "Dream Song #4" enacts a scene of sexual desire, not simply through the words, but through that whole mixture of language, sound, and presentation. And it includes the comic element that often attends sexual excitement—"What wonders is she sitting on, over there?" In its complexity, the poem is a symbol of feelings of intense desire and a parody of such feelings, a complicated parody because Berryman is mocking himself. But, if we allow ourselves, we are able to imagine Henry's feelings and ponder that black-haired, Latin beauty "filling her compact & delicious body / with chicken paprika"; we can duplicate, to a lesser degree, what the poet felt. We don't see Henry's desire—"I hungered back"—as a sign, as the word "sad" is a sign; rather, through the poem's enactment of sexual excitement, · we experience a definition of those words. This sense of feeling what the poet felt, among other things, gives us a sense of connection. If we have not behaved foolishly in a similar sort of way, we can at least imagine it; and briefly, we are lifted out of ourselves, out of our existential isolation. This symbolic presentation of the enacted emotion that a reader can experience is only possible through art. And this, says Langer, "is the point and purpose of artistic construction." It is this life of feeling and emotion that we often turn to in literature when we are considering our trajectories into the future, when we are wondering how another person did it, how another person felt.

We don't take these feelings from art as from a textbook. An exchange exists between the emotions we experience in art and those we experience in the world. We test what we learn; we measure its accuracy, if only imaginatively. What we find in art we validate in the world, and vice versa. As we do this, our insight into sentient life deepens, while such an exchange also widens our sense of possibility and of what is appropriate to the world—that is, a sense of the scope of sentient life and what is natural to it.

So what were Berryman's concerns? I expect his life was most dramatically affected by his father's suicide when Berryman was 12, and his dominating concern consciously and unconsciously was how to come to terms with that event. How he responded to it as a poet was affected by his ambition—"I didn't want to be *like* Yeats," he said in an interview, "I wanted to *be* Yeats"— as well as by his alcoholism and depression.[6] Through the years, like anyone, he had many concerns, some changing, some constant, but everything, I think, was seen in relation to his father's death.

In *Hope Abandoned*, which discusses Osip Mandelstam in the context of early twentieth-century Russia, his wife Nadezhda writes, "The poet's mode of thought is the product of all sides of his personality: the intellectual, physiological, spiritual, and emotional, a synthesis of what he perceives through his senses, his instincts and desires, and the higher aspirations of his spirit. All these can be bound together only by some dominant idea which shapes the personality. If there is no such idea, one will have, at best, a clever craftsman, a 'translator of ready-made ideas,' a mechanical nightingale. The unifying idea can be located at any level of the personality—in its deep reaches or on the surface."[7]

Her "dominant idea" is what I mean by a concern. It is the abstraction of an emotion or idea through which one's life experience is filtered. If one is a poet, one constantly seeks for metaphors with which to voice some aspect of that concern. Often, I think, it happens unconsciously, as with Ritsos observing that the buildings were like people standing together without exchanging glances. In Berryman's "Dream Song #4," we see the dominant idea appear at the end: "Where did it all go wrong? There ought to be a law against Henry."

This question and statement obstinately repeated itself in Berryman's brain like a tape loop just below consciousness, and it shaped the images to which he was particularly alert. I have no idea how he wrote this specific Dream Song, but, like many of the Dream Songs, I expect it was triggered by an actual event. People often find this sort of duplicity unsettling in poets. Berryman is in a restaurant having lustful feelings about a black-haired, Latin beauty, and at the same time he is watching himself having these lustful feelings. Then, at some point, as he is watching himself and thinking about what has skewed him toward this behavior, he thinks, coldly, "I can use this." This is how poems often come into being: the self detachedly watching the self.

One might prefer that the dominant idea have some philosophical or psychological merit, but Mandelstam says it "can be located at any level of the personality." She writes: "Mayakovski, for example, in his best verse, is a poet of adolescent rage. He screams and throws tantrums because the toys he wants are not immediately put in his hands. Like a child, he only hopes that one day, when it is too late, everybody will feel sorry for what they have done to him—'everybody' being the grownups who treat him so badly (and all women were grownups)."[8]

Vladimir Vladimirovich Mayakovski (or Mayakovsky) was born in 1893 and shot himself in 1930, seemingly out of disillusionment with the revolution and the Soviet government for which he had become a propagandist. The writing of his propaganda verse, Mandelstam says, "postponed his end, giving him a purpose in life and the sense of power so essential to a person of his temperament. His example shows that even at this level poetry is possible. What he put his faith in has proved to be an infirmity rather than a source of strength and . . . his tragedy lay precisely in his own weakness, which made it impossible for him to identify himself with real strength. The best he could do was to throw in his lot with his age, which was as infirm as he was himself."[9]

I quote this passage for two reasons. Even though this dominant idea can be located at any level of the personality, the greater its superficiality and, perhaps, self-centeredness, then the less its durability. For how long can one go on being a poet of adolescent rage?

This brings me to the second point. Over the years, I have had many students whose poetry was impelled by the complexities of adolescence. Once that phase and its problems had passed, quite a few either stopped writing or were at a loss for subject matter. Some turned into what Mandelstam dismisses as clever craftsmen, translators of ready-made ideas, mechanical nightingales. But there is another possibility that I will mention shortly.

If one is an adolescent poet—and the phase of becoming-an-adult can extend well past 18 or 21—one's subject matter will be obviously drawn from the complexities of this period in one's life. The poet dwells on those concerns and seeks out the metaphors to explain them, first for himself or herself, and then to turn them into art. It is the first step that can give a poem such power. Finding an outlet for that concern is extremely liberating. Not only is the concern once again given a voice, a new expression, but it once again seems to clarify itself to the poet with the illusion of understanding.

It is this energy, this appearance that, for the poet, the poem needed to be written that helps to convince the reader of the validity of the experience and its potential value. This is true of writing poetry at any age. If the poet can't convince the reader that he or she, to some large degree, *needed* to write the poem, the poem will rarely work, because the reader wants to believe that the experience, translated into art, will be of value to him or her as well. After all, there is that question: How does one live? No matter how much the reader may admire the poem as an object, the reader is also looking for metaphysical payback.

But for many adolescent poets the problems associated with adolescence either work themselves out or come to seem unimportant. It is then that many stop writing or start writing badly. Others, like Berryman, never leave that adolescent stage. Despite his great learning and deep seriousness, he remained, in part, an adolescent until his suicide at 58, and the sonnets and *Dream Songs* remain poems of adolescence, which contributes to their charm. I don't wish to psychoanalyze Berryman, but the shock of his father's death and the complexity of his reaction kept his father's suicide in the forefront of Berryman's brain all his life. This was exacerbated by his alcoholism: the constant self-medication that, if practiced attentively, freezes one at an early emotional age.

Other poets solve the problem of vanishing adolescence by reinventing themselves. Apollinaire, Neruda, Yeats, Rilke, Robert Lowell, Adrienne Rich, and others were able to redirect their concerns, their dominating ideas into seemingly new areas. I say "seemingly" because elements of the former concerns remain evident. The preoccupations of adolescence don't disappear; rather, they recede into the background or develop new meanings. Pablo Neruda's major symbol was a root (*la raiz*), but over the years the emphasis changed from a preoccupation with his personal origin to ideas about race and community—a more comprehensive and less personal conception of roots and origins. Yeats, in early poems, often uses the symbol of the rose. Then, in his thirties, the rose vanishes. But for many years afterward the rose continues to appear in his early drafts, only to be deleted.

Vladimir Mayakovski was the youngest of three children born in Baghdadi, Georgia, where his father worked as a forest ranger. When he was 13, his father died and the mother moved the family to Moscow. They were now poor, and at 15 Mayakovski was withdrawn from school. By that time he had become involved with radical socialist groups and was jailed on three occasions for subversive activity. When he was 16, he was held in solitary confinement in Butyrka prison in Moscow and began to write poetry. On release, he joined the Russian Futurist group and soon became its spokesman. His first publications appeared in 1912 in a Futurist manifesto, *A Slap in the Face of Public Taste*. It was a violent poetry often meant to shock. Mayakovski's adolescent rage was fueled by the dominant idea of unfairness. It was unfair that his father had died, unfair that he had been taken out of school. This sense of unfairness then evolved until it was directed at pre-Revolution society. It moved past the particular to become a social concern, but, in his thinking, life was still unfair, which led him to Bolshevism. What destroyed him, in Mandelstam's argument, was his realization that the Soviet government—the so-called solution—was worse than what had existed before.

Berryman, too, had this deep sense of unfairness that resulted from his father's death. But a suicide is different from a natural death. Children whose parents commit suicide often blame themselves. If they had been better children, more loving, more obedient, more something, the parent wouldn't have died—death being the ultimate rejection. Of course this is not rational; after all, they are children. Many of these children become emotionally arrested at that early age. The parent's suicide was the most tremendous event of their childhood, and they continue to revolve around it like the moon around the earth. Berryman, too, tried to move past the particular to a larger, social concern, but his sense of somehow having failed his father brought him back to that tragic center of gravity. It would be wrong to say that the deaths of Berryman's and Mayakovski's fathers caused their suicides: there is never one reason for something like suicide. But neither man was able to move past his father's death, an event reflected in their poetry.

This description oversimplifies the complexity of these men. It oversimplifies the trauma and their response to it. There is never a single cause. But each poet had a dominating idea of unfairness that was influenced by events he had experienced in childhood. In each case, the poet attempted to move past that personal concern to a larger sphere, but in each case that larger sphere continued to be filtered through the early trauma. This is common for writers, though the dominating idea needn't arise from a death. I can think of poets who were equally affected by the divorce of their parents or the death of a sibling or childhood sexual abuse. Nor does every poet require a trauma. Some writers, including Philip Larkin, were stutterers, and their work sought on paper the linguistic grace of which they themselves felt incapable when speaking. But Larkin was the child of older parents, which affected his ideas of love and marriage: in some poems his views were almost sappy, as in "Arundel Tomb" and "Whitsun Weddings," or antisocial, as in "Dockery & Son" and "This Be the Verse," while in between were conflicted poems like "No Road" and "Reasons for Attendance." The tension between these different attitudes about love was, for Larkin, a dominating idea.

W. B. Yeats's father, the painter John Yeats, was a passionate rationalist, empiricist, and atheist with an energetic and analytical mind that let him win any argument, especially with a child. Yeats's mother believed in ghosts, was intuitive, dreamy, and mentally fragile. Yeats the boy was constantly torn back and forth between the pair of them, since to embrace one was to be disloyal to the other. Is it any surprise that his dominating idea was that poetry arises from the tension of opposites?

Trauma itself is not the subject matter, nor is it the dominating idea, but it can give rise to the dominating idea—such as the idea of unfairness—and the poetry is a way to come to terms with that idea. It helps define it and give it expression. Nor does the trauma necessarily lead a person to poetry or cause poetry; that is a whole other subject. Childhood trauma might just as well lead to a career in the military or the priesthood or a life under a bridge with a bottle of Ripple.

The impulse to speak and the impulse to speak about something in particular are not the same. Many have the first without having the second. Whatever causes the need to speak about something in particular for a person in late adolescence needs to be strong enough to force the young writer to begin. The trauma, if there is one, may not even be obvious to him or her; all the poet knows is that *something* requires expression.

Need this motivating event be of a negative nature? Can't the poet be prompted by a powerful love of the natural world, as seems to have been the case with Wordsworth or Theodore Roethke? Perhaps, but as Philip Lar-kin said in an interview, quoting another writer, "Happiness paints white." Wordsworth as a young man was a supporter of the French Revolution, and his poetry was equally revolutionary. His poems about peasants and nature reflected those principles and formed an assault on the poetic taste of the pe-riod. Roethke's love of nature was bound to his sense of transience. Things die. We value the flower because its existence is fleeting. The apparent joy in their poems had dark foundations.

But it is not the negative nature of the motivating event that is important (if indeed it is negative), but rather the act of trying to come to terms with it, of trying to establish a life despite its power. Mayakovski's response to what he saw as unfairness was defiance; his poetry arose from the tension between the two. Berryman's poems that mention his father's suicide are not about the suicide itself, but about Berryman's struggle to deal with it, to grow beyond it.

Another kind of poetry found among young poets that seems beset by weakness derives from a passion to claim their histories, to identify who they are in the world, to write memoirs in verse. If the poems are able to tran-scend the poet's life to become meaningful to the reader's life, they can be successful. This, too, is a matter of the personal evolving into the societal, the subjective illuminating the objective. But often the poet, for various reasons, wants to keep the focus on the personal details of his or her life and not let them become metaphoric. The plums and peaches remain plums and peaches. These poems often reflect an almost poignant self-affirmation. Mostly they don't brag or claim uniqueness; rather, their writers' apparent motivation is to claim their own existential corner of the hearth. The difficulty is that such an ambition may interfere with the speaker's ability to function as the reader's representative, and so it may be more difficult for the reader to find his or her own life reflected in the life in the poem. And, often, the poet doesn't want this to happen, as it might draw attention away from the poet. So the reader, while he or she may admire the poem's form, intelligence, wit, and so on, is basically little more than an observer. This pleasure is short-lived and likely shallow.

The need to claim one's place in the world is most often a youthful enter-prise, and once that need is satisfied, the poet may stop writing, even though he or she might still have a desire to write. The exceptions are often prompted by the occurrence of some large event in adulthood that leads the writer to need to reestablish his or her place in the world: the death of a sibling or child, recovering from a great illness or accident, a divorce, a particularly intense love affair, a change in sexual persuasion, and so on—events that, in the poet's mind, give him or her permission or even a sense of obligation to speak. And certainly very good poems have been produced. The criteria continue to be those set down by George Saintsbury: "To have something to say; to say it under pretty strict limits of form and very strict ones of space; to say it forcibly; to say it beautifully."

To lose or be unable to express one's dominating idea can often lead to an emphasis on problematic innovation, usually accompanied by scorn heaped on anything seen as traditional. Nadezhda Mandelstam wrote, "The mania for innovation always leads to speculative traffic in arbitrary notions; and reliance on pure inventiveness invariably brings with it the spurning of man's accumulated riches, with all the fateful consequences this entails."[10]

Louise Glück discussed "speculative traffic in arbitrary notions" in her essay "Ersatz Thought" in the Winter 1999 issue of *The Threepenny Review*. She had been criticizing the use of the ellipsis, the fragment, the unnamed and unfinished to create a false sense of philosophic depth—the shimmering abyss. She then moved to non-sequiturs that she said have two uses: the first is "true non-relation," and the second is to turn non-sequiturs into a code so that the poem becomes "a diagram of systematic evasion."

> The mind skids from one thing to the next, anecdote to epiphany, with no visible or logical thread connecting its movement. The task of the reader, in poems of this sort, resembles the task of the psychoanalyst: listen closely enough to narrate the gaps, the unsaid, the center around which the said whirls, from and to which it departs and returns. The said, in this usage, is a shield; as the poem develops, the reader begins to piece together the deleted material: to the degree that the evasions and digressions compel in their resourcefulness (to the degree that the mind generating them interests us) the unsaid intensifies and quivers. And—the essential point—becomes increasingly specific. As in a murder inquiry: more and more possible subjects are ruled out. The difficulty is duration: how long can we pay attention to non-sequitur, attention focused enough to break the code.[11]

Such poems fail, according to Glück, when the non-sequitur is used *purely* as code, which "sentimentalizes" the poem, because "the only binding ra-

tionale one can devise is so vague, so inclusive, so elastic as to be banal."
This leads her to discuss apparent non-sequiturs: nongrammatical phrases and
the joining together of nonsensical fragments in which all chance of meaning
is denied and even mocked. And she points to a contemporary use of non-
sequitur that is neither code nor conversation that she identifies more with
John Ashbery's followers than with Ashbery himself. She writes,

> . . . these alternatives are not in themselves necessarily problematic, but their
> inherent opacities and elusiveness accommodate intellectual fraud. A model
> for the difference might be the difference between [Frank] O'Hara and Ash-
> bery, a shifting of interest from the moment to the idea of the moment, from
> speech to the abstraction of speech . . . from the palpable to the disembodied.
> It can be pulled off, this gesture; its dangers, however, resemble those of the
> [use of] the abyss. Like the abyss, it has a tendency to flatter the reader, who
> projects himself, by invitation, into the unintelligible, and reads in what he
> chooses.[12]

Glück then combines her discussion of the fragment with a discussion of
the non-sequitur and its rejection of the psychological in favor of the seemingly philosophical.

> It is eerie to watch this art develop; to see, on one hand, its immense security
> as to its scale and groundbreaking importance, and, on the other, the dazzling
> ease of its fabrication, once the principal tropes are in place. And to see the
> rigorously incoherent claim for itself of the stature of thought.
>   We have made of the infinite a topic. But there isn't, it turns out, much
> to say about it. Which leaves only the style of its saying.[13]

Though we will always have good and bad poems, the status of Homer,
Dante, and the rest of the canon is, I hope, secure. Nadezhda Mandelstam
spoke of a form or attitude of poetic innovation that spurned "man's accumulated riches, with all the fateful consequences this entails." Many of the poets
Glück mentions claim to have rendered the canon obsolete. As far as subject
matter is concerned, their poems replace subject matter with the *appearance*
of subject matter, or the poets may say that subject matter and/or accessibility
is unimportant, "with all the fateful consequences this entails."

This brings up another issue affecting subject matter, which deserves a chapter by itself, but will get only a page or two. This is the burden of the past, which, in fact, is the title of a book by Walter Jackson Bate, *The Burden of the Past and the English Poet,* which originated as a series of lectures delivered at the University of Toronto in 1969. The issue is simple. How is it possible to write when earlier poets have written great poems on the same subjects? Consequently, what is there left to do?

He quotes T. S. Eliot, who said, "Not only every great poet, but every genuine, but lesser poet, fulfills once for all some possibility of language, and so leaves one possibility less for his successors."[14] He quotes Goethe on the effect of Shakespeare's achievement: "Had I been born an Englishman and had those manifold masterworks pressed in upon me with all their power from my first youthful awakening, it would have overwhelmed me, and I would not have known what I wanted to do!"[15]

Bate gives many such examples and writes, "We could in fact argue that the remorseless deepening of self-consciousness before the rich and intimidating legacy of the past, has become the single greatest problem that modern art . . . has had to face, and that it will become increasingly so in the future."[16]

He then points to the great transitions in English poetry from the Elizabethans and Jacobeans to neoclassicism to romanticism to modernism. These new paradigms offered poets new opportunities, but they were accompanied by a certain amount of faultfinding in regard to the previous period, which made the great writers of previous generations more manageable. One sees this in late twentieth-century critical theory. By turning "humanism" into a pejorative term, theorists could dismiss the humanist critics who preceded them. By pointing to a canon full of "old white guys," they could dismiss the canon because it lacked racial, ethnic, or gender diversity. By arguing that previous claims about the efficacy of language as a tool of communication were mistaken or exaggerated, they could sweep aside something written in such language.

When no new paradigm declares itself, the alternative may be retrenchment or, as Bate writes, "given the massive achievement in the past, [poets] may have no further way to proceed except toward progressive refinement, nuance, indirection, and finally through the continued pressure for difference, into the various forms of anti-art."[17] Both Glück and Nadezhda Mandelstam wrote of these dangers.

Two great weapons that young poets have to combat the burden of the past are gall and ignorance. The first is a blessing, the second a curse. It is easy to avoid the burden of the past when one has read none of the great poets. A great many colleges facilitated this by removing literature survey classes and by replacing reading classes with writing classes. Gall, however, permits one to press forward despite the odds.

Starting in the mid-1950s three developments emerged, which, if they didn't form a new paradigm, offered ways of escape. First was the publication of Ginsberg's "Howl," the example of Walt Whitman, and the rise of the Beat Generation, as well as Charles Olson's influence, both in projectivist verse and as head of Black Mountain College in North Carolina. The second was the example of free verse established by Robert Lowell in *Life Studies*, accompanied by what has been called the confessional mode. Third was the great influx of translations by many accomplished poets. These developments offered ways of writing to set against the achievement of the modernists. And there were other developments—new formalism, language poetry, and so on. Most everybody writing today was deeply influenced by these changes of focus.

The burden of the past is a subject that young poets should consider in their pursuit of matter and manner. To my mind, the decision to write memoirs in verse is to pursue an ersatz paradigm, since it can produce poetry from which the reader is excluded. On the other hand, the differences in human psychology and the particularity of each person's subjective vision would seem to guarantee that no one poem will exactly repeat any other. All dead father poems are different. If we see each poem as the poet's struggle with his or her dominant idea, then, as Rilke said, subject matter becomes pretext. We are left with the self wriggling in its cocoon of existential isolation. As for the value of contemporary poetry, it is very difficult to make clear judgments about one's contemporaries. All that will be sorted out in the future, if there is one. The need is the constant attempt to master the craft, which, so long as it is not simply imitative, gives the poet some hope of succeeding when and if subject matter declares itself.

Many young writers spend sleepless nights trying to identify their subject matter without realizing that, if it exists at all, it has been there all along. One's concerns, one's dominant idea only needs to be accessed. Fortunately, we are subjective creatures. Our experience of the world is always filtered through the self and its vast complexity. Our concerns may be unconscious, but they are always with us. Rilke described in a letter his discovery that if he stared at something long enough, he would briefly forget his concerns and suddenly they would become lodged in what he was looking at, meaning that a metaphoric link formed between the object of his regard and his concern. In another letter he said that he tried not to wait for inspiration to happen, but just to start writing—say, a description of something—and that often the inspiration would come, by which he meant, again, that a metaphoric link would be established between the ostensible subject and a concern. The plums and peaches became more than plums and peaches.

Frequently we think that subject matter must be something profound, earth-shaking, but what is earth-shaking is our connection to other human beings and to the world. For instance, the trauma of death that results in an elegy presents us with a very simple relation. (Rilke's *Duino Elegies*, however, are anything but simple.) Yet what is complicated is not the dominant idea, but the vehicle, one that carries many other concerns under the wing of the dominating concern. And the vehicle is not simply the form, but the entire mix of form and content together. But that is another subject.

reconciling paradox

a paradox affects our relation to subject matter and subject matter's relation to a reader; that is, art can have no moral purpose, but it may have a moral function. Let us first consider moral purpose. In our vast intellectual, emotional, and metaphysical infrastructure, we have many ideas and beliefs that we hold because of our sex, religion, ethnicity, age, and all the rest—because of where we were born and how we were educated, because of our history, health, and even because of what we ate for lunch. This only begins to describe the many factors and influences, and we cannot keep these ideas and beliefs out of our work. Our ethical nature will be reflected in what we write. In fact it is to a large degree determined by this mass of underpinnings. But when I say that art can have no moral purpose, I mean that it cannot be purposefully inserted, that the work cannot be morally manipulated for some supposed greater good. But, indirectly, a work of art may have a moral effect on the viewer or reader.

As human beings we have many psychological constraints. We dislike things too blatant, too violent, too dirty. We may dislike obscenity, foul language, explicitly sexual descriptions. We dislike any evidence of racial, sexual, or ethnic prejudice. At times in workshops I have heard male students berated by female students because of their frankness in writing about male desire. Then there is the whole topic of political correctness.

An effect of these internal and external psychological constraints on a writer is to give the work a moral agenda, even when it is hardly intended, by the writer's taking pains to make sure the poem includes nothing offensive. Most poets not only want their work praised; they want to be praised for their work. The charge of incorrectness, even of immorality, may dash these hopes. And if they don't wish to be praised, they don't wish to be scolded, either. So they soften the rough places. Rage turns to dislike; lust to corporeal partiality. Or, if they can't remove the questionable parts, they make them obscure. Incestuous longings disappear; claws are sheathed.

In Chekhov's story "Gusev," a soldier dying of tuberculosis is being taken by ship back to Russia from the Far East with other sick soldiers. Gusev thinks of his home, but he is a man without depth or education, and his thoughts are ill defined, more like pictures than thoughts. We hear his opinions and the opinions of the men around him. Gusev does not seem like a bad man, but we know little of his moral makeup. At the end of the third part, we find these paragraphs.

> Gusev . . . was looking out the window. A boat, all flooded with blinding, hot sunlight, is rocking on the transparent, soft turquoise water. Naked Chinamen are standing in it holding up cages of canaries and shouting:
>
> "He sing! He sing!"
>
> Another boat knocks against the first; a steam launch passes by. And here is a third boat: in it sits a fat Chinaman, eating rice with little sticks. The water ripples lazily, white seagulls fly lazily over it.
>
> "It'd be nice to give that fat one a punch in the neck . . ." thinks Gusev, gazing at the fat Chinaman and yawning.
>
> He dozes off, and it seems to him that the whole of nature is dozing. Time runs fast. The day passes imperceptibly, darkness comes imperceptibly. . . . The ship is no longer standing still, but going on somewhere.[1]

I have taught this story several times, and each time some students are upset by the fact that Gusev should want to punch the Chinaman in the neck, that Chekhov would even permit such a sentiment into his story. It is my argument that such sentiments make the story successful.

Since our intellectual and metaphysical infrastructure is unconsciously set for or against whatever we read, what happens when we feel the writer

has manipulated his text, or has hoped to influence us with exemplary characters, or has toned down his or her situations, or has a moral or political
agenda? We reject it; we see it can be of no use to us. Or perhaps instead of
challenging the reader, the text soothes the reader, placates and flatters his
or her vanity.

We need Gusev to want to punch that Chinaman. We need him with all
his faults, all his humanity. If we feel he has been cleaned up, we turn away.
He is of no use to us. As Chekhov wrote in a letter to a young woman friend:

> To a chemist there is nothing impure on earth. The writer should be just as
> objective as the chemist; he should liberate himself from everyday subjectivity
> and acknowledge that manure piles play a highly respectable role in the land-
> scape and that evil passions are every bit as much a part of life as good ones.[2]

In Chapter 3 of Franz Kafka's *The Castle*, K. is hiding beneath the bar
next to the barmaid, Frieda, whom he met an hour before and who is the mis-
tress of the bar owner, Herr Klamm. The bar has closed for the night.

> [Frieda] began to tug at [K.] like a child. "Come on, it's too close down
> here," and they embraced each other, her little body burned in K.'s hands,
> in a state of unconsciousness which K. tried again and again but in vain to
> master they rolled a little way, landing with a thud at Klamm's door, where
> they lay, almost undressed, for each of them had torn open the other's clothes
> with hands and teeth, in the little puddles of beer and other refuse scattered
> on the floor. Three hours went past, hours in which they breathed as one, in
> which their hearts beat as one, hours in which K. was haunted by the feeling
> that he was losing himself or wandering into a strange country, farther than
> any man has wandered before, a country so strange that not even the air had
> anything in common with his native air, where one might die of strangeness,
> and yet whose enchantment was such that one could only go on and lose
> oneself further.[3]

It is striking that both Chekhov and Kafka contrast the rude behavior of
their characters with lyric images, how they follow the animal, as it were, with
the transcendent to make the animal even more vivid. In Chapter 4, K. and
Frieda are at it again.

. . . they reeled over and fell on the bed. There they lay, but not in the for-
getfulness of the previous night. She was seeking and he was seeking, they
raged and contorted their faces and bored their heads into each other's
bosoms in the urgency of seeking something, and their embraces and their
tossing limbs did not avail to make them forget, but only reminded them
of what they sought; like dogs desperately tearing up the ground, they tore
at each other's body, and often, helplessly baffled, in a final effort to at-
tain happiness they nuzzled and tongued each other's face. Sheer weariness
stilled them at last and made them grateful to each other. Then the maids
came in. "Look how they're lying there," said one, and sympathetically cast
a coverlet over them.[4]

Oddly, these scenes make K. convincing. They make him human; that is,
he is hemmed in by contradictions. And the purpose of the maids? They are
our representatives. They join us in the story as coconspirators and show us
how we are meant to feel. But if we thought that Kafka was sanitizing K., lay-
ing a moral grid across his novel, we would find it unacceptable. We also see
in the passages from Chekhov and Kafka examples of people trapped by their
human natures. K. and Frieda try to forget themselves, escape themselves each
by using the other, but of course they fail.

In my essay on Rilke in *Best Words, Best Order*, I describe him writing to his wife about Baudelaire's poem "The Carrion," in which Baudelaire
points out to his beloved a woman's decayed corpse by the side of the road.
He concludes by saying that while the worms will have his lover's body, his
poems will save the best about her. This is a common theme in love poems that
Baudelaire, to some degree, is satirizing. Rilke states that after Baudelaire's
poem no poet could turn away from any subject for reasons of propriety or
morality. He wrote,

Artistic perception had to overcome itself to the point of realizing that even
something horrible, something that seems no more than disgusting, truly exists, and shares the truth of its being with everything else that exists. Just as
the creative artist is not allowed to choose, neither is he permitted to turn his
back on anything: a single refusal, and he is cast out of the state of grace and
becomes sinful all the way through.[5]

Let's go further. In Rabelais's *Gargantua and Pantagruel,* published in the 1530s, we find a scene when Pantagruel's ship meets a ship full of sheep and sheep merchants. One merchant, Dingdong, insults Pantagruel's friend and squire Panurge, calling him a cuckold. Panurge takes revenge by bargaining for one of Dingdong's rams, buying it and then throwing it into the water. "All the other sheep," wrote Rabelais, "bleating and bellowing at the same pitch, began one after the other to leap into the sea after him: they pushed and shoved to see who would be the first to follow their companion. It was impossible to stop them, since as you know sheep always follow the leader, wherever he goes."[6]

Attempting to stop his sheep, Dingdong grabs onto the fleece of a powerful ram and is dragged into the sea.

And along with their master, Dingdong, went all the shepherds and other herdsmen, too, some of them trying to hold on to horns, some to legs, some clutching a fleece. But all of them were swept into the sea and miserably drowned.

Standing just outside the galley kitchen, Panurge picked up an oar—not to help the shepherds, but to keep them from climbing up onto the boat and escaping the general shipwreck. And he was preaching to them most eloquently . . . demonstrating to them . . . the world's infinite miseries, the good and the happiness of the other life . . . and promising each of them that he would put up a fine tombstone for them . . . when he returned from his trip.[7]

When Panurge's friend, Brother John, tells him that he still lost the 50,000 francs he paid for the ram, Panurge replies, "I've had one hell of a good time for my money. . . . No one amuses me for free, or at least without some acknowledgment. I'm not as ungrateful as all that, I never was and I never will be."[8]

In his essay "The Day Panurge No Longer Makes People Laugh" in *Testaments Betrayed,* the novelist Milan Kundera wrote,

People who cannot take pleasure in the spectacle of Panurge letting the sheep merchants drown while he sings them the praises of the hereafter will never understand a thing about the art of the novel.[9]

This is a knotty accusation, but it has to do with the idea that if art has a moral purpose, it may be no more than imagining that some subjects are inappropriate, which may be no more than thinking, if I am too frank, too clear, too direct, then people may dislike or disapprove of me.

Panurge's trick is one of many and probably not the worst. All of his actions are exaggerations of fairly conventional pranks that we either have done or might fantasize about doing. For instance, Panurge likes practical jokes and has dozens of pockets in which he keeps the tools of the trade. In one pocket he keeps models of small penises that he fastens to women's hats or the backs of their gowns. In another he keeps fishhooks so when in a crowd he can fasten men and women together; then, when they move apart, their clothes are ripped to shreds. In another pocket he keeps little packages of fleas and lice that in church he drops down the backs of the sweetest-looking ladies. In another he carries magnifying glasses with which to make men and women lose all control, drive them to a frenzy even in church, for, "as he used to say, there wasn't anything to choose from as between a woman who was crazy for religion and a woman whose ass moved like crazy."[10]

Such behavior is not unimaginable. And the moment we laugh, we admit complicity. We set aside our criticism of Panurge and his world, which may tell us more about our own righteousness than we care to know.

In his essay, Kundera discusses Octavio Paz's claim that humor "is the great invention of the modern spirit," that it begins with Rabelais and Cervantes, and that it is not mockery or satire, but "a particular species of the comic."[11] Paz also argues that "humor renders ambiguous everything it touches."[12] This is a matter of tone and surprise because the same may be said about horror: one doesn't know what will happen next. Consider our ambivalence to Jack Nicholson's character in Stanley Kubrick's film version of Stephen King's *The Shining*. In comedy and horror, the conventional rules of behavior and accepted laws of cause and effect have been set aside. We enter a place where anything might happen. That ambiguity, during the reading process, makes our response uncertain. Not only are we uncertain about what will happen next, but we are also uncertain how to respond to it.

Here is a poem describing human complexity that contains nothing that could be considered politically incorrect: an upside-down sonnet, "First Sight," by Bill Knott.

Summer is entered through screendoors,

and therefore seems unclear

at first sight, when it is in fact

a mesh of fine wires

suspended panewise

whose haze has confused the eyes . . .

What if we never entered then—

what if the days remained like this,

a hesitation at the threshold of itself,

expectant, tense, tensile

as lines that cross each other

in a space forever latent

where we wait, pressed up against

something trying to retain its vagueness.[13]

One sees here, in the use of syntax to direct argument, the debt that Knott owes to Philip Larkin. We have two sentences: one in the first stanza, which is a depersonalized statement, and one in the second stanza with the inclusive "we." At the end of the second stanza, the phrase "pressed up against" makes us realize that the waiting "we" is most likely a child. The idea the poem offers is that the promise, the latency, the very vagueness always holds out more than the actuality; and that the latency, the promise is increased by the blur caused by the thing that separates, in this case the mesh of fine wires. All of which takes us back to the "we's" question: What if we never entered? What if we had remained on the threshold of this promise? So the poem that begins with the expectation of pleasure turns instead to the expectation of disappointment, since only disappointment would lead to such a question. It reminds me of the Asian saying: Better than the vacation is the day before. It is a sad poem, and further rereadings give further meanings—the lines crossing each other become the lines of future possibility; the attempt to retain vagueness suggests the certainty of disappointment in the particular. All those sibilants in the first stanza: Do they represent bugs trying to get through the mesh, or do they represent confusion?

By taking a situation we have experienced, by using specific but slightly odd sense data to manipulate our memories, by making us participants in the poem with the inclusive "we," Knott leads us to calculate the gap between where we see ourselves at the moment of reading and the world of the poem. It is not that we identify with Knott, or at least that isn't the purpose, but we are meant to experience the situation, to be a child looking out a screen door in summer. Only a child has that eagerness to be outside and fantasizes about the pleasures that might be waiting. The purpose of the speaker is to give us access to the situation. As a result the poem makes us ask questions of ourselves, makes us confront issues of frustration and reward, pleasure and disappointment. Mostly in life we tell ourselves it is better to act, to take the chance—but perhaps, as is suggested here, it is better to do nothing, to not. And if you read enough of Knott, you learn that he constantly puns on "not"—to refuse, to deny, to back away, to not. But the poem is serious. It offers no ambiguity in the way Paz and Kundera use the term.

Here is John Berryman's "Dream Song #187":

Them lady poets must not marry, pal.
Miss Dickinson—fancy in Amherst bedding hér.
Fancy a lark with Sappho,
A tumble in the bushes with Miss Moore,
A spoon with Emily, while Charlotte glare.
Miss Bishop's too noble-O.

That was the lot. And two of them are here
as yet, and—and: Sylvia Plath is not.
She—she her credentials
has handed in, leaving alone two tots
and widower to what he makes of it—
surviving guy, &

when Tolstoy's pathetic widow doing her whung
(after them decades of marriage) & kids, she decided he was *queer*
& loving his agent.
Wherefore he rush off, leaving two journals, & die.
It is a true error to marry with poets
or to be by them.[14]

The ambiguity created by the humor is brought about by the details, the diction and tone, but also by the rhythms within and across the lines, the relation between stressed and unstressed syllables, syntax, a mass of little effects. This is all part of the surprise that keeps us uncertain how to respond until the last two lines when the humor is dropped and the poem makes a clear statement that connects back to the thesis, all the jazzing in between being examples: "It is a true error to marry with poets / or to be by them."

Berryman's humor also sets aside, temporarily, or keeps us from judging too quickly, the morality or immorality of a tumble in the bushes with the poet Marianne Moore. Unless we keep our moral axe always upraised for any hint of impropriety, we delay judgment because we can't determine Berryman's tone—the humor keeps it ambiguous. That delay allows us to reach the end without the intrusion of our moral indignation. By then we realize that Berryman's intention is not to make unpleasant remarks about the sexual unattractiveness of unmarried female poets; rather, he is discussing the dangers of art, while the last two lines refer more to the speaker than anyone else.

Kundera defines humor in literature as

... the divine flash that reveals the world in its moral ambiguity and man in his profound incompetence to judge others; [it is] the intoxicating relativity of human things; the strange pleasure that comes of the certainty that there is no certainty.[15]

Humor accepts no absolute truths. If Paz is correct with dating the rise of modern humor around 1500, perhaps we can link it to the challenges issued to the absolute truths of the Roman Catholic Church by the Renaissance and the Protestant Reformation. Think of the humor in *Don Quixote* that is created by the polar differences between Quixote and Sancho Panza—the ridiculous, though endearing, truths of the one; the harsh pragmatism of the other. But the issues of moral ambiguity and "the intoxicating relativity of human things" return us to the idea that art can have no moral purpose. Kundera defines the novel as "a realm where moral judgment is suspended." He writes:

Suspending moral judgment is not the immorality of the novel; it is its morality. The morality that stands against the ineradicable human habit of judging before, and in the absence of, understanding. From the viewpoint of the novel's wisdom, that fervid readiness to judge is the more detestable stupidity, the most pernicious evil. Not that the novelist utterly denies that moral judgment is legitimate, but that he refuses it a place in the novel. If you like you can accuse Panurge . . . , accuse Emma Bovary . . . —that's your business; the novelist has nothing to do with it.[16]

The novel (and poem) must be free of moral judgment because it must be able to permit access to the moral and intellectual world of the reader. Otherwise the poem or novel can't do its work. Kundera writes, "What is an individual? Wherein does his identity reside?" All novels seek to answer these questions. By what, exactly, is the self defined?

If the realm of the novel or poem isn't free of moral judgment, the reader won't trust the author's answers to those questions. Indeed, the reader won't become a participant in the answering process. And of course the reader judges; the reader always judges. But readers judge differently at different times, and in varying degrees of consequence. Teddy Roosevelt called Tolstoy's novella *The Kreutzer Sonata* the most obscene book he had ever read and had it banned by the U.S. Postal Service.

Charles Baudelaire begins his essay "On the Essence of Laughter" by brooding about the maxim "The Sage laughs not save in fear and trembling."[17] This leads him to think that Jesus Christ and God never laugh, that "the comic vanishes altogether from the point of view of absolute knowledge and power."[18] From there he moves to the position that "it is certain that human laughter is intimately linked with the accident of an ancient Fall, of a debasement both physical and moral . . . in the earthly paradise [where] it seemed to man that all created things were good. . . . As no trouble afflicted him, man's countenance was simple and smooth, and the laughter which now shakes the nations never distorted the features of his face. Laughter and tears cannot make their appearance in the paradise of delights. They are both equally the children of woe."[19] Consequently, "the comic is one of the tokens of the Satanic in man, one of the numerous pips contained in the symbolic apple."[20] He describes how we laugh when someone slips on the ice. "The poor devil has disfigured himself, at the very least; he may even have broken an essential member. Nevertheless the laugh has gone forth, sudden and irrepressible."[21] Such laughter is a boast of superiority. "All the miscreants of melodrama," he writes, "accursed, damned . . . [are] fatally marked with a grin which runs from ear to ear."[22] And he points to the rebel whose laughter is "the perpetual explosion of rage and suffering."[23] He then recapitulates:

> Laughter is satanic: it is thus profoundly human. It is the consequence in man of the idea of his own superiority. And since laughter is essentially human, it is, in fact, essentially contradictory; that is to say that it is at once a token of an infinite grandeur and an infinite misery—the latter in relation to the absolute Being of whom man has an inkling, the former in relation to the beasts.[24]

Laughter is the expression of a double—the clash of a sense of infinite grandeur and the recognition of infinite misery. As such, laughter is always subversive. There is no laughter in a courtroom or a police station, though at times those in power allow themselves a little wry humor just to flex a muscle. Laughter and the comic challenge the status quo, the moral law. They make it ambiguous and open to question, which leads us to reconsider our own body of definitions.

Look at this poem of Bill Knott's: "Performance-Art Piece."

First she slides a banana up my ass
almost but not quite all the way in
then deftly with a knife she slices
the rindtip that extrudes and when

the pithsweet meatus shows its white
cusp like a pearl between the moue
of a romeo in a cameo says Right
Hold it Okay now squeeze real slow

as she squats and eats the ivory
flesh emerging and smearing fused
her red lispberries while the yellow

skin remains within me to be used
as a kind of condom for the dildo
she has to ram in and out artfully.[25]

I dislike this poem; I find it offensive. In other times or places, it would be condemned. If the Victorians could ban poems by Walt Whitman, if the French could ban *Madame Bovary* and six poems from *Les Fleurs du Mal,* if the Russians could ban parts of Chekhov's stories, what would they have done to Mr. Knott?

Still, I keep returning to this poem. It is, for instance, if one can forget the content, a beautifully written sonnet. But mostly I return because I am interested in my response; I'm interested that I wish to tear it up. Because of the poem's confrontational approach, it is hard to see it as a "realm where moral judgment is suspended," while the fact that it is a single sentence and in present tense makes certain that the scene is enacted, not referred to. It takes place in front of us. It makes us voyeurs.

But again there is that element of comic ambiguity, which here is a matter of tone and diction—"pithsweet meatus," etc. Not once do we think it a realistic poem, that it is something the speaker experienced. What does the ambiguity reveal? We realize it is an angry poem. We see that it is not simply satirizing the traditional love sonnet, but it is attacking and casting judgment upon our definitions of poetry, as well as mocking our ideas about propriety and throwing them into relief. I find myself accusing Knott of violating poetic principles and principles of decency. But on early readings I failed to see that my very response might make this a successful poem. It took my whole fabric of belief and moral structure and gave it a shake. And included in the title, "Performance-Art Piece," is a question: Why isn't this art as well? Indeed, there is nothing about its form and execution that would lead us to reject it.

Knott, mostly by choice, has long been an outsider in the world of contemporary poetry. But the originality and oddness of his poems, as well as the outrageousness of quite a few, have also contributed to making him an outsider. His poem, among other things, is an attack on those ideas. Surely, Rabelais has worse obscenities; and perhaps Roosevelt's horror at Tolstoy's novella is no greater than ours is toward Knott. If we don't immediately reject the poem, we can see its very slyness, because by asking "why isn't this art as well?" the poem forces me to look at my definitions. I may still dislike the poem and find it obscene, but surely the questions it makes me ponder are valuable. And it can lead us to those questions that Kundera said all novels and poems seek to answer: "What is an individual? Wherein does his identity reside?"

For the past thirty years or so, much American poetry has been marked by an earnestness that rejects the comic. This has nothing to do with seriousness. The comic can be very serious. The trouble with the earnest is that it seeks to be commended. It seeks to be praised for its intention more than for what it is saying, and as such it is another way of inserting a moral purpose into one's writing. As may be supposed, poetry like this is far more discursive than nondiscursive. Either the nondiscursive has been scraped away, or it was never there in the first place. The poem's agenda, even if hardly conscious, is controlled by the left brain, and it functions outside of the aesthetic demands of the poem.

Much earnest poetry is so-called "I" poetry. The speaker, presumably the author, is writing about how he or she underwent some conflict or trauma, a dysfunctional childhood, bad marriage, unhappy situation: strife. Does the poem suggest it has been overcome? Perhaps. Or does the poet still suffer? Perhaps again. How are we meant to respond to it? Am I meant to commend the poet? This, too, is the sort of poetry that is being satirized by Knott's "Performance-Art Piece." I am recommending not that everybody write comic poems, but that more time go into investigating one's intention, that more thought go into choosing the tone and deciding whether to write in first person or another point of view, and to ask the reasons for the poem's being lyric, narrative, meditational, or whatever.

At the beginning I wrote that art can have no moral purpose but it may have a moral function. The comparison in art between the world of the reader and the world of the poem is a moral function. Baudelaire wrote:

Poetry has no other aim or object but herself; she can have no other. . . . I am not attempting to say that poetry does not ennoble morals—please understand me aright—or that its final result is not to lift man up above the level of vulgar interests; that would be a palpable absurdity. I am simply saying that if a poet pursues a moral aim, he will have weakened his poetic powers and it would not be rash to wager that the result will be a bad work . . . .and when an exquisite poem melts us into tears, those tears are not the proof of an excess of pleasure, but rather evidence of a certain petulant, impatient sorrow—of a nervous postulation—of a nature exiled amid the imperfect. . . . Thus the Poetic Principle lies, strictly and simply, in human aspiration toward a supernal Beauty, and the manifestation of that principle in an enthusiasm of the soul—an enthusiasm entirely independent of Passion, which is the intoxication of the heart, and of Truth which is the grazing ground of reason.[26]

What I like about this statement is it makes me argue with it. Indeed, some of my best conversations are with dead poets. But I, too, believe that we respond as we do to the perfection in art in part because art consoles us about our own imperfections. This can't happen if the poet has a moral agenda.

Traditionally, subject matter is seen as coming from three possible areas: from external sources, such as the gods or the muse; from pure intuition, that is, from deep within the unconscious; or it is made, that is, it is put together by the conscious mind using material from the unconscious. And I suppose there is a fourth method, which would be making the poem by chance methods— shutting your eyes and pointing to words in a newspaper. But let's forget about that fourth method. One writes through one's psychology. What a writer says about the world tells as much or more about the writer as about the world.

John Gardner in *On Moral Fiction* wrote about writing as a way of thinking. "What the writer understands, though the student or critic of literature need not, is that the writer discovers, works out, and tests his ideas in the process of writing. Thus at its best fiction is . . . a way of thinking, a philosophical method."[27] On the next page he added: "Moral fiction communicates meanings discovered by the process of the fiction's creation."[28]

So assume that subject matter comes from one of those three possible areas. The poet often begins with a vagueness in the brain, and then writes to discover why he or she is writing. This is what Gardner was talking about. In such a case, the best a poet can do is to stay out of his or her own way, to seek out and avoid areas of psychological constraint and avoid tampering.

Look at this poem by Ellen Bryant Voigt. It's called "Cow."

end of the day daylight subsiding into the trees lights coming on
in the milking barns as somewhere out in the yard some ants
are tucking in their aphids for the night behind
hydrangea leaves or in their stanchions underground
they have been bred for it the smaller brain

serving the larger brain the cows eat so we will eat we guarantee
digestion is the only work they do heads down tails up

for the maximum yield they won't have sex

they get some grain some salt they get their shots no catamounts

no wolves we fertilize the fields we put up bales of hay

oblivious one breached the fence last week the neighbors

stopped to shoo it back a girl held out a handful of grass

calling the cow as you would a dog no dice

so what if she recoiled to see me burst from the house with an axe

I held it by the blade I tapped with the handle where the steaks come from

like the one I serve my friend he is a water sign that likes to lurk

in the plural solitude of Zen retreat to calm his mind but when it's done

what he needs I think is something truly free of mind

a slab of earth by way of cow by way of fire the surface charred

the juices running pink and red on the white plate.[29]

The comic element in this poem is subtle to the degree that the comic element in Bill Knott's "Performance-Art Piece" is shameless. Like other poems with comic elements there is a sense of ambiguity that enters Voigt's poem, but what heightens the ambiguity is the poem's form, which we see before we begin to read. And what we see is worrisome. Where's the punctuation, where do sentences end, why no capitals, why this lineation? On the other hand, the poem has four stanzas of equal length, which is comforting. It suggests control. Then the title is reassuring: "Cow." After all, as we may tell ourselves, we know quite a lot about cows. Perhaps this allows us to approach the poem with more curiosity than dread. As for the lack of punctuation, W. S. Merwin does that, as did the great European poets Guillaume Apollinaire and Zbigniew Herbert. Punctuation was also rarely used by e. e. cummings, and he rarely used capitals. These are calming realizations.

Writers and readers are comforted by precedent, which is both a comfort and a curse. The comfort part should be obvious. Precedent attempts to imitate the qualities of an old armchair—half the springs are broken, and there's the clinging aroma of good cigars. That's why so many keep sighing over Longfellow (not to insult Longfellow). He's cozy.

The curse is more complicated. First of all, we don't like sudden and unexplained differences. Every substantial change in poetry in the last five hun-

dred years has been met by different degrees of indignation and dismay. John
Donne's contemporary, Ben Jonson, said that Donne should be hanged for the
liberties he took with the metrical accent. Donne wasn't truly celebrated as a
poet until T. S. Eliot wrote about him in the 1920s. Jonson also carped at Shakespeare for making a sham of Aristotle's rules of tragedy.

William Blake's contemporaries considered him mad, and his work was
mostly forgotten after his death in 1827. It was not until his biography was
published in the 1860s that he began to develop a readership; and it was not
until Yeats helped edit Blake's *Collected Works* in the early 1890s that his
work came to be widely known.

Keats was called a simplistic bumbler by reviewers of his day. His work
was branded as overly lush and self-indulgent. It didn't help that he was lower
class in a country as class conscious as England. His father had worked at the
stable of the Swan and Hoop, an inn in London, as an hostler, tending to the
guests' horses; while in his teens the future poet had apprenticed himself as an
apothecary and surgeon—positions just a tad higher than barber. With such a
background Keats could never be considered a gentleman, so how could he be
taken seriously as a poet? But from the beginning there were people convinced
of the greatness of his work, yet it wasn't until the mid-nineteenth century that
Keats's greatness came to be appreciated.

These writers and others, for one reason or another, were seen as violators of precedent, rather than innovators; and they were especially seen as
violators by people of their own generation. It's a difficult choice to be a vio-
lator if the poet wants the poem to be liked and admired. It's safer to follow
established conventions, with a certain individual flare of course. To go the
other way, one perhaps has to be a great egoist like Walt Whitman, or mentally disturbed like Christopher Smart, or perhaps outside of the tradition like
Keats, or a mild rebel, at least initially, like Wordsworth. In no case was their
violation seen as a conscious, artistic choice. Instead it was seen as a flaw in
their nature, a mistake.

When I first approached Voigt's poem, it wasn't with the delight of coming upon something new and unusual. I approached it with suspicion. As a
poem unlike any other, it seemed too peculiar. If poetry weren't only slightly
more popular than a good grasshopper race, people might respond with indignation, as Jonson responded to Donne and Shakespeare. But given poetry's present popularity most would respond with indifference. In any case,

precedent-breaking grew more common during modernism, although almost any dreary oddity could be pointed to as a work of genius. The trouble with so-called experimental poetry was that it was harder to read, which raised people's level of suspicion. But many critics today are adamant that anything that doesn't follow the rules of traditional form creates ephemera, while at the other end of the spectrum many critics are sure that any poem that *does* follow the rules is ephemera. Voigt's poem "Cow," oddly, seems to exist at both ends of that spectrum.

In Voigt's poem our first surprise is the manner of its telling: a block of type with only one capital letter—Z for Zen. However, with patience we can teach ourselves how to read it. We can identify the sentences and phrases even without punctuation; we determine where one starts and another stops. In addition, the first two lines are reassuring in their realism, even lyricism. Still, we may feel we're on iffy footing.

In the third line, we have those ants tucking the aphids in for the night, and then we have the aphids in the stanchions underground. This makes us readjust our relationship to the poem. We have found a comic and unrealistic element. Remember that Paz wrote, "Humor renders ambiguous all that it touches." So, again, there is mild discomfort.

The moment we find a comic element, the tone changes, and a tone we had thought we knew vanishes. The poem still may be serious, but it becomes lighter and trickier and could never be charged with earnestness. Indeed, because of the uncertain tone, we have, as yet, little idea what the poem is doing. Then in the fifth line is a questionable "it," which can mean the aphids are bred to be eaten or they are bred for the smaller brain or perhaps "it" refers to the cows. An advantage of the ambiguity is that it keeps us at a sufficient distance to allow the poem to do its work without our meddling. We read, but, as yet, have no reason to judge.

Then the questionable "it" resolves itself when we realize that as ants feed off aphids, so humans feed off cows, and both are bred for the smaller brain. So the pronoun can apply to both creatures. We may also notice the increasing use of play and surprise—features we began to notice even before we started reading when we saw the poem's peculiar appearance. Again there is a contest between the poet and reader: the reader tries to understand; the poet teases the reader with uncertainty. And in the beginning I feel the contest is one that I am losing.

But the ambiguity is created by more than comic elements. After all, every aspect of the form seems new to us. And not only do we love precedent, but we also love to categorize, and Voigt's poem seems to fit only the most general category: "Short piece of writing in English."

So along with trying to understand the content, we try to make sense of the form, which we should do with any poem. We have to learn how to read the poem, and if we can, we need to approach it without preconceived ideas. We need to set aside our bulwark of opinion, which we might feel is a dangerous undertaking. After all, our opinions exist to reassure us about the world and make it manageable, sort of.

In the second stanza, we find mildly comic elements in each line. Then in stanza 3, the comic elements become part of a comic narrative: last week a cow escaped and caused trouble. "No dice" is a comic bit I particularly like, because of its slangy aspect and how it takes me by surprise. But if I am trying to establish the poem's tone, everything is still up in the air.

However, the last stanza has a reduced comic element apart from the inferred contrast between the busy mind of the friend and the empty mind of the cow. There is still a lightness, but the lines grow increasingly serious as attention shifts from cow to friend. In fact, we see the poem isn't about cows at all, but about comforting a friend after he has finished a difficult task. And he is under a water sign; his emotions struggle with his wish to appear calm, which is presumably why he engages in Zen meditation. Then we have more subtle humor: the speaker tries to soothe the friend with the help of two other signs: earth and fire. This releases the friend from his burden: the juices run pink and red. They, too, are part of the water sign. Whatever had jammed him up has been cut loose. And what about *air*, one might ask. Thoughts come under the air sign, so earth and fire comfort or defeat water and air, I think.

This insertion of the four classical elements may seem a trifle arcane, but even if we understand none of the earth, air, fire, water business, we still see the subject shift from being about a cow to being about a friend and the need to free his mind, to soothe him. Surprisingly, the poem comes to be about friendship.

Yet, as I repeat, the poem isn't just about content, but about form and content together; and, as strange as it may seem, this content couldn't be presented with any other form. Change the form and the content changes with it.

As we dig further, we may notice that the final stanza is written in loose but easily identifiable iambs, especially in the last three lines. Then we see further iambic lines, as in lines 3 and 5 of the first stanza; lines 2, 4, and 5 in stanza 2; lines 2, 3, and 5 of the third stanza. And we see other little bits of iambic here and there to the degree that the whole poem could be called iambic. This, too, is surprising; I didn't see it the first time through, and maybe not even the second and third. After all, I am still trying to figure out how to read the poem, to figure out the tone, and I feel like a child clinging to the hand of a quickly moving adult.

We may also see that the rhythm is partly controlled by the iambs: the more purely iambic lines move much faster than the others, so our pace through the poem constantly changes. For instance, look at the speed of the last two lines of the second stanza and see how it is slowed by the emphasis on "oblivious" that starts the next stanza. In fact, that whole first line is slow.

Other formal or formal-like elements appear in the poem. For example, the rhythm is also affected by line breaks. In the third line, the abrupt break after "behind" gives great emphasis to "hydrangea." This is also true at the end of the first line of the second stanza: the extreme break after "guarantee" emphasizes "digestion." The line break after "neighbors" in the first line of stanza 3 puts great emphasis on "stopped." And there are other enjambed lines, though none so extreme as these. What we may also see is that many of these enjambed lines have comic possibilities. The word "stopped" that follows the line break at "neighbors" has such emphasis that, briefly, the entire poem stops. This is neatly done.

And there is more, such as the loose end rhyme: *on, behind, underground, brain* in stanza 1; *guarantee* and *hay* (very loose) in stanza 2; *grass, dice, axe* in stanza 3; and *luck* and *plate* as well as *done* and *mind* in the last stanza. These end rhymes also have partial rhymes within the body of the poem. I could go on to discuss alliteration, internal off-rhyme, assonance, consonance, and a lot of other stuff, but this seems sufficient. The point is that a poem that at first seemed confusing, subjectless, and lacking an identifiable rhythm changes on closer readings to a clear, rhythmic poem with a coherent subject. Some of our uncertainty about "Cow" comes from the comic elements in the first three stanzas, but all of that is resolved in the last stanza. Nothing in the poem can be anticipated due to its careful interweaving of form and content, while the pacing runs from slow to fast to slow over and over.

I said at the beginning of writing about this poem that it would probably offend both conservative and radical critics. After all, it combines experimental bits and traditional bits, which points out a weakness with categorization. To categorize is to diminish, and who knows where this poem would fit? On the other hand, the poem is hard to ignore. One can't dismiss it as simply sloppy, as critics did with Blake, Keats, Smart, Whitman, and many others. What I like about "Cow" is that the more I dig into it, the more complicated, understandable, and comic it becomes. It's like entering a house that we imagine to be a small house, but as we wander through its hallways, the house gets larger and larger. And I should say the form of this poem isn't an aberration for Voigt. She has written quite a few more that use the same or a similar form.

The poet—any poet—observes the world, inspects it, picks it up, pokes its soft places and hard places, then filters them through his or her sensibility, personality, and intellect, the vast brass tubing of the imagination, the ability to make metaphor and sweet-talk the impediments of language. All this is passed through the filter of self, where it becomes attached to the poet's primary concerns and dominant ideas. At last it emerges onto the page as a symbol, an illusion of virtual life for the reader to experience. Who would have guessed at the beginning of Voigt's poem that its dominant concern would be friendship?

Here is a final poem, "The Poet's Space," by Yannis Ritsos from 1963 and translated by Kimon Friar. It is the first in a series of twelve poems about the Greek poet C. P. Cavafy. Ritsos never knew Cavafy, who lived in Alexandria, Egypt, and died in 1933, but the poem describes the older poet, who was gay, sitting at his desk and greeting "the foolish adolescents" who came to visit.

> The black carved desk, the two silver candlesticks,
> his red pipe. He sits, almost invisible, in his armchair,
> keeping the window always at his back. Behind his glasses,
> enormous and circumspect, he scrutinizes whatever young man he's talking
>   with
> and whom he's bathed in light; while he himself remains hidden behind his
>   words,
> behind history, behind persons of his own creation, distant and
>   invulnerable,
> ensnaring the attention of others with the delicate reflections
> of the sapphire he wears on his finger and, thoroughly prepared,

savors the expressions of the foolish adolescents the moment
they moisten their lips with their tongues admiringly. And he,
cunning, voracious, carnal, the great innocent,
wavers with his whole being between the yes and the no, desire and
    repentance,
like a scale in the hand of God,
while the light from the window behind him
sets on his head a crown of forgiveness and saintliness.
"If poetry cannot absolve us"—he whispers to himself—
"then let's not expect mercy from anywhere."[30]

Ritsos's approach to a scene is always visual, and he describes Cavafy by
his objects (the black desk, the enormous glasses and sapphire ring) and his
actions: he scrutinizes, talks, savors, wavers. Even though Cavafy remains hidden, we see him in all his complexity—"cunning, voracious, carnal, the great
innocent" as he seduces the foolish young men, playing with them, educating
them, savoring their expressions as "they moisten their lips with their tongues
admiringly." Cavafy has both detachment and appetite, but still he wavers
"between the yes and the no, desire and repentance, / like a scale in the hand
of God," while his remark at the end refers to his wish for absolution in this
particular instance and then to the function of art in the greater world. Like
Baudelaire's description of laughter and tears, art had no place in the Garden
of Eden. It arises from our divided nature. Ritsos presents Cavafy as the maker
and the representative—the entire uncensored creature.

I don't believe that poetry can absolve us, and I'm not sure that Ritsos
or Cavafy believed it, either. But it's important that the character within the
poem believes it, a character that Ritsos calls Cavafy and who may in fact resemble Cavafy. But none of that matters. What matters is the presentation of
a divided nature with all the contradictions that that suggests. We see the great
Greek poet as a predator, unjudged and undefended, and the poem remains
beautiful.

Our subject matter and its existence on the page come out of that divided
nature. Is there someone of whom it can be said that he or she has no such flaw?
Of course not. We need not flaunt our flaws on the page, but neither should
they be excluded for reasons of modesty, ego, or political correctness. This can
be difficult to do. Many reasons exist why we might mute or distort our voices

out of psychological constraint, and where those constraints interfere with our work can be difficult to uncover. When one seeks the best word among many to put down in a poem, one must proceed by constantly challenging one's own veracity. How else will I find my path between what might be truth and what might be rationalization? After all, my rationalizations may try to convince me that the psychological constraint is an aesthetic choice. If I accept that—and my rationalizations spring from my most dearly held opinions—then I am allowing the poem to have a moral purpose.

In these three essays on subject matter, I have tried to describe what is required in the mechanics of the poem, poetry's source in the mind, and some pitfalls that will render it negligible. Much of this material will be expanded upon in the essays that follow.

four

aspects of the syllable

Since the first anthologies of English poetry were printed in the sixteenth century, a mild disagreement has persisted as to where the poem exists: in the air as a sound; on the page as a text; or in the reader's or listener's mind, nonexistent until it is perceived. For the purposes of what follows, I would like to define the poem both as a sound and as something fixed to the page, since the third alternative—that it isn't a poem until it is perceived—would seem suggested by the other two.

Literature and music are sequential arts, and we anticipate what is going to happen next by using our experience of the world and our experience of the particular art form. Literature can also create the illusion of time by presenting a narrative and then often using suspense to make us care about the narrative. We become invested in the question of what is going to happen. We anticipate the possible turnings, and the writer uses our anticipation as energy, sometimes rewarding it, sometimes frustrating it.

When confronted with the poem on the page, our anticipation begins before we read a word. The very shape of the poem leads us to make certain assumptions. Does the poem have symmetrical stanzas, asymmetrical stanzas, or no stanzas?; short lines, long lines, both short and long?; and are there unexplained gaps, spaces, and dropped lines? The presence of symmetrical stanzas can create a reassuring sense of control. We feel that nothing can go too wrong with such an imposition of order. Wallace Stevens consistently used a three-line stanza to create the impression of orderliness, in part to give the impression that someone was in charge, on material that used constant surprise and a wide range of diction. Traditionally, a poem without stanzas suggests a narrative, and a stanzaic poem suggests a lyric, though there are many exceptions.

When we hear a poem read, we usually can't tell if it is stichic (one stanza) or stanzaic, while unless the poem is written in a traditional form, it can be difficult to have a sense of the lines if the reader doesn't pause at the line breaks or if there isn't end rhyme. We begin our anticipation with the title, which may offer us a great deal of material, such as James Wright's "In Response to a Rumor that the Oldest Whorehouse in Wheeling, West Virginia, Has Been Condemned," or very little. Bill Knott has many poems called simply "Poem."

Our main tool in anticipating what comes next is the basic order of the English sentence: subject-verb-object. When we hear the subject, we anticipate the verb; when we hear the verb, we anticipate the object. Even if the sentence begins with something else, such as a prepositional phrase, we know that the subject and verb are coming. So if I begin a sentence with the words "The lion," you anticipate what the lion is going to do. If I follow the subject with a verb like "leaps," then tension is created that is based on knowledge. Lions are dangerous. If I said, "The kitten leaps," there would be little or no tension. Likewise, little tension would exist if I said the lion "sleeps" or "eats." But with the verb "leaps" you become more engaged. Now you wait for the object. Will the lion leap "on the red rubber ball" or "on the little girl running through the grass"? If it is the latter, the tension continues to increase. You want to know what happens to the girl. And here is the second tool that we have in anticipating what will happen next, which, very simply, is our sense of cause and effect. What is the effect of a lion leaping on a little girl? Nothing nice, I expect.

Our experience of the world—both direct and indirect experience, like reading or seeing films—has the ability to educate our sense of cause and effect. We are not born with this. A baby is impelled to learn it through discomfort: sensations of hunger or pain lead the baby to do something about it—to cry—and usually someone will come to alleviate the problem.

So, in the written arts, we deal with this information coming to us out of the future with our knowledge of the subject-verb-object order of the English sentence and by our sense of cause and effect. A poet or fiction writer must make his or her audience care about what comes next. What influences that caring is not just the subject matter but also the ordering of the information and the language selected to convey that ordering. And it isn't just the language, but the individual words and the qualities revealed by those words—not only in terms of meaning but also in terms of sound, which in many cases affects our sense of the meaning.

Paul Valéry wrote, "Ordinary spoken language is a practical tool. It is constantly resolving immediate problems. . . . On the other hand, poetic usage is dominated by *personal* conditions, by a conscious, continuous and sustained musical feeling. . . . Here language is no longer a transitive act. On the contrary, *it has its own value.*"[1]

As English speakers, we are blessed in our synonyms. Due to the Norman Conquest of 1066, thousands of Norman and Old French words were added to Old English, with the result that English has more synonyms than other Western languages. Another effect of the Conquest was the gradual loss of English inflections—all those word endings that one must memorize when learning other languages, which govern our sense of the subject, verb, and object by giving us information about gender, number, case, tense, and person. As Old English evolved into Middle English, these inflections began to disappear. Middle English was the language of the conquered people. It was spoken, rather than written down, and the word endings, the inflections, were gradually lopped off. The aristocracy spoke Norman and French, and until the Statute of Pleading in 1362 all court proceedings were written in Latin. After that date they were written in (Middle) English: Chaucer's English. Actually, in England in 1066 four major dialects were in use—Northumbrian and Mercian, which were linked together as Anglian dialects; Kentish, which was spoken in southeastern England; and West Saxon, which was spoken in southwestern and southern England. West Saxon was the dialect of the court of King Alfred in the ninth century, and it was the dialect of London, which was the seat of power. The English that we use today derives mostly from West Saxon, but those who spoke it after 1066 were the underclass, and how it was spoken or spelled or arranged was not determined by any established rules such as those that governed Latin and French.

The effect of the loss of inflections is the unadorned syllable and the result that English has more word endings than other Western languages. Because the presence of inflections means fewer word endings, it is easier to rhyme in languages like French, Spanish, and Italian than in English. This was quickly made apparent to Thomas Wyatt and Henry Howard, the earl of Surrey, early in the sixteenth century when they began to adapt the Petrarchan sonnet form to English use. In the Petrarchan sonnet the rhyme scheme is the same in the first two quatrains, so the author has to come up with eight words to fit two rhymes. In the English sonnet, as it developed, the first two quatrains didn't use the same rhymes, and the poet could use four rhymes with eight words. What is abba-abba in Petrarch became abab-cdcd in the English sonnet. This creates different expectations.

When we hear a poem, it comes to us in a string of mostly uninflected syllables. The third person singular verb adds an -s, the past tenses will add an -ed or -en, and the present participles will add -ing, but this is small potatoes in the vast warehouse of possible word endings.

When we read the first sentence of a poem on the page, rather than hearing it out loud, we have a more accurate idea of what might lie ahead because of the shape of the poem and because we might have noticed certain words farther on, but our basic experience is still syllable by syllable, and we ready ourselves for what is coming with our knowledge of word order and our sense of cause and effect.

If you imagine a stream of sound coming from a person's mouth, then syllables are junctures within that stream. The stream becomes segmented. Our word "word" derives from the proto-Indo-European for breaking off or biting off something. It goes back to the idea that we have a steady stream of preexisting sound, and we bite chunks out of it to make individual words. Well, what do we do with these chunks? We speak. The word "speak" derives from the proto-Indo-European for "strew," "sprinkle," "scatter," which have the same root. We scatter words as we might scatter straw or sparks. To speak, then, is to bite off pieces of sound from a stream of sound and scatter them in front of other people.

Neurolinguists use the word "chunking" to describe what happens when we process syntax. The term was coined by George A. Miller in his 1956 paper "The Magical Number Seven, Plus or Minus Two: Some Limits on Our Capacity for Processing Information," in which Miller wrote that our immediate or short-term memory has a capacity of "seven, plus or minus two, chunks" of information, a number which drops to about five when English monosyllabic words are used. As words come at us, we tend to process them in groups of five syllables, though we can teach ourselves to increase that number.

A syllable can have up to three parts, which, as *The New Princeton Encyclopedia of Poetry and Poetics* will tell you, are "onset," "nucleus" or "peak," and "coda."[2] In a three-part syllable the nucleus or peak is the vowel, and the onset and coda "are consonants or consonant clusters." Obviously a monosyllabic word is one syllable, while a polysyllabic word is made up of syllables which, by themselves, may or may not be words. A three-part syllable can be as different as the words "bit" and "through," "known" or "cat." A two-part syllable will have a consonant and a vowel in either order, such as "an" and "to." A one-part syllable is the single vowel: "a" or "I," for instance.

A syllable may be closed or open. If it ends with a vowel sound, the syllable is open—one can sound it indefinitely—but that vowel sound need not be a vowel, as is the case with the word/syllable "through." "Bit," "peak," and "root" are all closed syllables. We can't keep sounding them. There is also an in-between group of syllables ending in consonants that are neither completely open nor closed. These are syllables ending in labials, nasals, and sibilants. The words "hill," "shown," and "bits" can continue to be sounded even though they end in consonants, though perhaps not for as long as syllables ending in vowel sounds.

Although there are other aspects to syllables and their range of sounds, at the moment I wish to consider the effects created by being open or closed. Here is the poem "The Hill-Shade" by the Dorset poet William Barnes, who lived from 1801 to 1886. The designation "Dorset" is of consequence because his poems were mostly written in the dialect of that region, although this is not one of them.

At such a time, of year and day,
> In ages gone, that steep hill-brow
Cast down an evening shade, that lay
> In shape the same as lies there now:
Though then no shadows wheel'd around
The things that now are on the ground.

The hill's high shape may long outstand
> The house, of slowly-wasting stone;

The house may longer shade the land

    Than man's on-gliding shade is shown;

The man himself may longer stay

Than stands the summer's rick of hay.

The trees that rise, with boughs o'er boughs,

    To me for trees long-fall'n may pass;

And I could take these red hair'd cows

    For those that pull'd my first-known grass;

Our flow'rs seem yet on ground and spray,

But, oh, our people; where are they?[3]

Written in iambic tetrameter, the three six-line stanzas have a rhyme scheme that runs A-B-A-B-C-C. In the second stanza, the rhymes of the first four lines—*outstand, stone, land,* and *shown*—are off-rhymes of the C rhymes in stanza 1—*around* and *ground*—while the C rhymes of stanza 2—*stay* and *hay*—are full rhymes of the A rhymes of stanza 1. In stanza 3, the A rhymes—*boughs* and *cows*—are plural forms of the B rhymes in stanza 1—*brow* and *now*. The B rhymes in stanza 3—*pass* and *grass*—link with the sibilants of the A rhymes and are echoed by seven internal words in the first four lines of stanza 3, some being royal rhymes—*trees, rise, boughs, trees, these, those,* and *first*. Finally, the C rhymes of stanza 3 are the same as the C rhymes of stanza 2 and the A rhymes of stanza 1.

The subject of the poem is simple: things pass away and pass away at different speeds—hills very slowly, houses more quickly, people very quickly, a rick of hay even faster. But in the third stanza, Barnes makes a slight change: these things that pass away faster than human beings have no real specificity; this year's flower or cow is much like last year's. Human beings, on the other hand, are irreplaceable: "But, oh, our people; where are they?"

Barnes uses his open and closed syllables, as well as the rhymes that emphasize them, to create a metaphor for this transience. Within the body of the poem are many full and half rhymes of his end rhymes, while if you compare the first parts of his eighteen lines to the last parts, you see that in the first parts of his lines there are many closed syllables and in the very last parts there are none—as in lines 3 and 4, "Cast down an evening shade, that lay / In shape the same as lies there now." The nasals and sibilants fall into that in-between area and can continue to be sounded. So the syllables in each of the eighteen lines either move from closed to open or stay open all the way through.

The open syllable that receives increasing emphasis is the A rhyme of stanza 1—a long A—which is also used for the C rhymes of stanzas 2 and 3. This is heightened by the O-sound of the B rhymes of stanza 1—*brow* and *now*. That O appears often in the poem, setting us up for the "Oh" in the last line—an outcry of grief. Barnes first uses what is called a short O in phonics; then he mixes short and long O's as he prepares for the dramatic long O in the last line. Of course, how he pronounced these vowels in his Dorset accent is hard to tell, though some sense of it may be found in his dialect poems. In the poem "The Maid of Newton," the word "hay" is written to sound like "high" and "maid" to sound like "mide." In another poem, "Neighbor Playmates," Barnes inserts a W before the O in the words "rope," "more," and "stone" to give a sense of the pronunciation: "rwope," "mwore," and "stwone."

In "The Hill-Shade," Barnes's open syllables come to signify our mortality, our transience. They form the poem's dominant noise. The open syllable that ends the poem becomes a sound without closure. Its long cry still goes on. It is the speaker's articulation of our fate. At the beginning of the poem we have no idea of how Barnes is using open and closed syllables. But when we come to think about what, in the sound, makes the last line so strong, we understand.

Four features influence our sense of the syllable and consequently the word. These are stress, duration, pitch, and timbre. The first three are called the intonational features of sounds, while the fourth, timbre, is a sort of poor cousin often added to the list. Timbre is perhaps a weak label, and a better would be "quality," but "quality" has been used to describe durational stress, so that would be confusing. Timbre concerns the texture of the sound, its coloration, the resonant quality of a sound, whether it is rough or smooth, something in between, or something else altogether.

Three intonational features form the basis for three different metrical systems throughout the world. The Germanic languages use a prosody based on a stress system; the Romance languages use a prosody based on duration, as does Arabic poetry; while two thousand of the world's languages, many of them Asian, use a system based on pitch. As far as I know, there is no prosodic system based on timbre, but one can be imagined.

A syllable by itself is nothing. It lacks stress, duration, pitch, and perhaps timbre. Separately all syllables are equal. But put two syllables together and we see differences in their intonational features. The exception is when the two syllables seem about the same. For instance, two syllables might have the same degree of stress, as with "of the" and "rat pack." At times it takes a third or fourth syllable before we see the contrast, as in "of the rat pack" or "of the rat." When syllables occur in a line of poetry or prose—when they occur in a syllabic environment—then we quickly see that some are stressed and some unstressed. Every sentence—whether in poetry or prose, whether written in traditional verse or free verse—can be scanned and broken into feet. Traditional verse has repeating feet—iambic pentameter is five repeating iambs—while a free verse line may have any number of feet and none of them might repeat. But they can still be scanned. In poetry written in English, whether formal or free, one always deals with the relationship of stressed and unstressed syllables. One can't avoid it; it's built into the language. Indeed, English denotation can depend exactly on stressed and unstressed syllables. Consider, for instance, the examples "conTRACT" and "CONtract" (verb, noun), "minUTE" and "MINute" (adjective, noun). These differences can also be found in the British and North American pronunciation of the same word: BALLet and GARage in the British, ballET and garAGE in the American. In addition, the relationship between stressed and unstressed syllables can have an emotional dynamic—in a stream of syllables, the accented syllables tend to be more affective than unaccented syllables.

Now the idea of meter, even a particular meter, is an abstraction, and to impose the abstraction on the living poem can cause problems. In 1900 the Danish linguist Otto Jespersen argued in favor of what he called "the relative stress principle," that is, the principle that the degree of stress is influenced by a syllable's surroundings. He wrote, "The metrical value of a syllable depends on what comes before and what follows after it."[4] As a result, syllables we might think of as strong will become weak if placed between two stronger syllables, and syllables that are weak will become strong if placed between two weaker syllables. Also, the rhythm of a line might accent syllables that would not ordinarily be accented. Many volumes have been written on this subject, but for our purposes it is enough to paraphrase Jespersen and say that it is the relative stress that counts. His argument is also taken as evidence that there can be no such thing as a pure pyrrhic or pure spondee (the former being a foot of two unstressed syllables, the latter a foot of two stressed syllables). This may in fact be true, but what is important is the poet's intention and not the critic's quibble.

Often a difference may exist between metrical stress and speech stress. Metrical stress is the meter—an iambic pentameter line has ten syllables alternating between unstressed and stressed syllables. Speech stress, on the other hand, is how we might phrase the line in normal speech. The two need not be the same. Clearly they are the same in the first line of Milton's sonnet on his blindness: "When I consider how my light is spent." When we speak the line in a normal voice, it falls easily into iambic pentameter. The same is true of the first line of Philip Larkin's "Aubade"—"I work all day and get half drunk at night."[5] But the first two lines of Donald Justice's sonnet "The Poet at Seven" begin to emphasize the speech stress: "And on the porch across the upturned chair, / The boy would spread a dingy counterpane . . ."[6] You can sound out the iambic pentameter, but it creates a sense of artificiality. This is even truer of Philip Larkin's "The Explosion," the first three lines of which read: "On the day of the explosion / Shadows pointed from the pithead. / In the sun the slagheap slept."[7] Those lines and the rest of the poem are written in trochaic tetrameter, and those first lines are exactly trochaic—ON the DAY of THE ex-PLO-sion—but to read the lines emphasizing the meter creates an artificial, not to say comic, effect.

This indicates that a plain binary opposition of unstressed/stressed, short/long, high/low, and rough/smooth may work in prosodic analysis, but it is a simplification that can lead us to misread a poem. There are more than two degrees of stress. Computerized audio analyses have shown there can be hundreds. But in discussing syllables I want to use the Trager-Smith system I introduced in Chapter 1, which argues for four degrees of stress—primary, secondary, tertiary, and weak—noted 1–2–3–4, with 1 being the primary stress. This system is also an abstraction, and we could instead use three or five or ten degrees of stress, but the Trager-Smith system has worked well for some sixty years, and its four degrees will suit us for now.

As you may imagine, a syllable combination of weak and primary, 4–1, creates a lot of emphasis, though not as much as a spondee, while if the 4–1 pattern is repeated, it creates a casual or comic tone.

Here is a poem of Edward Lear's, "He Lived at Dingle Bank":

He lived at Dingle Bank–he did; -
He lived at Dingle Bank;
And in his garden was one Quail,
Four tulips and a Tank:

And from his window he could see
The ocean and the River Dee.

His house stood on a Cliff,–it did,
Its aspect it was cool;
And many thousand little boys
Resorted to his school,
Where if of progress they could boast
He gave them heaps of buttered toast.

But he grew rabid-wroth, he did,
If they neglected books,
And dragged them to adjacent Cliffs
With beastly Button Hooks,
And there with fatuous glee he threw
Them down into the ocean blue . . .

This uses only 4–1 iambs. In addition, the lines are shorter than the norm of pentameter, being in each stanza tetrameter, trimeter, tetrameter, trimeter, tetrameter, tetrameter. Also, something we will get to soon, the syllables are mostly syllables of short duration. One more point: Lear uses only one word of more than two syllables: *adjacent*. The effect of this is that the poem moves extremely quickly. The one exception is line 3 of stanza 4: "And dragged them to adjacent Cliffs." The long duration of *dragged* causes the sound seemingly to duplicate the subject.

Because of the 4–1 iambs and short-duration syllables, a number of words that are usually unstressed become stressed; for instance, *in* and *was* in line 3, *and* in line 4, *from* and *he* in line 5, and *and* in line 6. These are examples of Jespersen's relative stress principle at work. In addition, because of the meter and the one-syllable words, the speed of the poem shortens normally long-duration words to short-duration words, as in line 17: "And there with fatuous glee he threw." There are three obvious long-duration words in the line—*there*, *glee*, and *threw*. Such an arrangement generally creates comic lines, although there are exceptions.

Compare Lear's poem to the long-duration seventh line in Whitman's "Poets to Come" discussed in Chapter 1: "I am a man who, sauntering along without fully stopping, turns a casual / look upon you and then averts his face." Placing the Whitman line next to Lear's poem makes Whitman's line seem definitely sleepy. Also, Whitman uses all four degrees of stress instead of confining himself to just 1 and 4.

The use of these four gradations of stress is one way a poet can modulate his or her meaning. Looking again at Barnes's "The Hill-Shade," you see the iambic tetrameter of stanza 1 is nearly all 4–1, moving from weak to primary stress. This creates a casual tone. The speaker is making a rather offhand remark. But this 4–1 ratio changes in the next stanza, as the speaker begins to see a deeper meaning. So the first line of the second stanza is perhaps 4–1, 2–1, 2–1, 3–1. And this closer relationship between the stresses continues, although the last two lines of stanza 2 go back to 4–1 again.

But in the last stanza the speaker surprises in himself an even deeper meaning. I say "surprises" because the nature of the formal change makes it seem that a psychological change is taking place in front of us. It creates an illusion of immediacy and spontaneity. The deeper meaning and increased meditative quality of the last stanza is reflected in the stress ratios between the syllables. The third and fourth lines seem to be 4–1, 2–1, 2–1, 2–1 / 4–1, 3–2, 4–1, 3–2, while the last line becomes 3–1, 2–1, 4–1, 3–2. Others might see it a little differently, but the point is that one finds a clear difference in the stress ratios between the first and third stanzas, and this appears to be an incremental change indicative of the poem's growing seriousness. The change is used to modulate meaning.

Another way that stressed and unstressed syllables can modulate meaning is in the use of substitutions, replacing an anticipated foot with another to create a slight surprise. Look at the first two stanzas of Sir Thomas Wyatt's poem "They Flee from Me":

They fle from me that sometyme did me seke
With naked fote stalking in my chambre.
I have sene them gentill tame and meke
That nowe are wyld and do not remembre
That sometyme they put theimself in daunger
To take bred at my hand; and nowe they raunge
Besely seking with a continuell chaunge.

Thancked be fortune, it hath ben othrewise

Twenty tymes better; but ons in speciall

In thyn arraye after a pleasaunt gyse,

When her lose gowne from her shoulders did fall,

And she me caught in her armes long and small;

Therewithal swetely did me kysse,

And softely saide, *dere hert, howe like you this?*

It was no dreme: I lay brode waking.

But all is torned thorough my gentilnes

Into a straunge fashion of forsaking;

And I have leve too goo of her goodenes,

And she also to vse new fangilnes.

But syns that I so kyndely ame serued,

I would fain knowe what she hath deserued.[8]

Written nearly five hundred years ago, the poem uses an English that is still clear to us, although Wyatt's pronunciation would have been more French, with *chamber, danger,* and *remember* stressed on their last syllables, and *special,* meaning one time in particular, given three syllables. A courtier in the court of Henry VIII, Wyatt was imprisoned several times for brawling and sexual misconduct, and was also accused of treason. He died at the age of 39 in 1542. The poem is written in iambic pentameter, and the metrical substitutions are used to heighten the drama. Since Chaucer, who lived some 150 years before Wyatt, the five-foot decasyllabic line had emerged as the line of choice in English verse, though it didn't come to be called iambic pentameter until the end of the sixteenth century.

Wyatt's first substitution appears in line 2 where we find the trochee *stalking* instead of an iamb. This creates a little sonic metaphor enacting the tiptoe movement of the woman's foot: "With naked foot stalking in my chamber," as Wyatt describes the occasional nighttime activities in Henry VIII's palace. In the second stanza Wyatt shifts to a specific woman who enters his chamber dressed only in her nightgown. The substitutions in the last four lines enact this scene. In line 4 we have an iamb, spondee, pyrrhic, trochee and a final iamb: "When her loose gown from her shoulders did fall." In the next line Wyatt rather brilliantly puts the direct object "me" before the verb "caught," so this line too begins with an iamb and a spondee, then a pyrrhic, another spondee, and an iamb: "And she me caught in her arms long and small." The effect of these substitutions is to create sonic metaphors that show the nightgown slowly sliding from the woman's shoulders, and then, as naked as a jaybird, she steps forward to embrace Sir Thomas. Well, if you read the lines as he intended, they can take your breath. The next substitutions are the trochee "sweetly" in line 6 and the spondee "dear heart" in line 7, with a pun on "hart," meaning deer. These substitutions also modulate meaning by using stress-unstressed relationships to give the impression of physical movement.

Although duration as an intonational feature lacks the drama of stress, it is still useful in controlling meaning. Duration isn't affected by the length or brevity of the word so much as it is by the length of the syllables, the hardness or softness of the consonants, and whether the syllables are open or closed. Here is "Girl Help" by Janet Lewis.

Mild and slow and young,
She moves about the room,
And stirs the summer dust
With her wide broom.

In the warm, lofted air,
Soft lips together pressed,
Soft wispy hair,
She stops to rest,

And stops to breathe,
Among the summer hum,
The great white lilacs bloom
Scented with days to come.[9]

This is iambic trimeter and dimeter with a number of substitutions and exceptions. While the meter, rhyme, and open syllables affect the poem's slowness, it is primarily the duration of the syllables that creates a sense of lethargy and near stupor. The poem describes an adolescent girl dreaming of her future while supposedly cleaning the house, and the long-duration O's—*slow, young, move, room, broom, soft, among, bloom, come*—along with all the nasals—

among the summer hum—make the twelve short lines seem very protracted. You will notice the pattern changes somewhat in the second stanza, where there are fewer long-duration O's and nasals, and then Lewis returns to them in the last stanza. The effect is to create a further surprise while making sure we don't become exhausted by the poem's method too soon.

In Janet Lewis's poem we see the comic possibilities of duration, but the opposite effect is created in the last two lines of W. B. Yeats's "The Second Coming":

And what rough beast, its hour come round at last,
Slouches toward Bethlehem to be born?[10]

Written in loose iambic pentameter, the poem's long-duration O's and nasals enact the slouching movement of the beast. In addition, with "slouches" Yeats substitutes a trochee where we expect an iamb, using the same effect that Wyatt used with the word "stalking" centuries before. But Yeats's creature slouches, it doesn't stalk, and so he heightens our sense of the movement with syllables of long duration.

To return again to Barnes's "The Hill-Shade," we see that he uses an increasing number of long-duration syllables per line throughout his eighteen-line poem, ending with "But, oh, our people; where are they?" The words of short duration that predominate in the first stanza like *such, steep, hill, cast,* and *shape* are replaced in the last stanza with *bough, long, cows, known, ground,* and so on, all leading to the outcry "Oh" in the last line. Clearly, the syllables of short duration are not all the same length. "Steep" may be shorter than "shape," but both are considerably shorter than "bough" and "cow." The lengthening duration of the syllables in "The Hill-Shade" reflects the poem's growing seriousness, as well as a certain gloom, another long-duration word.

Pitch is a subtler feature of the syllable. Simply put, we have fifteen degrees of vowel pitch ranging from low *oo* to high *ee*. By pitch I mean frequency. The speed of sound is of course constant; it comes to us in waves. The shorter the waves, then the more waves occur in each second; consequently the higher the frequency, the higher the pitch. The highest pitch—*ee*—has the most sound waves per second. The lowest—*oo*—has the least. The fifteen vowel sounds may also be divided up into bass, tenor, and alto vowels.

Vowel sounds can have psychological effect, as can be seen by the low-pitched words *calm, cool,* and *soothe* as opposed to the high-pitched *scream* and *shriek,* but the effect may be nearly subliminal. Halfway up the scale of vowel pitch is a short U sound: Uh. In his book *Western Wind,* John Frederick Nims refers to this as "the shudder vowel," as in *ugh*—or *mud, blunder, bungle, chump, clumsy, crummy, runt, pus,* and *repugnant.*[11] But these are imprecise areas with many exceptions. For instance, *summer* and *comfort* also use the shudder vowel. And some of our fifteen sounds, like *boy* and *buy,* are diphthongs, where the second vowel lowers the pitch. However, as Nims goes on to say, the fact this is not an exact science doesn't keep it from being a useful tool in our study of poetry.

Consider Keats's "When I Have Fears":

When I have fears that I may cease to be

Before my pen has gleaned my teeming brain,

Before high-piled books, in charact'ry,

Hold like rich garners the full-ripened grain;

When I behold, upon the night's starred face,

Huge cloudy symbols of a high romance,

And think that I may never live to trace

Their shadows, with the magic hand of chance;

And when I feel, fair creature of the hour,

That I shall never look upon thee more,

Never have relish in the faery power

Of unreflecting love!—then on the shore

Of the wide world I stand alone, and think

Till Love and Fame to nothingness do sink.[12]

It is appropriate that Keats chose the Shakespearean sonnet to discuss his ambition, each quatrain with its own subject and beginning with "when," and then a concluding couplet. We also see examples of how he uses duration and stress to control modulation. For instance, the importance of the image in line 6—"Huge cloudy symbols of a high romance"—is indicated by the syllables of long duration, while the anxiety that the image creates in the speaker leads to the 4–1, weak-primary stress ratios in line 7: "And think that I may never live to trace." In any poem all four of these features—stress, duration, pitch, and timbre—will appear, but one may be stronger than others.

In the first line of the sonnet, Keats uses three syllables of the highest pitch: *fears, cease,* and *be,* while the two pronouns "I" are only two levels below them. Indeed, the first quatrain has many high-pitched syllables: *pen, glean, teem, piled,* "tree" in *charact'ry, rich,* and *ripe.* Keats is afraid he will die of the same disease that killed his brother, Tom, before he gets a chance to write the poems he longs to write. His hope of writing these poems is weakened by his despair. It is the latter feeling that comes to dominate the poem, and it is enacted by the slow change from high-frequency to low-frequency syllables.

For in the second quatrain we have none of the high *ee* sounds. He almost entirely abandons the alto range for the tenor range. Although he uses four I's, the dominant pitch is created by tenor A's and O's: *behold, face, cloudy, symbols, romance, trace, shadows, chance.* The anxiety that is indicated in the already mentioned metrical ratios of the seventh line heightens this despair, while in the first line of the third quatrain—"And when I feel, fair creature of the hour"—we see the whole range of pitch enacted from alto to bass. Then it stays low, and the dominating syllables are *look, on, more, power, love,* and *shore.* This pitch-change reflects not only Keats's despair but also his analysis, his very reasoning process, while his concluding couplet presents us with the lowest examples of pitch—"Of the wide world I stand alone, and think / Till Love and Fame to nothingness do sink."—a despair that is also affected by syllables of long duration. The very last word—"sink"—sounds low despite the 'i', because it comes at the end of a low-pitched line. In addition, the final 'k' drags down the higher 'i' as you can see if you compare *thin* and *think, sin* and *sink, win* and *wink.* The short 'i' of *sink* is the fourth vowel sound from the top in terms of frequency; it is the highest tenor vowel. The 'k', however, creates a small diphthong, adding a barely voiced "kuh" sound at the end of the word—the shudder vowel again. But even more the word "sink" reflects what Keats has done. The pitch has sunk from high to low, his hope has sunk, his expectations have sunk, and his life will sink. Keats uses the decreasing vowel pitch as a metaphor for his darkening emotional state.

Looking again at Barnes's "The Hill-Shade," one can see that he too uses vowel pitch to heighten his meaning. In Barnes's case, however, he uses the higher-pitch vowels toward the beginning of the lines and then lowers the pitch so that the end words have the lowest pitch. The first line of the second stanza descends bit by bit, right to the last word: "The hill's high shape may long outstand." The same is true of the last line of the third stanza: "The trees that rise, with boughs o'er boughs." Or many of the lines are low-pitched all the way through, like line 2 of stanza 2: "The house, of slowly-wasting stone," and of course the poem's last line: "But, oh, our people; where are they?" In addition, in keeping with the metrical lightness of the first stanza and its use of syllables of shorter duration, it is also in that stanza with the most high-pitched vowels.

For any of these sound features to work there must be contrast, and this is even truer of timbre. We have perhaps a sound of language in our ear, a sound that is modest and somewhat unassuming. This is the norm. It is the sound of daily discourse. For the most part it is serious, generally good-natured, and courteous. Timbre works best when set against that norm so that at the end of Yeats's "The Second Coming"—"And what rough beast, its hour come round at last, / Slouches toward Bethlehem to be born?"—the word "rough" is effective because its texture or timbre is far "rougher" than the other words in those lines.

In discussing timbre, we are somewhat at a disadvantage because words like *rough, smooth, sweet,* and *tart* are themselves metaphors for the harmonics, vibrations, and formants found in the resonant frequencies of the vocal tract. Yet we know it when we see it, and we can also often feel it. We can feel the vibration of the 'r', the explosive quality of 'b' and 'p', the dental pop of 'd' and 't', the liquid 'l's, the buzz of the nasals and hiss of the sibilants, the slight whistle of the fricatives like *fie* and *thigh*. Any language and especially a Germanic language activates the mouth.

These elements of texture are all to some extent suggestive of emotion. In the sounds themselves we can hear what we might imagine to be anger or melancholy or joy. Consequently one's use of timbre must be consistent with the emotional content of the poem. Indeed, it helps the writer modulate that emotion. Essentially, the sound must be consistent with the sense. But read the first stanza of Robert Lowell's "The Quaker Graveyard in Nantucket":

A brackish reach of shoal off Madaket

The sea was still breaking violently and night

Had steamed into our North Atlantic Fleet,

When the drowned sailor clutched the drag-net. Light

Flashed from his matted head and marble feet,

He grappled at the net

With the coiled, hurdling muscles of his thighs:

The corpse was bloodless, a botch of reds and whites,

Its open, staring eyes

Were lusterless dead lights

Or cabin windows on a stranded hulk

Heavy with sand. We weight the body, close

Its eyes and heave it seaward whence it came

Where the heel-headed dogfish barks its nose

On Ahab's void and forehead; and the name

Is blocked in yellow chalk.

Sailors, who pitch this portent at the sea

Where dreadnaughts shall confess

Its hell-bent deity,

When you are powerless

To sand-bag this Atlantic bulwark, faced

By the earth-shaker, green, unwearied, chaste

In his steel scales: ask for no Orphean lute

To pluck life back. The guns of the steeled fleet

Recoil and then repeat

The hoarse salute.[13]

This is not a voice of daily discourse, and we ask ourselves why. The beginning lines are dominated by a large number of harsh sounds: *brack, reach, Madaket, break, lent, night, Atlantic, Fleet, clutch, net, light, mat, feet, grap,* and *net,* which Lowell keeps up all the way through the stanza and then heightens again in the last three lines—*pluck, back, fleet, repeat, salute.* The harshness of these sounds is also increased by the fact that they are all closed syllables of short duration.

We can describe the sound quality of "ack" in various ways, all of which would be metaphors and examples of synesthesia unless we moved into the area of phonetics and psychoacoustics. But we immediately recognize the harsh quality of "ack," and we see how Lowell is carefully repeating that sound, or sounds similar to it. There is also the associative aspect of the sound, emotionally, psychologically, and intellectually. It is not a peaceful sound; it is violent and disruptive. The question is whether the sound is appropriate to the subject matter. For instance, it wouldn't be useful in a lullaby. You don't sing a baby to sleep at night going "ack-ack-ack." The poem, first published in 1946, is an elegy for Lowell's cousin who died at sea during the war. The timbre of the dominating syllables is meant to reflect, on its simplest level, the writer's anger, grief, and the violence of death, while describing the retrieval and subsequent sea burial of a drowned sailor. Lowell was a conscientious objector during the war (as mentioned in his poem "Memories of West Street and Lepke").

Lowell emphasizes timbre while also making great use of stress, duration, and pitch. He wants extreme contrasts, which reflect the turbulent sea and the emotion of the scene. In the first three pentameter lines, the iambs move from weak to primary stress with such violence that Lowell is forced to insert a useless word "still" in the second line to keep the rhythm from becoming exaggerated. Then at the start of the fourth line he breaks that movement with a pyrrhic and a spondee, while the violent enjambment of "Light / flashed" is meant to enact what it describes. Throughout the stanza Lowell uses a weak to primary stress ratio, breaking it with spondees and violent enjambments so that the meter seems about to fracture. And if you look at pitch, you can see that nearly every line uses both high and low, as in lines 8–10: "The corpse was bloodless, a botch of reds and whites, / Its open, staring eyes / Were luster-less dead lights." He uses duration similarly; that is, to create jarring contrast. In the first two lines we may stumble over "shoal" and "still" because they are of longer duration than the syllables in their immediate environment. Lowell wants to begin the stanza with great speed, which he complicates with a series of tongue-twisting sounds achieved by the harsh quality of the timbre. All of this is in keeping with his intention and his meaning.

The tone coloration of Barnes's "The Hill-Shade" is simpler and governed by low-pitch 'o' and 'a' sounds along with nasals and sibilants. After the jaunty beginning, the poem grows increasingly sonorous, and the pitch descends. Barnes uses few plosive consonants, preferring fricatives and softer sounds. There is none of Lowell's harsh "ack-ack-ack." This affects the tone, creating softness, gloominess, and melancholy, which is in keeping with his intended meaning and how he also uses stress, duration, and pitch.

A final point about Barnes is the meaning of his title, "The Hill-Shade." The word "shade" appears in the first two stanzas in its more conventional meaning: the relative darkness created by the interception of rays of light. But by the end of the poem the meaning evoked is of a ghost. This changes our sense of the title, expanding it to include the two meanings, with the greater emphasis being on the dead. It also answers the question posed by the last line: "But, oh, our people; where are they?" The shades of our people are all around us, whether literally, as spirits, or as memories. So Barnes takes the word/syllable "shade" and accustoms us to one of its meanings, and then surprises us at the end by changing his focus to a more powerful meaning, at which point we see that it existed in his title all along.

The real subject behind an analysis of the sonic features of syllables is modulation. How does a poet modulate his or her meaning? If you read a poem out loud, you use your own voice to modulate meaning. Your voice becomes like the band that gives life to the song lyric. But on the page, one of the ways to modulate meaning is by the sound features inherent in the syllable. Another is by the line break.

These four different sonic features all have different degrees of associative meaning or suggestion. If the poet doesn't pay attention to these features, then his or her poem will modulate meaning regardless, and it may not be the meaning that the poet wants. It has been argued by formalists that if a poet abandons traditional meter, then he or she also abandons the ability to modulate and create nuance. But this is incorrect. Surely it affects that ability, but, as I say, whether in free or traditional verse, one is always dealing with the relationship between stressed and unstressed syllables. With free verse, however, it is harder to modulate meaning, which is why the free verse poet must pay special attention to these other aspects of the syllable, to learn the ways it can be used to manipulate nuance. If not, the poet's expression becomes so generalized that it opens itself up to misreading.

That misreading, unluckily, is where the poem might exist. If, as speculated at the opening of this chapter, a poem isn't a poem until it is perceived, then that perception is left open to a large number of misinterpretations if the poet doesn't control his or her meaning. By learning how to use the intonational features available to the syllable, however, the poet is able to become more confident that his or her intended meaning will be the one perceived by the reader.

five

line breaks

he familiar distinction between poetry and prose is that prose has a justified right-hand margin and poetry has an uneven right margin. This is a
distinction often caused by the frustration of not knowing how to hit upon
anything better. During a period when all poetry was metrical, the uneven
margins were mostly determined by the line's metrical needs, rather than a
printer's customary practice. But with the introduction of nonmetrical poetry
in the mid-nineteenth century, the ragged right margin could no longer be
attributed solely to meter. In Walt Whitman's seven-line "The Cavalry Crossing the Ford," written in 1865, the line length varies between eight syllables
and twenty-three. Yet formal poems at this time also took liberties with line
length consistency. Matthew Arnold's "Dover Beach," published in 1867, is
mostly in iambic pentameter, but nearly half of the poem's thirty-seven lines
are written in dimeter, trimeter, and tetrameter. More importantly, no set order
governs the appearance of the non-pentameter lines. This is also true of other
nineteenth-century formal poets. Emily Dickinson's thirteen-line iambic poem,
"Safe in their Alabaster Chambers," moves between four- and eleven-syllable
lines. Again, no apparent pattern governs the line length. If Whitman's varying line lengths come as a surprise, we also see this type of surprise in formal
poets. Still, the question is often raised: What principles, if any, govern line
breaks, especially in nonmetrical poetry?

The two main reasons to have line breaks are rhythm and meaning. A third reason is the line break's visual effect, although this is slight compared to the other two. The visual effect of line breaks is most obvious in deliberately molded "shape poems," but the appearance of any poem on the page—both in its mass and line by line—will influence the reader in anticipating what lies ahead.

A poem's rhythm is by and large influenced by the fact that English is a stressed language. In a metered line, those stresses are arranged in a repeating pattern, but the alternation of stressed and unstressed syllables is also a major tool in nonmetered poetry. Here, however, the lack of regularity in the reoccurrence of stressed syllables keeps the reader from being able to anticipate when the stresses will appear. But in both metered and nonmetered poetry, the poet always deals with the relation between stressed and unstressed syllables, as well as the other aspects of a syllable that affect the rhythm of a line: duration, pitch, and sound quality.

The effect of the end of the line on meaning and how the line is broken is determined by how we imagine that line ending as an event. With metrical poetry, the line break creates a slight pause. If the line is end-stopped, indicating that it ends with a piece of punctuation or after a syntactic pause, such as before a prepositional phrase, then we hardly notice the line break, unless the poem uses rhyme or has a repeating metrical form and we have been counting stresses.

But if the line is broken where no punctuation or syntactic pause exists— if the line is enjambed—then we have an artificial pause, a brief hiccup in the flow of the sentence. A poem exists on the page as text and in the air as sound, and if we are not mentally evoking that noise, it can hardly be said that we are reading the poem at all. Once we accept the presence of enjambment, we can imagine different degrees of it from a line being lightly enjambed to radically enjambed. So a light enjambment might be a line break after a noun or verb; a stronger enjambment might be between an adjective and a noun or an adverb and a verb; a slightly stronger enjambment might be after a conjunction or pronoun; the most radical enjambment is after an article.

The strength of the enjambment is also influenced by other factors. For instance, does the sentence begin in the body of the line or at the beginning of the line; does it extend over one or more lines, or is it contained within the line? Each possibility will affect the accumulating rhythm and meaning. The

presence of meter and/or rhyme will also affect the strength of the enjamb-
ment, as will the duration, pitch, and sound quality of the syllables in a line.
Still, the most difficult enjambment is after an article, although successful ex-
amples exist. One might be William Blake's unrhymed sonnet "To the Evening
Star," published in 1787, in which the fifth line breaks after the article "the."
He also breaks two lines after "on" and "with."

What makes it difficult for a radical enjambment to be successful? The
reason in most instances is that it is not rhythmically credible. A poem in its
entirety has a governing rhythm, which we discover in the reading process.
Then different parts of the poem can have different rhythms, especially if the
poem has different stanzas. And these differences can be very great. Most
notable is W. H. Auden's "In Memory of W. B. Yeats," in which the first two
stanzas—thirty-one and ten lines—are written in very loose iambics with a
wide range of line lengths, and the third stanza—thirty-six lines—is written in
metrically tight seven-syllable quatrains. Yet Auden's third stanza feels appropriate to its subject. Although it comes as a surprise, the surprise isn't enough
to jar us off the page, to interrupt the reading process. In general, rhythmic
differences between stanzas point to differences in thought and/or emotion on
the part of the speaker. As soon as we recognize this connection, we are able
understand the reason for the rhythmic change. It becomes credible to us.

If something occurs in a single line that seems substantially different from
what has occurred before, there is the danger it will jar us off the page; that is,
we will stop reading to question what is happening. Most often this difference
is caused by an abrupt change in tone, and that change can occur in meaning,
syntax, diction, sound, and/or rhythm. Such a change throws into doubt our
assumptions about the poem. If we can't explain a sudden unprepared shift, it
can affect the poet's credibility. This can happen when breaking the line after
an article. If its surprise isn't quickly incorporated into the whole, it may interrupt the reading process. This is why it is much easier for the writer to get
away with something in the first line or sentence, rather than later, since in the
first line a tonal precedent has not yet been set.

The reader usually assumes that all aspects of sound and content exist
for a specific reason. That reason, as far as the reader is concerned, must fit
within a range of acceptable reasons based in part on reading experience and
in part on the reader's experience of the world. When T. S. Eliot's "The Love
Song of J. Alfred Prufrock" was published in 1915, the simile in the third line

so shocked many people that it made it difficult for them to read the poem: "Let us go then, you and I, / When the evening is spread out against the sky / Like a patient etherized upon a table . . ."[1] The comparison of the evening to a patient sedated on an operating table was sufficiently jarring to make readers turn from the page. As the third line of a 131-line poem, it could hardly be said that it constituted a change in tone, but it violated what many readers felt a poem should be, violated a definition based on their own, perhaps limited, reading experience. Our sense of inappropriateness, whether in form or content, affects us like this, and in many instances it forms an abrupt change in tone or a violation of some aesthetic judgment, but our response may be determined by our own shortcomings rather than the writer's.

Another way to talk about this sudden sense of the inappropriate, both in general and in terms of line breaks, is in terms of the reading process. We read by anticipating what will happen next. If everything we anticipate turns out to be true, we grow bored. If nothing turns out true, we grow frustrated. Consequently, the writer learns to play with our expectations, moving between the possible frustrations of obviousness and excessive obscurity, while still holding out the hope that the poem will ultimately give us the sort of reward our reading experience has taught us to expect.

The poet keeps our interest by using a multitude of surprises in form and content. To say something that the reader hasn't thought of constitutes a surprise, and to say something that the reader knows but in a new way can also be a surprise. Anything unexpected functions as a surprise—an idea, a word, a sound, a line break, and so on. The evening being compared to a patient etherized upon a table is definitely a surprise. But once the surprise has occurred, the reader tries to fit it into the whole. Does the surprise exist to heighten and expand our sense of the entire poem, or is it used for its own sake as a rhetorical device to give false energy to one part of the poem? An enjambed line is always a surprise; an artificial pause has been inserted where none was expected. A mild enjambment creates a mild surprise; a radical enjambment creates a stronger surprise. Right away the reader will try to determine the reason for this surprise, in terms of form and content. If no reason is forthcoming, the poet's credibility is in jeopardy. If it's a very little surprise, very little may be at risk. But if it is a large surprise, like breaking the line after an article, then the surprise is harder to justify and more will be jeopardized.

A poem, as we proceed down the page, moves back and forth between tension and rest. Enjambment creates tension; an end-stopped line creates rest. To establish a pattern and move away from it creates tension; to return to the pattern creates rest. There are many such examples. If the poet gives us one enjambed line after another, the tension will increase with each example until the poet relaxes the tension with an end-stopped line or until the reader turns away from the page. A radically enjambed line ("when I saw an / eagle disappear within a / reddening cloud . . .") can create an emphasis so strong as to be hardly credible. A reader will always ask (or subconsciously wonder), especially with nonmetered poetry, why the line was broken this way and not another. If the reader can't find a reason, either he or she is not looking hard enough or the writer hasn't provided one.

As must be apparent, any discussion of line breaks quickly leads to a wide variety of formal matters, but a few more general points should be made. A poem's sound is not a vehicle for its sense, nor does the sense form a pretext for the sound. One is not less important than the other; the poem is an equal blending of both, and one reads the poem for the experience of both parts together. If one is inflated over the other, the poem will suffer. A poem's sound—that mix of formal devices in both metered and nonmetered poetry—may and should be beautiful by itself, just as the poem's sense will carry meaning by itself, but together they have the potential to create something far larger.

One function of formal devices is to create a sense of nuance. When we speak, we create nuance not just with word choice, but with verbal emphasis, tone of voice, gestures, and facial expressions. A cocked eyebrow can turn a sincere remark into a sarcastic remark. In writing poetry, the poet has only the word itself, and so nuance can suffer. Much can be done with syntax and diction, but they are insufficient by themselves unless one engages in undue narrative detail. When reading work out loud, many poets add emphasis with their reading voice, but someone reading that same poem may easily miss it. And some poets will use italics, bold type, capitals, extra spaces, or accent marks, but, to my mind, each device draws more attention to itself as a device, rather than simply affecting nuance.

Manipulation of stressed and unstressed syllables, rhyme in all its full and partial varieties, consonance, assonance, alliteration, syllable duration, pitch, sound quality, rhythm, line length, and line breaks—all work to create nuance. A poem tries to enact an event, instead of only referring to an event off the page. The event of the poem happens before us and has all the drama of something that needed to be said. In any line the strongest positions, in terms of emphasis, are the first and last words. An enjambed line always gives particular emphasis to the last word of the line and the first word or words of the next line. To a lesser degree this is also true of an end-stopped line, since the conclusion of an end-stopped line most often concludes a thought, while the first word of the next line either qualifies that thought or begins a new thought. To read across line breaks as if they didn't exist is too erase those tools. In addition, the line breaks have these effects whether the writer wants them to or not. Often in the work of beginning poets the content of the poem says one thing and the form of the poem says something very different, because the writer hasn't taken control of the formal elements. As I say, the reader will ask why something has been done this way instead of that. If no answer is forthcoming, it can seem that the poet isn't in control of the medium.

Use of the artificial pause at the end of the line has been obvious since the late sixteenth century. Indeed, one also sees its use in Chaucer in the late 1300s, but it is most obvious when English evolves into the form with which we are most familiar. Some literary periods have used end-stopped and enjambed lines to create nuance and to affect rhythm more than others. The eighteenth century, with its preference for the heroic couplet, used enjambment less often, but with the Romantic period its application grew again as more emphasis was placed on verisimilitude and apparent spontaneity.

Then, with the rise of nonmetrical poetry, some uncertainty appears. All of Whitman's lines, as far as I can tell, are end-stopped. Wallace Stevens, when he read his poetry, never audibly broke the line. Marianne Moore, in her syllabic poetry, broke her lines according to her syllable count and very rarely for emphasis. And certainly other modern poets read across the end of their lines and didn't employ an artificial pause. But all through the twentieth century many, many poets, both those who wrote metrical verse and those who wrote nonmetrical verse, have used the artificial pause to create emphasis and nuance in the ways I have described.

But let's go back to an early example. Although Edmund Spenser, Sir Philip Sidney, Samuel Daniel, and others used the line break to create emphasis, we see it most dramatically in Shakespeare, and probably for no better reason than he was also a dramatist. Each sonnet enacts passionate declarations made directly or indirectly to a lover. Here is Sonnet 64.

When I have seen by Time's fell hand defaced
The rich proud cost of outward buried days,
When sometimes lofty towers I see down-razed,
And brass eternal slave to mortal rage;
When I have seen the hungry ocean gain
Advantage on the kingdom of the shore,
And the firm soil win of the wat'ry main,
Increasing store with loss and loss with store;
When I have seen such interchange of state,
Or state itself confounded to decay,
Ruin hath taught me thus to ruminate,
That Time will come and take my love away.
    This thought is as a death, which cannot choose
    But weep to have that which it fears to lose.[2]

First of all I should make five points. Shakespeare used more metrical substitutions and perhaps other formal devices than his contemporaries. This at times was held against him, and he was seen as violating the rules of poetry and drama handed down by Aristotle and the Romans. Instead, he was labeled, somewhat disparagingly, a "natural" poet, rather than a poet skilled in the formal rights and wrongs of writing. In "Il Allegro" John Milton called him "fancy's child [who warbles in] his native woodnotes wild." The proper poems of the time were the stately poems of Ben Jonson. But in his sonnets and other poetry, Shakespeare knew that a poem can't move at a single speed. If the meter and sound of the words reflect the emotions of the speaker, the poem must change pace. If the speed at which the information is released is always the same, as can sometimes happen in strictly formal poetry, then it is difficult to believe in the sincerity of the speaker. Line breaks and different degrees of enjambment are major ways to affect that pace.

Second, Shakespeare's sonnets are logical structures that seek to prove an argument. His particular sonnet form—three quatrains and a concluding couplet—lends itself to this. In Sonnet 64, we see the structure of his argument in the four "whens," each of which begins a line. Because of our knowledge of English syntax, we know that a "when" usually leads to something that means "in conclusion," which is indeed what happens in the closing couplet. "When/then" and "if/then" are used in many of the 154 sonnets, as are other opening words that conjure the form of an argument—such as how, as, since, so, what, who, and why. The effect is to set up syntactic expectations based on our knowledge of logic. Shakespeare also sets up expectations with his use of rhymes: A-B-A-B, C-D-C-D, E-F-E-F, G-G. When we reach the word "defaced" at the end of the first line, we know a rhyme will occur two lines later. The paradox of rhyme is that, although we have a sense of what the rhyming word must be, it still must be something of a surprise. If we guess the anticipated rhyme correctly—moon/June—we will be disappointed.

The trick of the sonnet—if we can say that poetry has tricks—is how to transcend the constraint of 140 syllables by creating an illusion of space. By using initial words like "what," "if," and so on, Shakespeare increases the danger of claustrophobia. Syntactically at least, we believe we will find no surprises. Like any poet, Shakespeare is working against our expectations. We anticipate what will come knowing he has only 140 syllables with which to work his magic and that he has further reduced his range of possibility with words that establish a logical structure. And we have his rhyme scheme for which there are clear expectations. Shakespeare's trick is like Houdini's: How will he get free of the chains with which he has wrapped himself?

Third, it is difficult to speak of one formal device without mentioning the devices around it; this is especially true of line breaks. A poem is not simply a noise; it is a rhythmic structure. That rhythm, by necessity, connects syllables together, meaning that to look at a syllable or a word by itself, in isolation, creates a distortion. We think we know what an iamb is, but its appearance in a line or several lines can change significantly. How it works is dependent on its aural environment.

Fourth, we have the rhythm of the sentence and the rhythm of the line. These are not necessarily the same. In metered poetry the interaction of the differing rhythms of the sentence and the line has been called counterpoint. Formalists have argued that it does not exist in nonmetered poetry, but once one accepts the presence of an artificial pause at the end of a line in both metered and nonmetered poetry, then we see that counterpoint always exists, even though it may be harder to control in an environment without metrical repetition and consistent line length. Counterpoint, like other formal elements, contributes to the entire formal organization of the poem—the poem as structured sound—as well as highlighting and contributing to the meaning. The sounds of a poem are mostly processed by the right brain, while meaning and a poem's discursive elements are processed by the left. In Sonnet 64, several instances exist where the sound stands in metaphoric relation to the sense. Not only is that aural metaphor processed by the right brain, but also its information corroborates the discursive information. The potential for an equal engagement by the left and right sides of the brain in working out the poem's total experience is what can make poetry so powerful as an art form.

Lastly, as I said in Chapter 4, we can't understand what the poet is doing if we see stressed and unstressed syllables as forming a binary system. To know what is happening, we need to imagine at least four degrees of possible stress, with one being the primary stress and four the weakest. In addition, we will also see the interactions of the other three aspects of the syllable: duration, pitch, and sound quality. The noise of this sonnet—the rhythmic sculpting of a sound of a certain duration—establishes something by itself, something that we call beautiful, but it also works with the content to create a sense of nuance. It works to enact the content.

What is perhaps most noticeable in Shakespeare's first line—"When I have seen by Time's fell hand defaced"—is the metrical substitution in the fourth position, the appearance of the spondee "fell hand." Many argue that spondees don't exist, that it is impossible to have two exactly equal stresses side by side. This hardly matters. What we see is that Shakespeare wanted two stresses of approximate strength next to one another. In fact, we have three stresses because the spondee is preceded by an iamb: "by Time's." Shakespeare also wished to make the stress on "Time" stronger than the following spondee. After all, "Time" is the actor and "fell hand" is the tool. He does that by making "Time" a half or three-quarter rhyme with "when" and "seen," so that "Time" seems louder in our ears. He also increases the word's stress with the capital letter, an obvious visual effect.

Sonnet 64 is about a form of despair, and right away the poet is setting up his emotional apparatus. We may also see it in the second position iamb "have seen." Imagining four degrees of stress, this iamb might be 3–4, while the preceding or first iamb might be 2–4. Now why is he doing this?

Metrical light verse or comic verse often uses a rapid succession of 4–1 iambs or anapests. The first quatrain of a poem by Edward Lear begins:

How pleasant to know Mr. Lear!
Who has written such volumes of stuff!

Some think him ill-tempered and queer,
But a few think him pleasant enough.[3]

And here is a comic quatrain sometimes said to be about death. It is also said to have been recited by John Brown to Dr. John Fell, Dean of Christ Church, Oxford, in the late seventeenth century. Mr. Brown presented it as a nearly instantaneous translation of an epigram by Martial.

I do not love thee Doctor Fell,
The reason is I cannot tell,
But this I know and know full well:
I do not like thee Doctor Fell.

One might imagine the language of contentment and complacent social intercourse to be a succession of mild 3–1 and 3–2 iambs. But we assume that a serious poem, or comic one, was written out of some governing intentionality, and that need will be reflected in the form; hence the use of substitutions, enjambment, the changing speed in the flow of information, all the many devices available to us.

The energetic regularity of the light examples just quoted is opposite to the effect of the first four lines of Sonnet 64, where one finds four spondees, a clash of hard syllables, seven long-duration syllables in the second line—"The rich proud cost of outward buried days"—and the third line, where only two of the five feet are iambs: "When sometimes lofty towers I see down-razed." "Towers," by the way, is read as one syllable.

These are examples of time out of joint. Each of the four lines is end-stopped, although the slight hesitation at the end of the first line and the iamb that begins the second give extra emphasis to "rich proud cost." Starting a sentence or phrase at the head of the line lets the rhythm build up over a greater distance, which in this case helps establish the solemnity and brooding quality of the poem's first twenty syllables. The third line retains the tone of the first two, while changing the rhythm and threatening to abandon iambics altogether. But the fourth line returns us to the meter with five 4–1 iambs: "And brass eternal slave to mortal rage." The line expresses anger, but, unbeknownst to us, Shakespeare is also setting up the fifth line and the first of the poem's two enjambments.

The second quatrain leaves the depredations of "Time's fell hand" to begin a metaphor about the battle between sea and land. The quatrain's first line—"When I have seen the hungry ocean gain"—is metrically similar to the previous line: five 4–1 iambs. Here, however, they mimic the movement of the waves, but they wouldn't have as strong an effect without the previous line, since line 5, instead of starting a new rhythm, maintains a rhythm begun ten syllables earlier. The result is to make the fifth line stronger. We can see some of this effect in the repetition of "when I have seen." I said that in the first line those iambs were 4–2 and 4–3, but the presence of the 4–1 iambic structure of line 4 leads us to read the fifth line similarly, making "When I have seen" 4–1, 4–1. These estimations are inevitably relative, but if one hears a difference between the first two instances of "when I have seen," one tries to discover the nature of Shakespeare's intention.

The fifth line builds its power as we move past the familiar phrase—"when I have seen"—to a new one personifying the ocean—"the hungry ocean gain." Shakespeare again uses the trick he used in the poem's first line: he strengthens a word by rhyming it with two previous words in the line, so that the final word "gain" is strengthened by "when" and "seen."

Then comes the enjambment. Shakespeare inserts an artificial pause between the verb and direct object. The result, combined with the accumulating iambic rhythm of lines 4 and 5, is that the word "advantage" receives terrific emphasis: "Advantage on the kingdom of the shore." Then the rest of the line seems to trail away with two apparent pyrrhic (unstressed) feet: "on the" and "of the." But the line is perfectly iambic, even though two of the stressed syllables—"on" and "of"—carry only slightly more stress than the two unstressed syllables that follow them. Indeed, it seems as if two groups of three unstressed syllables appear in the middle of the line. These reflect the weakened wave, now hardly more than a slosh of water.

Shakespeare in these lines is enacting the scene. The iambic rhythm of line 5, already heightened by the same rhythm in line 4, mimics the rhythm of the approaching waves. Then the closest wave curls and hesitates, a moment mimicked by the intensified "gain" and the pause of the enjambment. Next the wave comes crashing down—that's the heavy stress placed on the first word of the next line—"advantage"—especially on the second syllable "vant," where the letter 'n' is repeated after appearing five times in line 5. The foam scuttling up to the shore is enacted in the line's apparent pyrrhic feet. The scene of the approaching wave that breaks and hurries weakly onto the shingle is perfectly enacted by the meter, sound quality, and, especially, the enjambment.

The second quatrain enacts a battle. The ocean attacks the shore, and in the third line with the beginning pyrrhic, pyrrhic, spondee, and trochee—"And the firm soil win of the wat'ry main"—the shore fights back so the line's last five syllables—"of the wat'ry main"—echo the rhythm in line 2, but now, instead of referring to the beaten shore, they refer to the defeated waves. But as the last line of the quatrain suggests, all that is gained in the battle is exhaustion. The shore rejects and takes from the ocean; the waves return and take from the shore.

The third quatrain keeps up the pattern and repeats the beginning of the first two quatrains: "when I have seen." All is in a constant state of flux, decay, and destruction, which reminds the speaker that Time's fell hand will also take his love away. This leads to the poem's second enjambed line, which ends the first line of the concluding couplet: "This thought is as a death, which cannot choose . . ." Although this is a perfect iambic line, the metrical stress in each of the five feet is different with the only 4–1 iamb—"a death"—being in the third position. Here Shakespeare sets up the enjambment differently. After the line's strongest iamb occurs the poem's only caesura—the comma between "death" and "which." The effect is to insert a longer pause, a hesitation that is repeated in the enjambment by the larger hesitation between "cannot choose" and "But weep."

What is the consequence of this rumination? The speaker weeps, weeps at the very paradox that to have some cherished, transient something, in this case his lover, means also having the fear—indeed, the knowledge—that he will eventually lose him. In this couplet, Shakespeare also needs something to set against "death," an event more powerful than mere tears. The emphasis that the enjambment places on "but weep" raises its emotional value. The hesitation of the enjambment italicizes the words that follow. The stronger the emotion, the stronger must be its setting, its aural environment. That setting need not be created by enjambment; we can see how Shakespeare also created it with meter and sound quality; but the breaking wave in line 5 would not be enacted if "advantage" were placed in the middle of the line, nor, perhaps, would we believe in the tears if "but weep" appeared in the middle of a line. This would make "but weep" appear offhand and insincere.

But the enjambment in line 13 has another purpose, which is the double meaning of "choose": "This thought is as a death, which cannot choose." The first meaning states we have no choice over death—it will take us no matter what—and there may be the suggestion that death itself has no choice, that it is the tool of some greater power. But after the enjambment, with the words "to weep," our minds correct themselves, and we proceed to the end. Yet that correction doesn't erase the first meaning; rather, we carry it with us as a secondary meaning. Again, if one were to rebreak the line to read "but cannot choose but weep to have," the double meaning would be lost, as would the emphasis on "but weep."

An effect of nonmetered poetry is that it makes it more difficult to control nuance. In metered poetry, an unemphasized iambic pentameter line can be used as the norm in such a way that any substitution creates emphasis and thus nuance. Of course, the effect of a stressed syllable is still available in nonmetered poetry, but not usually in a repeating pattern. But ordinary speech, unless it has a large number of Latinate words, still has a fairly even division between stressed and unstressed syllables. This is the norm. The practitioner of nonmetered poetry can use this norm to create nuance just as metered poetry can create nuance.

Many poets who use meter and many critics who favor meter believe that without the regulation of meter no enjambment is possible, that one reads across the enjambment without the slightest hesitation. Thousands of examples show this is not the case. There is still the visual experience of the line break and the act of readjusting one's eyes to the beginning of the next line, which produces a slight pause. Although this pause is brief, it is enough to modify rhythm and counterpoint, while elements of stress, pitch, duration, and sound quality can be used to make it stronger. This seems so obvious as to be beyond the necessity of argument.

Indeed, because nonmetered poetry can lack the range of emotional effects found in metered poetry, it makes the enjambed line with its artificial pause even more important, and, aside from rhythm, it functions much like an artificial pause in conversation; that is, to create emphasis and nuance. Historically, one sees the artificial pause becoming more focused as an issue in the late 1950s. Once Robert Lowell, John Berryman, and others of that generation changed from writing metered poetry to nonmetered poetry, then the poets of the next generation, who were in their twenties and thirties and whose early poetry had been metered, began to reexamine the effect of line breaks. Many like James Wright, Sylvia Plath, Alan Dugan, Donald Justice, Galway Kinnell, W. S. Merwin, and Adrienne Rich in their new nonmetered poetry continued to use the line break as a definite pause; others didn't. A literary generation spans about fifteen years, and most poets of the next generation also used the line break as a pause. Mary Oliver's line breaks were influenced by James Wright's.

Unfortunately, many poets of the following generation—the fourth after Lowell—who write nonmetered poetry no longer seem to have the example of metered verse within the ear, with the result that many of their lines appear flaccid and lack any apparent reason why a line is broken this way rather than that. Their lines often read like prose. But a line break is always a formal choice, and the result of a formal choice appearing gratuitous is an immediate loss of authorial credibility.

James Wright published two books of metered poetry: *The Green Wall* in 1957 and *Saint Judas* in 1959. Then he published his first book of nonmetered poetry, *The Branch Will Not Break,* in 1963. This was followed by six others, although about a dozen metered poems are scattered through these later books. He died of cancer at the age of 53 in 1980.

Many reasons exist for Wright's change from metered to unmetered verse: the example of friends like Robert Bly and Theodore Roethke, his translations of Pablo Neruda and Cesar Vallejo, and the example of Lowell and Berryman. That time in Wright's life is best described by Donald Hall's essay "Lament for a Maker," which serves as the introduction to Wright's complete poems, *Above the River.* Hall describes Wright as having the best ear of any poet of his generation and the ability to remember thousands of lines of poetry.

Although Wright used enjambed lines in the nonmetered poetry of *The Branch Will Not Break,* he didn't use them with the confidence that he developed later, and it is in subsequent books that the best examples of enjambed lines are to be found. Along with his line breaks, Wright was a genius of using phrasing to speed and slow the poem to create emphasis and surprise. Here is "Rip" from *Shall We Gather at the River:*

It can't be the passing of time that casts
That white shadow across the waters
Just off shore.
I shiver a little, with the evening.

I turn down the steep path to find
What's left of the river gold.
I whistle a dog lazily, and lazily
A bird whistles me.
Close by a big river, I am alive in my own country,
I am home again.
Yes; I lived here, and here, and my name
That I carved young, with a girl's, is healed over, now,
And lies sleeping beneath the inward sky
Of a tree's skin, close to the quick.
It's best to keep still.
But:
There goes that bird that whistled me down here
To the river a moment ago.
Who is he? A little white barn owl from Hudson's Bay,
Flown out of his range here, and lost?
Oh, let him be home here, and, if he wants to,
He can be the body that casts
That white shadow across the waters
Just off shore.[4]

Wright was born in Martins Ferry, Ohio, a mill and mining town on the Ohio River. He left home when he joined the army as a teenager, and the setting of the poem refers to a return visit. The poem's twenty-four lines range from one syllable to fifteen syllables, and that changing length goes far to vary pacing, rhythm, and emphasis. Working in conjunction with this varying line length is the syntax of the poem's eleven sentences. These have little syntactic similarity except for sentences two through four, each of which begins with the pronoun "I."

Although nonmetered, the poem is informed by Wright's work with meter, and he constantly manipulates the relationship between stressed and unstressed syllables. The first line, a ten-syllable line, has an iamb, two anapests, and an iamb; the second line, a nine-syllable line, has a spondee, trochee, and two iambs, the second iamb having a feminine ending. Then he throws off any possibility of consistent meter with a three-syllable line, which can be read as three stresses. But with these lines he has established his use of stressed and unstressed syllables so in line 5—"I turn down the steep path to find"—we hear the two double stresses "turn down" and "steep path" enacting within the line the speaker's physical movement. From this point on we can see Wright using stressed syllables and unstressed-stressed ratios to create nuance.

The enjambments of the first and second lines work to emphasize the meaning of the words beginning the next lines, so that both "that" and "just" are particularized, as are the two final words: "casts" and "waters." Wright also establishes his variation of short and long phrases to affect rhythm. Line 1 is one long phrase, lines 2 through 4 use five short phrases of equal length, and line 5 repeats the long phrasing of line 1 to the extent that it also ends with an enjambed verb, "find," while the enjambment in line 5 emphasizes the river and that last moment of sunset. The long first sentence with two enjambments also builds tension, which is at last relaxed with the short one-line sentence of line 4.

The language of the poem is simple and unadorned. The tone is nostalgic and even somber with the one active moment being the exclamation "Oh" in the last sentence. One of Wright's great strengths, which was influenced by his friendship with Theodore Roethke and John Logan, was a willingness to tread the edge of the sentimental. His use of "Oh" is indicative of this: the strong interjection introducing affective content. This was another influence on Mary Oliver, who often uses "oh" in a similar manner.

If one rewrote the poem as a prose paragraph, the language would be flat and uninteresting. The line breaks with their enjambment, and the rhythm they help to create, keep that from happening. The enjambment in line 7—"I whistle a dog lazily, and lazily"—strongly emphasizes the bird that begins the next line and which introduces the poem's dominant symbol.

The rest of the lines, except one, are mildly enjambed at best, although the enjambments within the two long sentences—the first beginning with "Yes" and the second with "Oh"—go far in controlling the rhythm as well as directing our attention. In addition, the mild enjambment of line 11—"Yes; I lived here, and here, and my name . . ." helps to create tension by further delaying the verb "is" that occurs after two short modifying phrases in line 12: "That I carved young, with a girl's, is healed over, now." And, of course, the enjambment also emphasizes "name."

That enjambment, with the three caesuras in line 12, redirects the rhythm and expands the meaning of the sentence. In fact, one can say that four-line sentence has ten caesuras and reflects the speaker's emotional tension that he must relax with the one-line sentence that follows: "It's best to keep still." An effect of this long, hesitating sentence is that the word "name"—the final word of line 11—adds to its denotative meaning a range of connotative meanings. It no longer means simply "James Wright" but also a whole complicated history with which he has to come to terms and which he hopes to put to rest. This gives a double meaning to line 15—"It's best to keep still"—which we realize also means: It is best not to wake it; it is best to let it rest in peace.

The last significant enjambment is in the third line from the bottom—"He can be the body that casts"—which repeats the movement of the poem's first line. It also repeats the first line's function of setting up a group of short phrases, so, rhythmically, the poem ends as it began. But by breaking the twenty-second line at the word "casts," Wright, an avid fisherman, can enlarge the meaning of "casting a shadow" to include "cast" in terms of throw or hurl, as well as casting a line in hope of getting something back, which is self-knowledge, which ultimately is the poem. We may also see a suggested meaning "to cast a statue," which he can use in the sense of "to fix in memory."

None of the formal devices call attention to themselves. Wright makes a poem that seems realistic and offhand to give a sense of verisimilitude and spontaneity. Yet his intention is to set up the symbol of the barn owl and its apparent white shadow. Is it the ghost of who he was, the ghost of his name? Wright leads us to think about this, and such a reading informs the title, so that we see "Rip" as meaning "requiescat in pace" or "rest in peace." We also realize that the "it" beginning the poem refers to the shadow of the barn owl. The speaker responds to the sight of the shadow by shivering. Ostensibly, he shivers because of the onset of evening chill, but our reading experience tells us it is more complicated than that. The speaker is shivering in the presence of the mystery. Then, like Dante at the beginning of the *Inferno*, he turns down the steep hill to seek out who he has become. The descent even includes Wright's version of Cerberus: "I whistle a dog lazily . . ."

Wright's poem is as complicated, formally, as Shakespeare's and uses as many formal devices. But we may not realize that until we sound it out and begin to ask why he has done what he has done. One of the first elements that demands our question of why is the enjambment in line 1, which emphasizes the white shadow and which opens the door to the poem's mystery. Rebreak the line any other way and that power is lost.

Another master of the line break is the fine contemporary poet Thomas Lux. He is able to control the rhythm of the sentence and set it against the rhythm of the line to the point that it results in a kind of syncopation. He is also such a master of surprise that it is practically impossible to anticipate where a sentence is going, much less the poem itself. Although Lux primarily writes in free verse, the poem "A Little Tooth" is rhymed in iambic tetrameter, which isn't at first apparent due to the interaction between the sentence and enjambed line.

> Your baby grows a tooth, then two,
> and four, and five, then she wants some meat
> directly from the bone. It's all
>
> over: she'll learn some words, she'll fall
> in love with cretins, dolts, a sweet
> talker on his way to jail. And you,
>
> your wife, get old, flyblown, and rue
> nothing. You did, you loved, your feet
> are sore. It's dusk. Your daughter's tall.[5]

Either each line break occurs at the end of the syntactic phrase and then surprises us with a continuation, as is the case with lines 1, 2, 4, and 7, or the continuation is far from what we might have guessed, as with lines 3, 5 and 8. The six sentences range in length from two words to twenty-two. The most radical enjambment is in line 3, which is heightened by the stanza break, but the enjambments in lines 4, 5, and 7 are competitive. In the first stanza the iambs are nearly all 4–1; in the second stanza most iambs are still 4–1 except in lines 4 and perhaps line 6, while in the third stanza the iambs soften to 4–2's and 3–1's. The poem begins slowly with a string of long-duration syllables in the first line. The second line uses several long-duration syllables at the start, but then the rest of the poem seems to increase in speed to the very end. The speed is also affected by the use of shortening sentences and a shorter distance between the caesuras.

Of his rhyming words three are open—*two, you,* and *rue*—three are closed—*meat, sweet, feet*—and the labials are somewhere in between—*all, fall,*

tall. This mix of long and short, open and closed syllables, along with the tetrameter and enjambments also add to the sense of speed. And that, in part, is
what the poem is about: your life is over before you know it, a fact suggested by
the words "It's dusk." The couple has reached the evening of their lives.

Lux likes noisy poems. The individual words employ a wide range of
sounds that are emphasized by the trochaic substitutions in lines 4, 6, and 8.
The poem seems a perfect example of form joined to content to create something far larger than either could be separately.

Another contemporary poet who skillfully uses line breaks to create nuance and affect rhythm is Louise Glück. Indeed, with many of her poems one
can read the line breaks before reading the whole poem and learn much about
the poem's emotional import. In her essays she has written about the influence of George Oppen and C. P. Cavafy on her work, fostering a simplicity
of speech that at times borders on minimalism. This has many virtues, but a
major one is that any word or turn of phrase that even slightly departs from
the norm takes our attention. Read "Gift" from *Descending Figure,* published
in 1980.

Lord, You may not recognize me
speaking for someone else.
I have a son. He is
so little, so ignorant.
He likes to stand
at the screen door, calling
oggie, oggie, entering
language, and sometimes
a dog will stop and come up
the walk, perhaps
accidentally. May he believe
this is not an accident?
At the screen
welcoming each beast
in love's name, Your Emissary.[6]

The poem has six sentences in fifteen lines. The first three have a total of
nineteen words and are balanced against the last two sentences, which also

have nineteen words. Both nineteen-word groups directly address the Lord, while separating them is a twenty-six-word sentence that gives the poem's brief narrative. An effect of the simplicity of diction is to draw attention to the polysyllabic words—*recognize, ignorant, language, accidentally, accident, welcoming,* and *Emissary*—and, as we read, we realize these are the poem's most important words and help to direct us to Glück's intention.

Working against the simplicity of diction are the line breaks. Eleven of the poem's fifteen lines are enjambed, and each enjambment expands the poem's information. In fact, eight of the enjambments carry double meanings as they refer to the words that precede them in one way and to the words that follow them in another. For instance, we read the first line by itself—"Lord, You may not recognize me"—as an expression of modesty, suggesting the speaker is so small and inconsequential that the Lord may have overlooked her. The second line—"speaking for someone else"—corrects this misapprehension. We realize that the speaker in fact spends a lot of time speaking to the Lord, but, somewhat selfishly, only about herself; and this is perhaps the first time, ever, she has spoken to the Lord about someone else. But the enjambment and second line don't erase the first meaning; rather, it carries it along as a secondary reading, and we continue to see the speaker as modest. In terms of form and content, every good poem teaches us how to read it, and this is our first lesson.

The third line again uses this doubling device, though to a lesser degree. The perceived reading is "I have a son. He exists." Then, after the enjambment, we are given the modifiers—"so little, so ignorant." The hesitation of the enjambment and the resulting emphasis on line 4 is made even greater by the fact that line 3 is iambic trimeter with three 4–1 iambs. Rhythmically, we don't expect a hesitation. The first short sentence of two iambic feet—"I have a son"—sets an example which we think will be repeated with "he is," but instead we have the enjambment that emphasizes the following line with great stress on "so." And from this we see that "so little, so ignorant" is the very reason the Lord is being addressed: the son is not simply small; he is fragile, delicate, and beloved. Technically, one could have a semicolon, rather than two separate sentences, but this would weaken the emphasis. And if Glück had said "I have a small and ignorant son" or "I have a son who is small and ignorant," the effect of the enjambment would be destroyed.

The rhythm created by Glück's enjambments and end-stopped lines separates the poem from prose. They also make it possible to suggest a tentativeness and modesty in the speaker's address to the Lord, the uncertainty of speaking for someone else and the humility that comes from speaking to so vast a figure. The enjambments also create a nuance that doesn't exist if we remove them, and they direct us to her intended meaning, especially in the long, middle sentence where we find the poem's two most important enjambments. The first separates lines 7 and 8—"*oggie, oggie,* entering / language, and sometimes." By emphasizing "language," the poet first surprises us with her sense of priority and then directs us to what will form a major part of the subject. The child is not simply learning about language but about the *power* of language, which, for any poet, is of paramount interest. And just as the crucial enjambment of line 3 was strengthened by iambic trimeter and the pause before the initial iamb of line 4, a similar device is used here. Line 7 is trochaic trimeter—two trochees and a dactyl—heightening the emphasis on "language," another dactyl.

The second important enjambment, perhaps two enjambments, occur within the long sentence between lines 10 and 12: "the walk, perhaps / accidentally. May he believe / this is not an accident?" The hesitation between the words "perhaps" and "accidentally" opens up all sorts of new information; it is here we realize the speaker is talking about the power of language by suggesting the dog's appearance is not accidental; that the speaker herself does not wish to see the visiting animal as accidental, but as purposeful and indicative of the Lord's concern and even, for the speaker, of the Lord's existence. In addition, line 11's line break, which puts emphasis on "this," expresses the hope that the child will come to believe not only in the power of language, but also in the Lord. And what is the nature of this Lord? We see that in the final enjambment in line 14 and in the last line: "welcoming each beast / in love's name, Your Emissary." The Lord is equated with love, and the parent's hope is for the child to become an emissary of that love; that is, to love language, to love the world.

As in James Wright's poem, and unlike Shakespeare's sonnet, these formal devices are not immediately apparent. In fact, some would say they are not "formal" at all. Yet taken together, they constitute much of what separates poetry from prose. In "Gift" the nature of the syllables, the relationship between stressed and unstressed syllables, and the nature of the line breaks create a rhythmic whole that presents an experience we find valuable by itself, but which also presents information to complement and expand the basic information of the words. Rewrite Glück's poem with end-stopped lines and it would read as prose, while if the same were done to Lux's poem, it would still read as a poem, though a much weaker one.

With all four poems we gain access to this information only by asking why the poem is doing one thing rather than another. These questions lead us to the poets' intention, and that awareness leads us back into the poem's form, with the result that what happens is a sort of conversation between the reader and the writer. In such a way, the reader experiences, though to a lesser degree, what the writer had experienced and what led the writer to write the poem. In such a way, the reader becomes a participant in the creative process. To ignore or not to make use of the enjambment's artificial hesitation is to make this participation, this very power of language and communication, less possible.

context and causality

the poem in its finished state, as it appears on the page, presents to the reader the effects of a series of causes in both form and content. In terms of the content, those causes, which lie outside the poem, make up the context of the poem. Yet even the form, in that it reflects the content in terms of sound and rhythm, also constitutes the effects of a series of causes.

The word "context" from the Latin means the weaving together of different elements. The word "textile" has the same root. In poetry what is being woven together are thoughts, ideas, memories, emotions, and sense data, as well as those elements of sound and rhythm that make up the form. For the purposes of our discussion, we may call them all concepts—images, sounds, and emotions, all of them—because they must be intellectualized in order to be put into language. They are there not by accident, but because we decided to use them.

So the reader is presented with a series of effects on the page and a series of causes off the page, and by inferring the nature of those causes the reader comes to an understanding of the context, and from understanding that context the reader can infer the poet's intention—that is, the reason or reasons why the poet wrote the poem. Sometimes this is very simple; sometimes it is difficult; sometimes it is impossible, because not even the poet will know all the reasons that led him or her to write.

Again, for the purposes of our discussion we may say there are two distinct contexts. There is the foundational context, which joins the original generating ideas, and there is the immediate context, which joins the immediate causes leading to the effects that form the poem. An illustration of this is the elegy. Here is the first stanza of John Berryman's "Dream Song 18: A Strut for Roethke":

Westward, hit a low note, for a roarer lost
across the Sound but north from Bremerton,
hit a way down note.
And never cadenza again of flowers, or cost.
Him who could really do that cleared his throat
& staggered on.[1]

Theodore Roethke died on August 1, 1963, at the age of 55. He taught at the University of Washington and died of a heart attack in a friend's swimming pool on Bainbridge Island in Puget Sound. Roethke's father and uncle owned a large greenhouse in Saginaw, Michigan, and Roethke grew up around that greenhouse. In "Dream Song 18," the foundational context is Berryman's decision to write the elegy, which is itself the effect of a cause: a specific death. But the immediate context is the body of information being referred to in this first stanza. Westward, the Sound, and Bremerton refer to where Roethke died. The "cadenza" of flowers is a nod to Roethke's youth and to the many nature references in his poems, but, more exactly, "cadenza" is a musical solo played near the end of a classical work, which, again, may be taken as a reference to Roethke's death.

"Hit a low note" suggests a New Orleans jazz funeral, and "Him who could really do that" refers to Roethke's own great ability as a musician/poet, while "roarer" joins the music, the poetry with the manic boisterous energy for which Roethke was well known. That ability and personality form the cause of which "roarer" is the effect. To understand a poem we must ask questions of it. To ask "why 'roarer'?" leads us to infer something about Roethke. Indeed, we ask a question at nearly every point—why "Westward," why "low note," why "Sound," etc.?—and either from the poem or from educated guesses we deduce the correct answers and arrive at an understanding of the immediate context, which leads us to infer the foundational context:

Roethke's death and Berryman's decision to write an elegy. As for the poet's intention, it may include this foundational context, but the intention is mostly driven by emotion, which here, obviously, is Berryman's grief, admiration, and affection for a friend and fellow poet.

If we knew nothing about Theodore Roethke, we would still understand this is an elegy for a friend, but we wouldn't understand some of the references in the first stanza—"Westward," Bremerton, and the rest. We wouldn't know the causes of these effects, because they depend on extraliterary sources. How much a poem should depend on extraliterary information is a constant source of argument. In this particular poem, however, the extraliterary information may increase our understanding, but isn't necessary for a basic grasp of the context.

Yet if we understand a poem by asking questions of it, we only have a certain toleration for being unable to find those answers, a certain toleration for obscurity. This is different for everyone, and it depends on various factors: experience, patience, education, even good health. In the revision process, the poet needs to take these matters into consideration, since the reader's frustration means that for this particular reader the poem has failed.

Every poem written exemplifies a causal relationship. We are presented with a number of effects, and we have to infer the causes in order to conclude the nature of the immediate context, which then may lead us to the foundational context and the poet's intention. The immediate context is made up of everything that affected the poet's choices in the writing of the poem. These are ideas and emotions, but it can also be affected by whether the poet got a good night's sleep. Clearly, we won't be able to establish everything that is part of the immediate context, but neither is everything—such as a good night's sleep—particularly important.

If the reader can't get past the effects to the causes, then there is no way that he or she can fully understand the poem. This may be the reader's fault, the poet's, or both. The poet, at some point in the revision process, has to become cognizant of that chain of causality open at each point of the poem and decide what to do about it; that is, to decide how clear he or she wants to make it.

In an elegy, the chain of causality is usually obvious. In other poems, it may be less so. Here are the first four lines of Yeats's sonnet "Leda and the Swan":

A sudden blow: the great wings beating still
Above the staggering girl, her thighs caressed
By the dark webs, her nape caught in his bill,
He holds her helpless breast upon his breast.[2]

The poem begins in the middle of an event. Were it not for the title, we would have little idea of the immediate context: a girl has just been jumped on by a large bird. One could write a poem about Big Bird on Sesame Street going berserk and begin it with Yeats's first stanza. But Yeats doesn't want us to ponder the nature of the context; he wants us to move forward to consider the future effects of this event, its ramifications, which we can't do if we are mentally fussing about Big Bird and Miss Piggy. So he grounds us with a title to let us know immediately what is going on. We know, from sources outside the poem, just who owns those wings: Zeus has taken the form of a swan.

Any poem has a conflict that may be no more than the poet trying to see clearly or express something precisely, or it may be as violent as Leda's rape and all the violence it sets in motion. It is by thinking about the conflict that the reader enters into and imagines the world of the poem, and sets in motion an investigation that makes the poem both affective and meaningful. In order to engage the reader, this conflict will require some thought, since it is by asking questions that one enters the poem and the poem avoids being simply anecdotal. But inexperienced writers can confuse the conflict and the context. It may be useful for the conflict to have some degree of obscurity, but it is not useful that the context be obscure. In Yeats's poem, what would be gained by wondering who is doing what to whom? It is nearly impossible to work out the conflict unless we have a sense of the context largely because that context gives us the chain of causality. By having a sense of or being able to deduce what led up to the conflict, we are better able to understand its ramifications, better able to see those effects become causes themselves.

We are always caught up in the fluidity of time. The events of the specific moment in which I write are the effects in a causal chain that goes back to the Big Bang and perhaps before. And these events, which now slip past, become causes that influence or determine a whole range of imminent effects, which, the moment they are realized, themselves become causes. Every sentence reflects that drama: the subject leads us to anticipate the predicate, which leads us to the direct object and so on.

The poem, as we often hear, seeks to freeze a moment or a series of moments of time. A chain of events has led up to it and a chain of events or
outcomes can be inferred from what occurs in the body of the poem. And,
as we often hear, the poet begins to write when something happens to move
him or her to such a degree that he or she is unable to remain silent and so
the poet, to paraphrase Philip Larkin, creates a small machine out of words
which sets off this same emotion in another human being, anytime or any-
place. This causal event may be an actual event—for instance, a death. It may
be a remembered event. It may be an idea or an abstraction. It may be entirely
or partly invented. And, as Larkin says, it is the *emotion,* not the event, that
is important, so the event that the poet uses to present the emotion may not in
fact be the actual causal event. Often an inexperienced writer may think it is
the event that is important, but that is not the case. The poem is not a memoir.
The event is only a vehicle for the emotion, and a completely imaginary event
may do as well or better.

Yeats doesn't write "Leda and the Swan" from an interest in bird-girl relations. He forms an argument that the effects of the rape—through the birth of
Helen of Troy, the Trojan War and its consequences—were made violent by
the violence of the initiating event. This is also part of his belief in the cycles of
mankind; the two thousand years of violence, which began with Leda and the
swan, was replaced by an opposite two-thousand-year cycle brought about by
the birth of Jesus. To Yeats's mind the violence in and around World War I was
proof of the start of another violent cycle—"And what rough beast, its hour
come round at last, slouches to Bethlehem to be born?"[3] The seed, or one of
them, that began the poem (and this is rank speculation) might have been the
death in the war of the son of his friend Lady Gregory. But even if this wasn't a
seed, it was probably some personal experience like this. So some event out of
the violence of the times found its release in the poem "Leda and the Swan."
It is unimportant to the poem to know what prompted it, except insofar as
the event moved Yeats to do something about it. What we care about is the
word "moved," because it is the emotion, rather than the initiating event, that
infuses the poem.

Now one might call that unknown event the poem's foundational context:
some violent event occurred that moved Yeats to place it within his philosophical system of repeating cycles, which led him to dwell upon the previous violent cycle that began with Leda and the swan. But there is rarely one

single event; rather, we often find a combination of events, a mixture of physical, emotional, and psychological concerns. The poem was published in 1928 when Yeats was 63. During these years, and up to his death in 1939, Yeats had had a number of affairs. According to his biographer R. F. Foster, Yeats saw his sexual life as energizing his creative life, and consequently he was very concerned about his potency, or lack of it. In 1934, while having an affair with Margot Ruddock, a twenty-seven-year-old actress, singer, and poet, Yeats underwent a Steinach sexual rejuvenation operation performed by Dr. Norman Haire, the Harley Street sexologist. This was no more than a unilateral vasectomy, but several years later Yeats told friends that the operation had been a great success.[4] Yeats didn't write "Leda and the Swan" because he envied Zeus's sexual power, but his concern about sexual potency was one of the factors that led to the writing of the poem; it was one of the causes of which the poem is the effect. There is no need to know this to appreciate the poem. What is important is the strength of emotion that derived from this and other sources. The poem takes its life from that emotion, but the source or sources of that emotion are irrelevant.

All poems begin with personal events, but the poem needn't be about what happened. Myths, biblical tales, events out of history—we know hundreds of examples where such stories are used as metaphors to serve as a vehicle for an emotion about which the poet was unable to remain silent. Here is a sonnet titled "Leda" by Rilke. The translation is my own.

> When the god in his great need passed inside,
> he was shocked almost to find the swan so beautiful;
> he slid within it all confused.
> But his deception bore him to the deed
>
> before he could put that untried creature's
> feelings to the test. And the opened woman
> saw at once who was coming in the swan
> and knew he had but a single purpose,
>
> which she, confused in her refusal,
> was no longer able to deny. The god came down
> and pushing aside her weakening hand
>
> . . .

loosened himself into the one he loved.

Then only—with what delight!—he felt his feathers

and grew truly swan within her womb.[5]

Rilke's poem could hardly be more different than Yeats's, but it is the same story, and the immediate context is established by the title. Yet for Rilke what became important was what the god learned from the event. Leda is more an afterthought than a victim. And there are two rapes: the penetration of the swan by Zeus and the penetration of Leda by the swan. And as Zeus is shocked and confused to find the swan beautiful, so Leda is shocked and confused by what she finds the swan to be. Then, in the last half of the sestet, Zeus's sense of displacement within the swan and Leda's sense of displacement with Zeus are resolved, and Zeus, through his delight, grows "truly swan within her womb." His god/swan sperm fertilizes her egg, and after a suitable period of time, she hatches two eggs from which emerge four children—Helen and Clytemnestra in one, Castor and Pollux in the other—all of whom have divine attributes. Leda was the granddaughter of Ares, the god of war, one reason that the rape led to the Trojan War.

Was this a story that excited Rilke? No, the emotion already existed and he needed a vehicle. "Leda" was the third poem in *New Poems: The Other Part*, published in 1908. A previous book, titled simply *New Poems*, had appeared in 1907. Both books charted his attempts to find a new way of writing. Instead of waiting for inspiration to strike, he would begin to write about a subject, and the inspiration would appear after he had begun. He had learned this way of working from the great sculptor Rodin, for whom he was employed as secretary, because Rodin often worked in clay before he knew what he wanted to make and then, once he was engaged, inspiration would strike and the subject would reveal itself. (*New Poems: The Other Part* is dedicated to Rodin.) I discuss this in an essay on Rilke in *Best Words, Best Order*; Rilke writes about the process in letters from this time, and in one he states that subject matter is always pretext, meaning that when writing about Leda he is not writing about Leda.

The first poem of the 1908 book is "The Archaic Torso of Apollo." It and the next five poems, which are drawn from myth and biblical tales, work symbolically to define for Rilke the creative process and how and when the poem comes into being. For instance, in the fifth poem, "The Island of the Sirens,"

Odysseus is fretting about how to tell King Alcinous and his court about his meeting with the sirens so they will see what he saw, feel what he felt. Should he raise his voice and frighten them and use clever turns of phrase? But then he understands his mistake, and instead he chooses the method of the sirens themselves: to sing the song that rises barely above the silence. And this, for Rilke at this time in his writing career, meant choosing tone and syntax over the noise of rhetorical effects. As subject matter this is hardly riveting, but the emotion that his discovery gave rise to was an emotion Rilke could use. What it needed was a vehicle, and he chose that moment when Odysseus is telling the king and his court the story of his travels.

Initiating impulses drawn from different aspects of writing and making art might seem trivial to someone who isn't a poet and even to many who are, which is why in a letter Rilke describes any poem's motivating impulse as a "personal insanity" that the reader need know nothing about. In "Leda" one can interpret the swan as the poet's muse or his poet-self or an impulse to write without yet knowing the subject—"he slid within it all confused"—and then the violation of Leda symbolizes the act of writing, of putting words on paper, and in that very act of writing the poem appears: "Then only—with what delight!—he felt his feathers / and grew truly swan within her womb."

One can take this further. About ten years before this time Rilke's lover, Lou Andreas Solomon, convinced him that if he was serious about being a poet he had to change all the shoddy and sloppy aspects of his personality. Among other things, she made him change his handwriting, and so he studied penmanship and calligraphy, using different writing instruments, even quills. You see where I am going with this. The swan is the pen and Leda is the paper; the poet violates the blank sheet of paper with black marks. It hardly matters if Rilke consciously meant this or not, though I think it's a strong possibility. What Rilke found was that he could access his strongest emotions, even if they derived from seemingly trivial causes, and then place those emotions in metaphors to serve as their vehicles.

So to return to context, the foundational context is, in part, Rilke's discovery of a metaphor to serve as a vehicle for a specific emotion that he has experienced. The immediate context is the story of Leda and the swan. How do we understand "great need" in the first line? Within this immediate context, we understand it as referring to burning sexual desire. And the words "passed inside"? They refer to Zeus entering into the swan, but they also foreshadow the swan's penetration of Leda. In each instance, we ask what or why, and our knowledge of the context provides us with an answer. If we did not know the story, we would be mightily confused.

As for the foundational context, we would have no idea of it unless we read Rilke's letters and studied his other poems. And we don't need to know the background to appreciate this particular poem; rather, we trust Rilke as a poet; we trust the validity of the emotion; we understand, if we think about it, that the whole business symbolizes an affective aspect of Rilke's life, something that forms the foundational context and supplies the necessary emotion to write.

Another chain of causality should be considered. We understand the first line as the effect of a cause, but why is it the first line? Why does the poem begin here rather than someplace else? What if Rilke's poem began "And the opened woman / saw at once who was coming in the swan / and knew he had but a single purpose"? It would be the same story, but a different poem, one in which Leda rather than Zeus is the focus. Or what if it began: "The god came down / and pushing aside her weakening hand / loosened himself into the one he loved"? Then the focus is on the narrative, the very melodrama of the situation, with little room for the god's sudden sense of self-awareness and self-discovery.

In asking why Rilke begins the poem where he does, we seek out causality of motive. It is that question that leads to the poet's intention, while the first line is the effect of that motive. Gradually, our increasing knowledge gives us a broader sense of context. "The god in his great need passed inside"—we stop reading the line denotatively and begin looking for larger meanings. And as we ask why he puts the first line first, so we ask about the second and third and so on, because by questioning the poem's structure, we are discovering its strategy, which again can lead us back to the context and the poet's intention.

This is something we must also do as writers—to ask ourselves why we put this first and that second and so on, because, as I said, we are often writing to discover why we are writing. A simple revision tool is arbitrarily to begin our poem at another spot to see how it affects the whole. Such an action does wonders to help to clarify our purpose.

The Imagist poet H.D., Hilda Doolittle, also wrote a poem titled "Leda," which appeared in her 1921 book *Hymen*:

Where the slow river
meets the tide,
a red swan lifts red wings
and darker beak,
and underneath the purple down
of his soft breast
uncurls his coral feet.

Through the deep purple
of the dying heat
of sun and mist
the level ray of sun-beam
has caressed
the lily with dark breast
and flecked with richer gold
its golden crest.

Where the slow lifting
of the tide,
floats into the river
and slowly drifts
among the reeds
and lifts the yellow flags,
he floats
where tide and river meet.

Ah kingly kiss—
no more regret
nor old deep memories
to mar the bliss;
where the low sledge is thick,
the day-lily
outspreads and rests
beneath the soft fluttering
of red swan wings

and the warm quivering
of the red swan's breast.[6]

Here the violence has disappeared. Zeus is no longer a predator. The colors and mass of long-duration syllables create a languorous opulence that is the very opposite of Yeats, while the actual rape—because we know there must be a rape—is reduced to a single word: "fluttering." As for Leda, she seems to have been transformed into a day lily. The story has been stripped of its drama, and if it weren't for the title, we would be hard pressed to know what the scene described.

What is the tone? Are we meant to take "Ah kingly kiss" at face value? I would say so. At least it is in keeping with the other poems in *Hymen*, most of which are named after women and goddesses in Greek mythology. "Kingly" is defined by the immediate context, which is established by the title, and must refer to Zeus. But who has been spared additional regret and old deep memories? It must be Leda, for whom it is important that nothing "mar the bliss," but this doesn't sound like the teenage Leda encountered in myth. Indeed, if there is congress with anything, it would seem to be with the day lily that "outspreads and rests / beneath the soft fluttering," though I expect that H.D. meant water lily, because a day lily is another plant altogether. Another linguistic confusion is the line "where the low sledge is thick." What is sledge? I went through half a dozen dictionaries and the word had two basic meanings, which you can already guess: a heavy hammer usually wielded with two hands, and a sled, or sleigh. The only meaning connected to a river is an obsolete term: a water sledge driver, which is an apparatus designed to pound wooden pilings into the muck along a shoreline or riverbank. Yet it is hard to imagine that the phrase "the low sledge is thick" refers to such an apparatus. So I decided, not with a high degree of certainty, that she wanted a word to suggest *sludge*, mud, ooze. If we see it as mud, then it implies psychological information about Leda's past, or rather the Leda of H.D.'s imagination, which also links with "no more regret / nor old deep memories." But if the words "regret," "old deep memories," "bliss," "low sledge," and even "day-lily" are so many effects, which they must be, then they point to a series of causes I can only guess about.

H.D. had an active and complicated sex life. She was engaged twice to Ezra Pound before the age of 20. For thirty years she lived with the English novelist

Bryher (Annie Winifred Ellerman), while married for part of that time to the poet Richard Aldington; and during those years Bryher married and divorced two of H.D.'s lovers. H.D. dedicated *Hymen* to Bryher and her own two-year-old daughter Perdita, whom she had not by her husband, but by the Scottish composer and music critic Cecil Gray. H.D. had many affairs and often wrote about the attractions and difficulties that accompanied intense heterosexual and lesbian desire. One might guess that the lines about regret and "old deep memories / to mar the bliss" refer to such a lifestyle, but such an assumption is a possibility, not a probability. In fact, the lines refer to unspecified causes outside the immediate context, and by remaining inaccessible they remain rooted in the private. One might say that the causes behind the effects in Rilke's "Leda" are also rooted in the private, but all the material in Rilke's poem can be explained by information on the page, rather than requiring information off the page. This is also true of Yeats's poem, but it is not true of H.D.'s poem. The "regret" and the rest of it are symptoms of an unknown condition. I should add that H.D. began reading Freud in 1909, became a patient of his in Vienna in 1933, and later wrote a tribute to Freud. I say this because if one guesses that "low sledge" has a Freudian interpretation, it most likely does.

I said at the beginning that a poem presents us with a series of effects not only in its content, but also in its form. The hard consonants, spondees, short-duration syllables, the high-pitched vowels in Yeats's first line—these formal elements and others are the effects of Yeats's controlling idea that violence begets violence. Not only are they sounds, they are concepts. In H.D.'s "Leda" the long-duration vowels, the slow rhythm, the preponderance of low-pitched vowels and soft consonants are also concepts that refer back to her controlling idea, which is less apparent because her stated desire not "to mar the bliss" lacks a clear immediate context. But in both cases (we can say nothing about the vowels and consonants in Rilke's poem because it is a translation) the sounds and rhythms have been intellectualized. They have been chosen to give specific information about the immediate and foundational contexts.

But I would like to compare H.D.'s poem to an untitled poem by Anna Akhmatova dated 1911, written when she was 21 or 22. It was translated by Lyn Coffin.

Memories of the sun fade as my heart grows numb—
The grass is yellower, too.

The wind toys with what snowflakes have already come—
So few, so few.

In narrow canals, there's already nothing that flows—
Water stands still.
Nothing happens here, nothing grows—
It never will!

Against the sky, the willow lifts its skeletal life,
Its see-through shawl.
Maybe it's better that I'm not your wife,
After all.

Memories of the sun fade as my heart grows numb.
What's this? Darkness in town?
Maybe! And during the night, winter may come—
And settle down.

                                                              —1911[7]

Two extraliterary pieces of information, which you probably know if you know her work, are that the town in question is St. Petersburg, Russia, a city of many canals often referred to as the "Venice of the North"; and that it has a near-arctic climate, with snow cover at least six months of the year, below-zero temperatures from November through March, and, at its darkest, less than five hours of daylight.

As with H.D.'s poem, we assume that the quality of the natural detail has been determined by the speaker's emotional state. In H.D.'s case it is languorous, sensual, opiated. In Akhmatova's case—we can't discuss the formal aspects of the translation—the details and tone suggest winter dread. In H.D.'s poem, we are given little cause to explain the language. Yes, we have the context of Leda and the swan, but the approach is the opposite of Yeats's approach and very different from Rilke's. Yet we don't know why.

Akhmatova, however, inserts one vital sentence in the third stanza: "Maybe it's better that I'm not your wife, / After all." Those words become the filter through which we see the entire poem. As emphasis, she twice gives us the line that establishes the tone, the second time being after the phrase

"I'm not your wife": "Memories of the sun fade as my heart grows numb."
With the second reading, we see the line differently. It becomes the effect of
an emotional cause, rather than of a physical cause, which leads us to see that
all the details can be read as effects of emotional causes, so the last three lines
suggest a yearning for death, even suicide. This gives the poem two very different but complementary readings.

We don't need to know more about the people than is established in one
sentence: "Maybe it's better that I'm not your wife, / After all." That and
our experience of the world are sufficient. We don't know everything, but we
know enough. It is the cause of which the rest of the poem is the effect. As it is,
we read that one sentence in a variety of ways. They have just gotten divorced,
or they can't get married because one or both are already married, or she
wants to be his wife but she knows it would never work so she is trying to talk
herself out of it, or maybe she thinks what she is saying is completely false,
or maybe he has rejected her, or she has rejected him. The effect is to make us
think about the sentence more deeply, to let it become an object of contemplation, to have us move back and forth between the sentence and the rest of the
poem; to create, as it were, a dialogue between them. This would happen to
a lesser degree if the sentence were rephrased to contain only one meaning,
and as a result, the poem would affect us less. The very ambiguity forces us to
spend more time with the poem, to draw from it a variety of nuance.

What would happen if we removed the sentence? Then we would have
only gloom and no context. Since we know that all perception is affected
by the psychological state of the perceiver, we would guess that the gloom
indicated the speaker's inner condition, but it would be a symptom only. We
would have no cause. Worse, the gloom would be presented as a given, as if it
were part of the speaker's natural condition, as if she were born with gloom.
But even if that were the case, what could the reader do with it? How could
the reader respond when he or she could neither identify nor imagine? We
could do little more than say, "Cheer up."

This tells us something vital about the role of the reader, and, by implica-
tion, the duties of the poet. Does one want the reader to be a witness or a participant? The witness can appreciate many aspects of the poem: form, craft,
intelligence, and wit. But, ultimately, he or she won't care, and consequently,
he or she won't remember. This is the price of inaccessibility. The poem becomes ephemera. To be a participant, the reader must come to understand the

nature of the conflict, the context, and the chain of causality. If the poem is a symbol of affective life, that symbol needs to be more than perceived. It needs to become an object of contemplation; the reader needs to see, or imagine, his or her own life within it. We, as readers, are always in search of our own stories. Achilles sulking in his tent, King Lear rejecting his favorite daughter—the context allows us to see our lives in those situations and so imagine and understand, to empathize with the suffering of the protagonists. And if we don't have the context, we have nothing.

seven

a sense of space

One of the most important elements in a poem is a sense of space: a poem must give the impression that it is larger than its actual size would suggest. Through the use of metaphor, connotative meanings, and a variety of formal elements, a good sonnet gives a sense of space within fourteen lines and 140 syllables. It seems unconstrained by the apparent limits of its size. Similarly, one of the effects of the line break is that by emphasizing the first and last words of the line, as well as by using the pause offered by enjambment, the break widens the possibilities of a sentence. Again, there is a sense of space.

Varieties of syntax are another way of creating a sense of space. We read by anticipating what will come next; as mentioned earlier, when we hear the subject, we expect the predicate, and so on. Any variation can create tension by making the reader uncertain of the sentence's direction. A simple example is to put a word or phrase between the subject and predicate: "George, being of sound mind and body, as well as being given to a regimen of daily exercise impossible for other men of ninety-five, *did* such-and-such." As the modifying phrases continue, the tension builds while we try to imagine what sort of main verb might possibly follow.

Most, if not all, elements of form contribute to this sense of space, but the ideal result is to create a poem or story that seems more than the sum of its parts. What I want to focus on here are sentences, using examples from two writers: the first paragraph of Henry James's story "The Middle Years," published in *Scribner's Magazine* in 1893 when James was 50, and William Butler Yeats's poem "Her Praise," which he wrote in 1915, also at the age of 50. Henry James is helpful because he uses many syntactic effects that are also used in poems. He is expansive and slow, while poems tend to be compact and move much faster. This helps us see these effects more clearly. I'll first give the entire paragraph and then speak of individual sentences.

The April day was soft and bright, and poor Dencombe, happy in the conceit of reasserted strength, stood in the garden of the hotel, comparing, with a deliberation in which, however, there was still something of languor, the attractions of easy strolls. He liked the feeling of the south, so far as you could have it in the north, he liked the sandy cliffs and the clustered pines, he liked even the colourless sea. 'Bournemouth as a health-resort' had sounded like a mere advertisement, but now he was reconciled to the prosaic. The sociable country postman, passing through the garden, had just given him a small parcel, which he took out with him, leaving the hotel to the right and creeping to a convenient bench that he knew of, a safe recess in the cliff. It looked to the south, to the tinted walls of the Island, and was protected behind by the sloping shoulder of the down. He was tired enough when he reached it, and for a moment he was disappointed; he was better, of course, but better, after all, than what? He should never again, as at one or two great moments of the past, be better than himself. The infinite of life had gone, and what was left of the dose was a small glass engraved like a thermometer by the apothecary. He sat and stared at the sea, which appeared all surface and twinkle, far shallower than the spirit of man. It was the abyss of human illusion that was the real, the tideless deep. He held his packet, which had come by book-post, unopened on his knee, liking, in the lapse of so many joys (his illness had made him feel his age), to know that it was there, but taking for granted there could be no complete renewal of the pleasure, dear to young experience, of seeing one's self 'just out'. Dencombe, who had a reputation, had come out too often and knew too well in advance how he should look.[1]

Here is the first sentence: "The April day was soft and bright, and poor Dencombe, happy in the conceit of reasserted strength, stood in the garden of the hotel, comparing, with a deliberation in which, however, there was still something of languor, the attractions of easy strolls."

The sentence's complexity is found in many of James's third-person sentences, especially in his later writing. It can be a pleasure or an aggravation, but it gave him great control over the pacing, and it allowed a keenness of nuance rare outside of poetry. The first paragraph of "The Middle Years" has twelve sentences, thirty-seven commas, and one semicolon. James used these commas to call attention to important words, used them in fact as line breaks are often used in poetry. They work mostly to modulate emphasis, but they also work rhythmically, because rhythm, too, was important to James.

James's complex-compound sentence begins with an independent clause; the tone is straightforward and somewhat optimistic—"The April day was soft and bright." Rhythmically, we notice the clause is four iambs, which contributes to its lightness. The second independent clause also begins with an iamb—"and poor"—but then the tone changes and the rhythm is overthrown. The second independent clause has seven commas, which ensures no consistent rhythm can be established. This rhythmic disruption, as it were, arises directly from the word "poor."

Dencombe is "poor" because of his health, but also because he is deceived; that is, he is "happy in the conceit of reasserted strength." The word "conceit" gives a lot of information. It may refer to vanity, to imagery, to illusion, to deception, to an extended metaphor or trope, and more. James's phrasing opens the word to a range of connotative meanings—Dencombe is not simply "conceited"—and we continue reading in part to determine the specific meaning.

Although we don't know it yet, "The Middle Years" is about illusion and self-deception. James's rhythmic shift in the second independent clause anticipates this. All is not well with Dencombe.

The modifying phrase between the subject, Dencombe, and the verb, "stood," the following dependent clauses and string of prepositional phrases create tension by delaying verbs and direct objects, but they also in their progression and rhythm imitate the languor of Dencombe's thought, a languor that gives evidence of his ill health. All of this delay and deliberation leads to a slightly humorous direct object: Dencombe is imagining "the attractions of easy strolls."

So far we know little about Dencombe, who seemingly has been ill, but he is observed with some complexity. He feels confident about his strength, though, as he stands in the garden comparing possible strolls, he has a niggling fear that even an easy stroll might be too much. As with a classic Latinate sentence, James's second independent clause accumulates meaning until it reaches its most important words: "easy strolls." This, after all, is the object of Dencombe's thought, while the "soft and bright" April day provides the occasion. James's sentence keeps us from being able to anticipate its direction and controls the speed at which we read it, while the word "poor" provides us with suspense enough to care about that direction.

James could have begun with any type of sentence, but he began with the most complicated. There are four types classified by structure: a Simple Sentence, which contains one independent clause and no dependent clauses; a Compound Sentence, which contains more than one independent clause joined by linking words and/or punctuation, but with no dependent clause; a Complex Sentence, with at least one independent and dependent clause; and a Complex-Compound Sentence, which contains two or more independent clauses and at least one dependent clause.

All offer possible difficulties, and a simple sentence with a single action and at minimum two pieces of information can be the weakest. Each sentence is a container that must have a subject and predicate, but if each container has only two pieces of information—People cheered. The boy sang.—then the ratio of information to apparatus is very low, while the amassing of sentences each with only two pieces of information can be stultifying. The mind readjusts itself for each new container. This is why we talk to small children in simple sentences: it makes it easy for them to process the information. But to write anything complicated in simple sentences may lead to frustration. The reader's expectations are rushing ahead, and the information comes in a drizzle.

The simple sentence has many uses, but it is a sentence's ability to utilize complex forms that facilitates complex thought. On the other hand, the very brevity of a simple sentence can make padding and unnecessary information apparent to the writer. This may not be so obvious in more complicated sentences. I would like to discuss this a moment before returning to James.

There are two general types of padding and unnecessary information: rhetorical and contextual. In the first, one or more words are used primarily or only as emphasis. In the second, the added information is redundant or inappropriate. And you can imagine how certain examples could be both at the same time.

A common form of rhetorical padding is the use of intensifiers, which tend to be adverbs functioning as submodifiers to create emphasis where no emphasis is needed. These include words such as *still, even, some, yet, very, just, clearly, only, finally, quite, somewhat, rather, fairly,* and so on. They are rarely necessary and are especially damaging in a poem when, in rereading, they appear as chaff. I use them all the time, and then, slowly, I take most of them out. Often they reflect the insecurity of a writer who worries that he or she hasn't gotten the point across and so has added rhetorical emphasis. But if more is needed, it will take more than an intensifier to communicate it.

Another form of intensifier more obvious in poetry than in prose, though common in both genres, is an unnecessary one-syllable adjective placed before a weak, one- or two-syllable noun. There are variations on this theme, but this is the basic form. They may be unnecessary quantifiers—*big, deep, loud, bright*—that work as sound and may suit the needs of the form, but are unnecessary for the sense. Obvious examples in prose are "free gift," "closed fist," and "true fact." Each is redundant, but the double stress creates the illusion of drama and substance. The use of a rhetorical double stress is particularly damaging in poetry because the reader sees its purpose so easily. The ideal in poetry is to use a word that functions equally on the levels of sound and sense. This clearly doesn't happen when a word exists only for its sound value.

The inexperienced writer needs to question each modifier to make sure it has actual contextual value. The effect of intensifiers that contribute nothing to the meaning can lead the reader to doubt the writer's credibility, while the awareness of unnecessary padding in a few places can cause the reader to grow suspicious of other places, thereby weakening the reader's suspension of disbelief.

One way to avoid unnecessary information is to examine one's sentence by rewriting it in its simplest form and then comparing it to the original. This allows the writer to investigate each addition and to establish which, if any, are needed. James's sentence could be rewritten as "It was a nice day and Dencombe decided to go for a walk." In comparing this to the original, it is difficult to see what in his long sentence doesn't contribute to the whole. We also realize that the short version is descriptive and the long version is dramatic.

One refers; the other enacts. James's sentence has two intensifiers—*however* and *still*—but the first creates a sense of precision, while the second is used in the meaning of "there remained," that is, Dencombe continued to suffer from his illness. Both are necessary. Third, by seeing just how the writer has expanded upon the simple version of his or her sentence, we develop a better idea of the writer's intention.

The twelve sentences making up the first paragraph of "The Middle Years" each repeat the accustomed model of subject, predicate, object, yet they do not seem repetitive due to variations in length and structure. In fact, they follow a pattern. I have written elsewhere that fiction and poetry create patterns of tension and rest that affect pacing and the reader's expectations. These are more common in poetry, where one may find patterns using a wide variety of formal devices, but in both fiction and poetry the use of obscurity creates tension, while clarity creates a rest; a long sentence will create tension and a shorter sentence will create rest. This is a common function of a simple sentence: it can create a rest. If one long sentence follows another and another, the increasing tension may lead the reader to turn away from the page.

James follows his first sentence with two shorter sentences, which are made up of five independent clauses that divide into seven short phrases of more or less equal length. He also returns to the iambic rhythm of the first independent clause. "He liked the feeling of the south, so far as you could have it in the north, he liked the sandy cliffs and the clustered pines, he liked even the colourless sea. 'Bournemouth as a health-resort' had sounded like a mere advertisement, but now he was reconciled to the prosaic." One effect of the iambic rhythm is that it allows James to give emphasis to those Latinate words that don't fit the rhythm—*advertisement, reconciled,* and *prosaic*—which let us read those words ironically and to understand, if we care to, that Dencombe is definitely not reconciled to the prosaic.

Bournemouth is a port on the southern coast of England, which can enjoy mild temperatures. But by being England it remains familiar; that is, prosaic. The first sentence presents us with a paradox clarified in the second. The tone is the same as in the paragraph's first independent clause, "The April day was soft and bright," while the paradox is mildly humorous: the presence of the south in the north. The sentences use three intensifiers: *even, mere,* and *now.* Each gives information about Dencombe, and the sentences would be weaker without them. The fact he likes "*even* the colourless sea" tells us about his present weakened condition and his aesthetic sensibilities when in better health; and by placing "even" after "like," instead of before, he stops the iambic rhythm, which otherwise would dominate the entire sentence. In addition, by moving "even" to an unexpected place, he is able to intensify it, which stresses its importance.

Also important is the staccato effect of the seven short phrases, which forms a rhythmic bridge between the first complex-compound sentence and the next: "The sociable country postman, passing through the garden, had just given [Dencombe] a small parcel, which he took out with him, leaving the hotel to the right and creeping to a convenient bench that he knew of, a safe recess in the cliff." The extended sentence dramatizes the physical movement as the five commas change the rhythm and vary the phrase length, while the words "creeping" and "safe recess" remind us of Dencombe's fragility. The only intensifier is "just," which serves to indicate this action immediately precedes the first sentence of the story. We still know nothing about Dencombe, nor do we know anything about the parcel.

The fifth sentence provides a rest. "It looked to the south, to the tinted walls of the Island, and was protected behind by the sloping shoulder of the down." Again, the short phrases are roughly iambic, while "protected" suggests Dencombe's fragility. The sixth is a complex-compound sentence that surprises us by becoming a question: "He was tired enough when he reached it, and for a moment he was disappointed; he was better, of course, but better, after all, than what?" You see how the short phrases within these two sentences provide a rest for the long sentence that precedes them? In addition, the interrogative takes us by surprise and stops the forward movement of the narrative. Most often, in something other than a simple sentence, an interrogative can take us back to the beginning of the sentence to understand the nature of the question.

Dencombe answers his question with a short complex sentence: "He should never again, as at one or two great moments of the past, be better than himself." The sentence forms a paradox—how can one be better than oneself?—but James renders it especially important by the staccato phrasing of these three sentences, so the paradox strikes Dencombe with the weight of revelation.

The island referred to in the fifth sentence is Brownsea Island within Poole Harbor, and the "down" that lay behind Dencombe is now a golf course.

The staccato phrasing dramatizes the action. Dencombe is out of breath and increasingly anxious; the commas in these sentences enact his breathlessness. They tell us that Dencombe is no longer "happy in the conceit of reasserted strength," which leads him to the revelation that he would never again be better than himself. He doesn't feel well. The paradox is obviously based on an illusion—to feel better than oneself—which returns us to the notion of self-deception, suggested by the use of the word "conceit" that hints at the story's main themes.

In the sixth sentence "enough" is an intensifier, while in the second half of the sentence "of course" and "after all" are also intensifiers. All seem necessary, while the second and third heighten the sense of breathlessness. We are also, as it were, experiencing Dencombe's process of thought. Physically and mentally, he has a faltering step. The language, the manner of the telling, dramatizes what is told.

The eighth sentence changes the pattern. It begins with another short phrase—an independent clause with an iambic rhythm—but the second half of the sentence is two times longer and rhythmically different, signifying its special importance: "The infinite of life had gone, and what was left of the dose was a small glass engraved like a thermometer by the apothecary." The sense of the infinite he had had when young has been replaced by specific markings, while the metaphor of the thermometer again brings up Dencombe's questionable health.

What we may also see is that James's simple direct statements—for instance, "the April day was soft and bright," "he liked the feeling of the south," "he liked the sandy cliffs," "he looked to the south," and "the infinite of life had gone"—are generally iambic, while the active and introspective phrases overthrow that iambic rhythm. This creates one sort of rhythm for the descriptive and another for the dramatic. The interplay between the two rhythms helps to give the paragraph a complexity that holds our interest. There is no sense of rhythmic redundancy.

One might also say the simplicity of these opening phrases lures us into the sentences' complexity. If the sentences began with complicated phrases, our reading experience would be different, while the increased difficulty might make us resistant.

Dencombe in sentence eight is approaching a bigger revelation, a conclusion, which is the logical consequence of his thought. But James delays the revelation with a bit of description in the ninth sentence that functions as a metaphor that announces what comes next. "He sat and stared at the sea, which appeared all surface and twinkle, far shallower than the spirit of man." The staccato effect is like a drum roll, while the twinkling surface of the ocean provides a sense of immanence. The tenth sentence gives us that revelation, while answering the unstated question, "What is deeper than the sea?" It again changes the pattern and is the shortest sentence in the paragraph, a simple sentence followed by a three-word appositive: "It was the abyss of human illusion that was the real, the tideless deep."

All that he had valued, Dencombe realizes, was illusion. As readers we can again see how James has prepared for this revelation with that modifying phrase in the first sentence, "happy in the conceit of reasserted strength," as well as the illusion of being better than oneself. The paragraph, in fact, could end at this point—after all, this is the paragraph's most important sentence— but James is interested in psychology, not melodrama. He needs to lighten the tone. In addition, we have no context. Who is Dencombe, and what is in the package?

The eleventh sentence is the longest in the paragraph and most complicated, while the last sentence returns us to the pattern of short phrases. "He held his packet, which had come by book-post, unopened on his knee, liking, in the lapse of so many joys (his illness had made him feel his age), to know that it was there, but taking for granted there could be no complete renewal of the pleasure, dear to young experience, of seeing one's self 'just out.' Dencombe, who had a reputation, had come out too often and knew too well in advance how he should look."

Dencombe is an established writer, and we soon learn that the package contains his newest novel, titled *The Middle Years*. Yet the two sentences remain ambiguous; no novel is mentioned.

In the eleventh sentence, James delays one adjective ("unopened") and two verbs ("to know" and "of seeing"). He speeds and slows the pace of the sentence with a relative clause, several prepositional phrases, a parenthetical phrase, and other subordinate clauses, ending with the two important syllables "just out," which, with "come out" in the last sentence, suggest a debutante at her first ball, a suggestion reinforced by the modifying phrase "dear to young experience." "Just out" form the sentence's most important words in terms of what is happening. It is Dencombe's wish to inspect this first copy of his novel that has led him on an "easy stroll"—another illusion—to a bench on the cliff facing the sea. The scene itself is symbolic. He is staring from a cliff at the abyss of human illusion.

The complexity of the sentence reflects the complexity of Dencombe's thought. A simple rephrasing might be: "He held his unopened book, glad that it was out, but he no longer felt pleasure in being published." To compare this to the original is to see James's intention and his method. Dencombe is ambivalent, and the sentence's eight commas help enact this ambivalence. There is a shift at the end with the words "just out" and "seeing one's self" to an emphasis on appearance based on reputation and to reputation based on appearance—nothing is said about the quality of the book—and this returns us to the "abyss of human illusion." Dencombe knew too well what his appearance should be; he knew how he "should look." The irony allows us to read these words in different ways, so we cannot establish if his perception is wisdom or self-deceit.

However, the quotation marks around "just out" show them as an ironic reference to a formal dance to which debutantes are invited for the inspection of eligible bachelors. That makes the last sentence mildly comic. Dencombe has often been in the position of a debutante. He has a reputation and has never been chosen. "Reputation," in this instance, has a negative meaning. Dencombe is diminished by this sentence; he is made less tragic by his illusion. He appears slightly foolish. He is more interested in how he looks or plays the role of author than in how the book is received. James undercuts the possible melodrama of sentence ten to present Dencombe with more complexity in the form of another paradox: Dencombe is both wise and deluded.

This paragraph may not be to one's taste, but it is brilliantly made. There is no sense of repetition, despite the repeating subject-verb-object structure. The verbs are simple, and James often uses the verb "to be." One often hears teachers telling writing students to vary their syntax and use active verbs. James does neither. Other words are also simple, and none of the carefully placed polysyllabic words seem ornamental. As George Orwell cautioned in an essay, "Never use a long word when a short word will do," and James would seem attentive to that. What strikes us as different about James's style are the long and complicated sentences, and that is because literary fashion in the United States was so affected by the lean, terse journalistic style of Ernest Hemingway.

The complexity of the sentences, and paragraph as a whole, is caused partly by the thirty-seven commas and their effect on pacing; partly by the rhythmic shift between simple descriptive phrases and dramatic or enactive phrases, and also by the complexity of tone. We don't know how seriously to take Dencombe. On one hand, there is his revelation in the tenth sentence— "It was the abyss of human illusion that was the real"—and on the other he is compared to an overexposed debutante. There is also a complexity caused by our ignorance—we know nothing about Dencombe and learn about him only in little bits, while by the end of the paragraph we see there are two Dencombes: the appearance, or illusion, and the reality, which even Dencombe has trouble sorting out.

What creates the sense of space in James's paragraph? Most obviously, there is a sense there is more to be known. The paragraph begins in the middle of things with questions immediately raised about past and future. Nothing is concluded. Our information is partial, in a state of flux, as James moves between the external and internal, the quantitative and qualitative, all of which keeps us asking questions and being unable to anticipate where James is going. This is also the effect of contrast and paradox. Dencombe is poor and happy, wise and deluded. There is the feeling of the south in the north; the safe recess in a cliff; the one or two great moments of being better than oneself; the sea being shallower than the spirit of man, a spirit composed of human illusion; to be a debutante too often, like being a virgin too often. These contrasts and paradoxes raise the question: How is this possible? And this question heightens the more important questions: Who is Dencombe, and what is his problem?

Other elements in this paragraph deserve mention. The twelve contrasting sentences give the story's basic range of sentences. Of what is to come, only dialogue forms the exception. If some very different kind of sentence appeared later in the story, it would create a change in tone. Perhaps James might want that, but if he didn't, then that change of tone could affect his credibility. Likewise, this first paragraph presents a range of diction. Anything substantially different that appeared later in the story could again change the tone and damage his credibility.

Did James consciously map out this paragraph? Yes and no. His work from the 1860s and most of the '70s is entirely different. The sentences are shorter and descriptive. They contain none of the psychology or subtlety found in the long sentences. They don't enact. James's decision to write longer and more complicated sentences was completely conscious. And after this story, the sentences kept expanding until, in his last novel, there are sentences two pages long. These sentences lengthened for a reason we see in this paragraph. Some of it was probably unconscious, but only because he had worked out those elements in previous books.

Where does James begin in his narrative, and why does he choose this spot? We learn in the fourth sentence: the postman has just given Dencombe an important package, and he wanted to go someplace private to inspect it. The story is about Dencombe's relationship to his work and his illusion, or conceit, that restored health will give him another chance to write something really first-rate. But at the very end Dencombe tells his doctor, who is also his friend and who greatly admires Dencombe's work: "A second chance—*that's* the delusion. There never was to be but one. We work in the dark—we do what we can—we give what we have. Our doubt is our passion and our passion is our task. The rest is the madness of art."[2]

We understand at the end that the first sentence was written with the end in view. The partial subject of the story—conceit and delusion—is one that Dencombe comes to grasp only moments before his death. This is the arc of the story—an arc that doesn't seem to be an arc until the story is finished.

Poems may be built similarly. Here is William Butler Yeats's "Her Praise." The manuscript copy of the poem is dated January 27, 1915.

1- She is foremost of those that I would hear praised.

2- I have gone about the house, gone up and down

3- As a man does who has published a new book,

4- Or a young girl dressed out in her new gown,

5- And though I have turned the talk by hook or crook

6- Until her praise should be the uppermost theme,

7- A woman spoke of some new tale she had read,

8- A man confusedly in a half dream

9- As though some other name ran in his head.

10- She is foremost of those that I would hear praised.

11- I will talk no more of books or the long war

12- But walk by the dry thorn until I have found

13- Some beggar sheltering from the wind, and there

14- Manage the talk until her name come round.

15- If there be rags enough he will know her name

16- And be well pleased remembering it, for in the old days,

17- Though she had young men's praise and old men's blame,

18- Among the poor both old and young gave her praise.[3]

Yeats had first titled the poem "The Thorn Tree," but then changed it to bring it into line with other poems he had written about Maud Gonne: "Her Anxiety," "Her Courage," "Her Courtesy," "Her Dream," "Her Race," "Her Triumph," and "Her Vision in the Wood." A passionate Irish nationalist, Maud Gonne was also well known for her charitable work with the poor, but she had retired from public life after her marriage to Major John MacBride on February 21, 1903, when she was 37. Then Gonne separated from MacBride in 1905, charging him with drunkenness, cruelty, and having adulterous relations with one or both of the two girls in her care: her nine-year-old daughter Iseult and her sixteen-year-old half-sister Eileen Wilson. The separation was a long legal process. In October 1906, Gonne went with Yeats to a performance at the Abbey Theatre, but when they arrived Gonne was hissed at by a number of MacBride's supporters. She rose up to her full height and glared at them imperiously, but Yeats was appalled. The words "old men's blame" refer to this, as well as to other occasions.

By the time the poem was written, Maud Gonne had been living in France for some years; during the war she and Iseult worked in hospitals nursing the wounded. But in Ireland, according to Yeats, she had been mostly forgotten or held in disfavor, except by the poor. This is what the poem discusses. The speaker—Yeats—tries to get his friends—Ezra Pound and Dorothy Shakespear—to talk and praise, but they only wish to discuss their own concerns. So Yeats discovers a beggar by a thorn tree who remembers Maud Gonne and is glad to talk about her.

Originally the poem ended with these two quatrains.

A man comes hither because of the harsh wind

I am certain that where he finds the thorn he will stop

To shelter a while, that puts it into my mind

To turn the talk until her name has come up.

And being but a ragged man he will know her name

And be well pleased remembering it, for in old days
Though she had young man's praise and old men's blame
Among the poor both old and young gave her praise.[4]

Yeats's work didn't come easily. He would often begin with a prose version or description of the subject and then grind out the poem with, as he
said, "[an] intense unnatural labor that reduces composition to four or five
lines a day."[5] To his friend Katharine Tynan, he wrote, "I envy your power
of writing stray snatches of verse. I cannot do it at all. With me everything is
premeditated for a long time."[6] And in another letter to Tynan about the writing of "The Wanderings of Oisin": "It beset me day and night. Not that I ever
wrote more than a few lines a day. But those few lines took me hours. All the
rest of the time I walked about the roads thinking of it."[7] Often as he walked
he would "speak" the poems he was working on "in a loud chanting voice."[8]
His early drafts attest to his labor, a dozen or so pages beginning with hesitant
scrawls far from the finished poem.

Personally, I find this an odd way to work: to begin with a prose paraphrase. No matter how emotional the poems may be, most begin as intel-
lectualization. Instead of beginning intuitively, they begin discursively. The
subjects found in "Her Praise" weren't original for Yeats. He had written
about them before and would again. Indeed, "Her Praise" was the first of
six consecutive poems in *Wild Swans of Coole* on Maud Gonne in middle
age, being, in the words of John Unterecker, "vehicles for [Yeats's] persistent
theme of time's treachery."[9] Earlier poems like "When Helen Lived" and
"Fallen Majesty," from *Responsibilities*, also refer to Gonne being unfairly
criticized and forgotten; and in the extracts of his 1909 diary published as
The Death of Synge, Yeats wrote on July 8: "I dreamed this thought two
nights ago: 'Why should we complain if men ill-treat our Muses, when all
that they gave Helen while she lived was a song and a jest?'"[10] In his lecture "The Irish Dramatic Movement" Yeats refers to a Gonne-like "famous
country beauty": "I have spoken to old men and women who remembered
her, though all are dead now, and they spoke of her as the old men upon the
wall of Troy spoke of Helen."[11] Yeats uses this same simile to describe how
Gonne was remembered.

I mention these details because I want to show Yeats not as a Nobel lau-
reate, but as someone for whom the business of writing poetry didn't come

easily, who had much anxiety about its possible success. One might think that a poet of his stature would write with great confidence. Instead it was a constant struggle.

So when Yeats wrote his paraphrase, he had a number of specific memories to draw upon, some referred to in other places. He also had a list of images he might incorporate that would be applicable in the specific instance and also reference some aspect of his philosophical and mystical beliefs. He would also, in many cases, make a list of the rhymes to use in the still unwritten poem. And of course he had his knowledge of and expertise with the English metrical system. So he had a number of pieces of the upcoming poem already in hand and a number of ways in which they could be used.

I have said elsewhere that one writes a poem, in part, to discover why one is writing the poem. Yeats didn't do this. Instead, he began with the subject, and sound and image came later. Then, when he had his paraphrase with his images and rhymes close at hand, he went in search of language. The poem's first sentence echoes the paraphrase: "She is foremost of those that I would hear praised." The simple declaration has great authority. Although the line is iambic pentameter, it is not obviously iambic and at first seems closer to prose.

But as I've said in other chapters, one needs to see the English metrical system not simply as a binary system—that is, stress, no-stress; rather, one needs to imagine at least four degrees of stress. To force the first line of "Her Praise" into a binary system would be to exaggerate it, making a pyrrhic and spondee of the first two feet and turning the anapest that concludes the line into three stresses. But the first two feet are both iambs—one weaker, one stronger—while the concluding anapest can be seen as 4, 4, 2 in terms of stress. In fact, the entire poem displays what might be called a loose iambic, though Yeats will follow a loose line, like the first one, with a strong iambic line, like the second: "I have gone about the house, gone up and down . . ." He also does this in lines 8 and 9: "A man confusedly in a half dream / As though some other name ran in his head . . ." where line 9 has great iambic emphasis.

For the previous fifteen years, Yeats had tried to free his poetry from the artificiality he saw in the poems he had written in the 1880s and '90s. "My work has got far more masculine," he wrote Lady Gregory in 1903. "It has more salt in it."[12] And his book *Responsibilities* (1914) concluded with "A

Coat," where his old way of writing is called a coat "Covered with embroi-
deries / Out of old mythologies" and ends ". . . there's more enterprise / In
walking naked."[13]

To describe all that influenced Yeats in these changes would make a long
list, but one influence for plainer speech was Ezra Pound, who had helped
Yeats with a number of poems. Yeats was spending his second winter with
Pound and his wife Dorothy Shakespear in Stone Cottage in Sussex when he
wrote "Her Praise" and the two poems about Maud Gonne that followed
it, "His Phoenix" and "The People." James Longenbach in *Stone Cottage:
Pound, Yeats and Modernism* wrote that the poems were "quite specific in
their references to Yeats's living condition with Pound and his wife" and
had elements of the "unclouded precision" that Pound tried to encourage in
Yeats's poetry.[14] It was Pound's desire, Longenbach wrote, "to purge Yeats's
work of its dreamy nostalgia and push it toward the precision of Joyce's 'realism.'"[15] He had also "grown tired of Yeats's fixation on Maud Gonne,"[16]
and one can imagine times when Yeats tried to turn the conversation to Maud
Gonne and Pound insistently turned it elsewhere. All three poems were sub-
mitted to *Poetry* magazine with a note from Pound at the end of January and
were accepted.

Other influences on Yeats's pursuit of a simpler language were the plays he
wrote for the Abbey Theatre. In his lecture "The Irish Dramatic Movement,"
he said, "We were to find ourselves in a quarrel with public opinion that compelled us against our own will and the will of our players to become always
more realistic, substituting dialect for verse, common speech for dialect."[17]

One sees in this remark Yeats's ambivalence to what he called common
speech, with the word "common" suggesting a value judgment. Yeats hated
public opinion, which he believed was ignorant and fickle, and, as he said in
his Nobel acceptance speech, Ireland was a country ruled by public opinion.[18]
It was public opinion that had caused Maud Gonne to be booed. It was ig-
noble and violent, the very antithesis of the voice of an enlightened aristocracy
that Yeats was coming to value.

As a result, while Yeats continued to simplify the syntax and diction of
the poems along the lines of Pound's suggestions, he also made sure that his
language couldn't be mistaken for common speech. Richard Ellmann in *The
Identity of Yeats* describes how Yeats first "worked to . . . rid himself of ar-
chaisms until he was about thirty-five [and then] spent the next fifteen years

reviving some of them."[19] But he didn't add them like salt and pepper as he had once done. Instead, they are placed to create slight changes in tone.

We see an instance of it in lines 14 and 15 of "Her Praise": "Manage the talk until her name come round. / If there be rags enough he will know her name," where the changes in diction are in keeping with the old beggar. "If there be rags enough" is an example of this slightly archaic phrasing, as is the subjunctive "come." More importantly, these two lines were late additions, and they replaced the lines: "To turn the talk until her name has come up. / And being but a ragged man he will know her name . . ." In those lines, Yeats rejects a new usage—such as "until her name has come up"—for an older one. I'll return to these lines again.

Yeats formal intention in "Her Praise" is to create a sense of common speech through diction and syntax and yet work against common speech with meter and sound. We right away notice the end rhyme, but more striking is what Unterecker calls "Yeats' growing interest in functional repetition . . . echoing interwoven words (foremost, uppermost, foremost; praise, praised, praise, praised, praise, praise; book, books; talk, talk, talk; name, name, name; new, new, new; old, old, old; young, young, young)."[20] And he might have added the repetition of "there" in lines 13 and 15. One also finds a mass of internal rhymes and off-rhymes; for instance, in the first four lines we find: *most, those, praised, house, has, -lished,* and *dressed.*

Equally significant is Yeats's use of a dominant vowel sound: the long O that occurs one or more times in nearly every line. There are fifteen degrees of vowel pitch or frequency: seven bass vowels, five tenor vowels, and three alto vowels. The long O used by Yeats is the second lowest. He also repeats other bass vowels, such as those found in *book, bought,* and *bough,* but the long O is a constant, and it functions like a drone in music, a sound heard through the entire piece. This long O drone helps to create an emotional tone. It is somber in a way that tenor and alto vowels are not. It seeks to reflect the frustration and grief of the speaker.

In the first ten lines, we have a one-line simple sentence followed by an eight-line complex-compound sentence, followed by a repetition of the first sentence. The long sentence allows Yeats to accumulate the sound of the drone to accompany the speaker's increasing frustration. To break these eight lines into shorter sentences would create a staccato effect, but Yeats wants the speaker's frustration to build until he is driven from the house.

The continuing drone within the long sentence with its conjunctions and repetitions allows this to happen. The long sentence also creates tension. One wonders when will it ever end. Yeats also uses this sentence to imitate the process of going about the house, using a series of subordinate clauses to suggest the length of time spent in this futile endeavor. Then Yeats uses a transitional line, "I will talk no more of books or the long war," which again emphasizes his key repeating sounds.

And then comes a misstep in the earlier version of line 12: "A man comes hither because of the harsh wind." We notice an older diction in the use of "hither" and there is no long O. What has Yeats done? We all, as writers, have a series of default moves—phrasings and language we have used in the past that satisfy the needs of the sound and feel correct, but which diminish the sense. Usually we turn to a default move out of impatience. We want something now. These five or so lines seem like such a move.

Of course, I am only speculating about what Yeats did, but in the earlier version the rhyme "wind" and "mind" uses tenor vowels, and he changes it to "found" and "round," which have the bass vowels so prevalent in the poem. He also takes the emphasis off the wind and gives it to the thorn tree, making it a spondee in line 12: "But walk by the *dry thorn* until I have found." With that change, the dry thorn takes on a sexual resonance that would have appealed to Yeats. Thirdly, the speaker becomes more active. Instead of waiting near the thorn tree for someone to show up, he searches until he has found "some beggar sheltering from the wind." And instead of *thinking* about *turning* the talk, as he had done back in line 5, he now *manages* the talk, while the enjambment of line 13 gives special emphasis to "manage." The speaker takes charge here. There are other changes. He rephrases the second, third, and fourth old lines to cut down on the weaker little words. The second line, which had been thirteen syllables, becomes eleven syllables, and he starts it with the intensifier "some," with its bass vowel, and changes "man" to "beggar."

However, the second part, while better, still has a familiar ring to it, unlike the first part, which was written with the clarity Pound liked. But with repetitions, internal rhymes, and the long O drone, as well as meter and end rhyme, Yeats was able to expand the possibilities of language, to avoid what he saw as common speech.

As I said earlier, actual language is always a diminishment of the meaning that the writer intends. Written language, in that it lacks vocal emphasis and physical gesture, can be even more of a diminishment. What we see in these examples of James and Yeats are ways in which writers might work against this diminishment with structural elements; that is, syntax, types of sentence, rhythm, and sound. In James's case these elements create specificity and nuance. This is also true with Yeats, but in using the internal rhyme and long O drone, Yeats is also able to give his language the appearance of common speech without sacrificing the musicality and rhythms that he wanted.

closure

In human affairs, the word "closure" means putting something behind us; in a successful poem, it can mean the invocation of something ahead. This apparent paradox points to one of a poem's greatest strengths. The poem doesn't end; rather, it gives back meaning with each rereading. Without such an ending, the poem is in danger of suffering closure in the conventional sense. It won't transcend its syntactic closure; it won't be more than the sum of its parts.

A lyric poem is a symbol of affective life, the realm of feelings. It was written because the poet has experienced an emotion about which he or she was unable to remain silent. The poet bears witness to that emotion and attempts to recreate it in the reader by presenting pertinent information equally in form and content. That act of bearing witness is what draws us to the poem as readers. If we don't find that emotional dynamic, we may take pleasure in other elements, such as form, intelligence, quality of writing, strength of imagery, and so on, but none will take the place of the symbol of affective life. Indeed, if we grasp that symbol and the other elements are poorly executed, we will still value it more than a poem in which the reverse is true.

In a good poem we expect the emotional dynamic to transcend the particulars of the poet's life in order to speak to the reader's life. The reader doesn't come to the poem out of curiosity about the poet, but in search of evidence for his or her own life. However, the poet must do more than bear witness to an emotional dynamic, which is why Philip Larkin said that a poem must be theatrical in operation. If the poet is writing because he or she is unable to remain silent, we expect the strength of that emotion to energize the poem. In the making of the poem, that emotion is translated into the poem's theatrical dynamic. This doesn't mean that the poem must be loud, but it must live up to the promise of its speaking.

The poem as symbol shares a symbol's characteristics: it is nondiscursive; it is a product of the right brain; it is more than the sum of its parts; and it usually presents its information through sense data. In a poem, unlike an anecdote, the reader's question—"What does this mean?"—is not fully answered by its syntactic closure. We have a sense of more, and so we move past the syntactic closure to reread the poem in search of the scope of that "more." But no matter how much we reread, the poem continues to defy paraphrase. It remains dynamic, a living thing. Like any successful symbol, it continues to give back information, to transmit meaning. We may tire of it, but we can never exhaust it.

Look at Billy Collins's "The Dead" from *Sailing Alone Around the Room:*

The dead are always looking down on us, they say,

while we are putting on our shoes or making a sandwich,

they are looking down through the glass-bottomed boats of heaven

as they row themselves slowly through eternity.

They watch the tops of our heads moving below on earth,

and when we lie down in a field or on a couch,

drugged perhaps by the hum of a warm afternoon,

they think we are looking back at them,

which makes them lift their oars and fall silent

and wait, like parents, for us to close our eyes.[1]

We find here, as with any poem, four types of closure. The most obvious is visual closure—the shape of the poem on the page—which we notice even before we begin to read: ten lines, two and a half quatrains.

The second is syntactic closure: the place where the sentences end. In Collins's poem, we read two sentences. The first occupies the first quatrain. The second is the rest of the poem. But it is more complicated than that. The second sentence could logically close at the end of the second stanza: "they think we are looking back at them." The continuation with a relative clause forms a mild surprise, while the end of the poem, the final period, receives further emphasis with the last four words. The sentence stops; the people stop, they die.

The poem is a deceptive conditional. It depends on the condition of the last two words in the first line, "they say": a vague outside authority is being acknowledged. This condition is reinforced by "perhaps" in line 7 and "they think" in line 8. Syntactically, we see that Collins is presenting us with a metaphor. In saying "They say," he is saying "It is as if."

Collins is a genius of tone. We are seduced by his relaxed manner, his seemingly offhand observations. The people in his poems aren't doing anything important—they are putting on their shoes, lying down on a couch. He starts with general actions and moves to the more specific: "drugged perhaps by the hum of a warm afternoon."

The third type is narrative closure: the story comes to an end. Often this is a literal narrative with a sequence of events that reach a conclusion. Many lyrics, however, lack a conventional narrative; or rather, it can only be inferred: for instance, a man walks to a chair; he relives emotional pain; the man gets up and leaves the room. One narrative is the inferred time between the experience of the pain and recalling of the pain. The other is walking to the chair, sitting, and then leaving the room. All the poem needs is the man recalling the pain. The rest is cut out, but it can still be inferred.

So with narrative closure there also comes a point when the poem's information is complete. Although Collins's poem has narrative elements, it is primarily lyric. But with its last words—"to close our eyes"—its information is finished. Nothing more could be added.

The fourth type of closure is contextual closure, which we expect to find in the last two lines. After all, this is where the other types of closure are leading. Something has happened to "make" the dead stop rowing and "wait"; and then Collins slips in that simile "like parents."

So is that when the poem closes? Is that when we stop reading? Don't we ask, How is this like parents?, and doesn't this lead us back into the poem?

Indeed, we reread the poem through the lens of those last two lines to answer the question, What does this mean? But we don't get a simple answer. The dead are always waiting for us. They watch us close our eyes in the way a parent watches over a child falling asleep. They wait for us as a parent waits for a child to come home. Then we see more connections. The simple diction and syntax, the repetitions resemble the language that a parent uses with a child. The tone seems kindly. Nothing is hurried. The dead row slowly; we are drugged by the hum of a warm afternoon. Reading and rereading, we discover the nature of the poem's emotional strength, the complexity of its artifice; we come to see the poet's intention. But we still can't paraphrase it. There is always more.

Syntactic closure may be divided into two general categories: discursive and nondiscursive.

The discursive is joined with the logic of the syntax and proceeds through analytic argument. In fact, it might be said that every poem contains an argument or is structured like an argument. It seeks to convince us of something. Collins presents his thesis in his first line—"The dead are always looking down on us . . ."—and then he presents his evidence. But discursive closure makes use of deductive or inductive argument; we are given a series of propositions and a conclusion. The truth of the conclusion is a logical consequence of the propositions. We find this in many Shakespearean sonnets: three quatrains that begin with "if" or "when" and a concluding couplet that begins with "then." While poems using discursive closure may use nondiscursive material—image, simile, metaphors, and so on—that material doesn't necessarily form part of the conclusion.

Heather McHugh's "I Knew I'd Sing" from the book *To the Quick* is a modern example of discursive closure.

A few sashay, a few finagle.
Some make whoopee, some
make good. But most make
diddly-squat. I tell you this

is what I love about
America—the words it puts
in my mouth, the mouth where once
my mother rubbed

a word away with soap. The word
was *cunt*. She stuck that bar

of family-size in there
until there was no hole to speak of,

so she hoped. But still
I'm full of it—the cunt,
the prick, short U, short I
the word that stood

for her and him. I loved the thing
they must have done, the love they must
have made, to make
an example of me. After my lunch of Ivory I said

vagina for a day or two, but knew
from that day forth which word
struck home like sex itself. I knew
when I was big I'd sing

a song in praise of cunt—I'd want
to keep my word, the one with teeth in it.
Forevermore (and even after I was raised) I swore

nothing—but nothing—would be beneath me.

I find this poem an amazing joining of form and content. We also see, though perhaps not immediately, that the poem is written in iambics. But the slight conflict between speech stress and metrical stress in the first three lines briefly takes our mind off form. Although we may not notice at first, the first line is iambic tetrameter. Yet if you read the iambs as iambs, it would sound unnatural and forced. Then line 5 begins an obvious iambic meter with 4–1 iambs.

However, a difficulty with 4–1 iambs is they can create a galloping rhythm, so she interrupts them briefly in line 7 with an anapest: "in my mouth." "Into" would be the more accurate word at that spot, but if she used "into," she would make a perfect line of iambic tetrameter, and the poem would go galloping forward through five more lines of 4–1 iambs. This would create a metrical exaggeration reminiscent of Edward Lear. So she stops the iambs again in line 12 with a pyrrhic and spondee in the second and third positions. Then the iambs gallop off again to line 20 ("an example of me. After my lunch of Ivory I said") where we have anapest, anapest, trochee, iamb, iamb, anapest. Then it is iambic again to the last line, which is trochee, trochee, anapest, iamb with a feminine ending.

Another element that mildly conceals the iambs is a varying line length between two and seven feet, which appears in no set order. That variation makes it difficult for the reader to find a consistent rhythm, which would be more likely with lines of the same length. Yet what mostly distracts are the line breaks, the majority of which are heavily enjambed, for instance lines 2 through 7. Then she gives a short rest and starts enjambing again until line 11, where she gives two end-stopped lines. The rest of the lines to the end are enjambed.

A third element to distract us is that nearly all of those enjambments create a surprise with the first words of the next line. Those words are unexpected and may carry double meanings: for instance, the penultimate line ends with "I swore," while the next seems to say she never swears. The enjambments also distract us by presenting a stop-and-go movement that keeps us from settling at any one place. Another distraction is the humor that interrupts our forward movement. It consistently appears throughout the poem, creating more surprises.

A fifth element that catches us up are the puns and double meanings. We have a slight pun on the phallic bar of soap in line 10. Then there are double meanings in lines 12, 14, 15, perhaps in 23, in 26 with the play on vagina dentata, and then in the last two lines. That's a lot of word play.

In addition, there is quite a lot alliteration and internal rhyme. The whole form of the poem works as surprise and distracts us from the rest, until, perhaps, we go through the poem a second time. The first time through is all roller coaster.

The words in the poem are mostly simple, but we don't notice that unless we look. Indeed, we have no time. But paraphrase the poem and put it into a prose paragraph, and you'll find a rather uncomplicated narrative anecdote with a discursive ending. This, too, she conceals at first; the narrative doesn't begin until line 7: "once / my mother rubbed / a word away with soap." Yet the second time through we see that her love of language derives from that one offensive word and how the mother responded.

The anecdote begins with a motivating event; the mother tries to teach the daughter a lesson. And what is the consequence of this? It didn't work. Not only didn't it work, but it leads the daughter—another consequence—to take a position opposite her mother's. The consequence that appears in the last two lines is a discursive statement that arises out of a logical sequence: I did this; my mother did that; and in consequence I did this.

One result of the formal complications in the poem is to create a sense of space, which I discussed in Chapter 7. McHugh packs these twenty-four lines as a butcher packs a sausage, but the mass of formal elements together with the narrative creates no feeling of confinement in the six four-line stanzas. We lose a sense of time and space. Many of McHugh's poems do this.

An apparent benefit of free verse poetry is that it contains a higher degree of verisimilitude than formal poetry. Billy Collins's "The Dead" is seemingly written in the plain speech of everyday intercourse, while the formal elements in McHugh's poem suggest artifice although she, too, uses the diction of plain speech. I say "seemingly" in Collins's case because his last two lines are iambic pentameter, which gives them rhetorical stress.

Here is another discursive poem: W. S. Merwin's "Going" from *The Shadow of Sirius* (2008):

Only humans believe
there is a word for goodbye
we have one in every language
one of the first words we learn
it is made out of greeting
but they are going away
the raised hand waving
the face the person the place
the animal the day
leaving the word behind
and what it was meant to say[2]

In reading these eleven lines, the obvious formal element is the lack of punctuation (long typical of Merwin). But with the poem's final word "say" we hear its rhyme with "day" in line 9. Looking more closely, we notice the rhyme with "away" that ends line 6, as well as long 'a' assonance in lines

5 through 9: *made, away, raised, waving, face,* and *place.* Merwin uses the long 'a' to create a pattern in five successive lines, a pattern that he abandons in the penultimate line and returns to in the last line, which creates added emphasis. The effect of the rhyme is to tie the end firmly to the rest of the poem and to place rhetorical stress on the poem's final word. Perhaps the ending is true or false, but the rhetorical stress encourages us to believe it is true. The rhetorical stress indicates the word's importance, and we look at it closely to discover the nature of that importance. This can lead us to the word's connotative meanings. The word "goodbye" doesn't simply mean "I am leaving" but comes to be an acknowledgment of all that was left unsaid. It may also recall that "goodbye" is a contraction of "God be with you." The poem could syntactically end with the ninth line, but the last two lines form a commentary on what came before, a commentary that leads us back into the poem.

Again we are presented with a number of propositions and a conclusion. The context seems tied to the syntax, but the rhetorical stress on the final word raises a question about Merwin's intention, and we reenter the poem in search of an answer. What at first seemed a simple matter of visual, syntactic, and contextual closure being joined together becomes complicated. The poem has no narrative, but the poem's discursive structure and discursive conclusion strengthens the poem's meditative aspect because of its causal progression and conclusion.

Here is "Inpatient" from Jane Kenyon's *The Boat of Quiet Hours* (1986):

The young attendants wrapped him in a red
velour blanket, and pulled the strapping tight.
sedated on a stretcher and outside
for the last time, he raised his head and sniffed
the air like an animal. A wedge of geese
flew honking over us. The sky leaned close;
a drop of rain fell on his upturned face.
I stood aside, steward of Grandma's red-
letter New Testament and an empty vase.
The nurse went with him through the sliding door.
Without having to speak of it we left
the suitcase with his streetclothes in the car.[3]

Kenyon's poem is all narrative with no commentary and seemingly no metaphor. The discursive syntactic closure receives only slight rhetorical stress—the off-rhyme between *door* and *car*. However, in lines 5 through 10 the off-rhymes *geese, us, close, his, face, vase,* and *nurse* serve to set up *case* and *clothes* in the last line. We may easily overlook these rhymes, but they create an emphasis that the poet felt was needed. Kenyon, like Merwin, establishes a pattern of off-rhymes that is dropped in the penultimate line and returned to in the last line. That pause in the penultimate lines gives the final voicing of the off-rhymes greater impact.

As for the poem's discursive argument, the title presents a condition and the narrative gives evidence to support that condition. Yet as we read, we see the nature of that condition change. Then, in the last line, we realize that the man is an "inpatient" because he is never coming out. He has gone to the hospital not to be cured, but to die. The word is being used as a metaphor. When we understand this, the narrative seems to shift and we reenter the poem in search of its contextual closure.

There are, I expect, as many types of closure as there are poems, but all will fall into those categories of discursive and nondiscursive, with many using elements of both. But in free verse there is danger that the discursive ending may be seen as no more than a remark. A way to avoid this is to use one or more formal elements to create rhetorical emphasis. The off-rhymes in Kenyon's last line link it to the rest of the poem to create a sense of the appropriate, which is almost subliminal. That emphasis makes us more likely to investigate the last statement, leading us to understand why the clothes are being left in the car and to discover the muted elements of grief.

What one finds in poems using discursive closure is a shift at the end. The subject matter can appear to be buried by the form, as with McHugh; or there is a change of focus, as with Merwin; or there is an unexpected clarification, as with Kenyon. And certainly there are other sorts of turns. This must happen. We read by anticipating what is coming next. In a discursive poem, the logic forms an inexorable progression.

McHugh wants to write a poem about a self-revelation that brought about the writing of poetry; Merwin wants to write a poem about the failures of language; Kenyon wants to write a poem about the death of a loved one. These poems achieve their meanings and convince us by appearing to go in one direction but then making a turn to arrive at a place that we come to realize was their destination all along. They are deceptive. They are operating theatrically.

To grasp the nature of the poem's contextual closure we have to reread it to see how the answer that struck us as a surprise was there all along. The rhetorical intensifiers stress the importance of the end—it is more than just a remark—and we reenter the poem to understand that importance. For instance, rereading Merwin's poem we see the word "believe" in the first line differently. Reading the poem the first time, we may pass over it or see it as meaning "feel" or "realize" or "know." Reading the poem a second time, we see it as meaning credulous, foolish to believe. Once we read the poem with that altered sense of context, we see its details differently. The fact that there is one in every language points to our inability to express the sentiment accurately. "One of the first words we learn" underlines the irony that we still don't have it right. "It is made out of greeting"—"God be with you" was both greeting and farewell.

In Kenyon's poem, and to a lesser extent in McHugh's, the nondiscursive material takes on more weight with rereading. Metaphor, symbol, and image are nondiscursive. Their accuracy can't be proven by logical methods. They are nonpropositional and noninferential. Kenyon's images "A wedge of geese / flew honking over us. The sky leaned close; / a drop of rain fell on his upturned face" are all indicative of grief. What was at first merely descriptive becomes metaphoric. We come to understand this on subsequent readings in pursuit of the poem's contextual closure.

In McHugh's case the twelfth line—"until there was no hole to speak of"—refers to the vagina, while "to speak of" says the hole (cunt) was mostly removed, as well as saying that because of the soap there was an inability to speak. In the fourteenth line the words "I'm full of it" refer to genitalia, to language, to exaggeration, deceit, or what we mean when we say, "You're full of it." And there are still more metaphors based on word play.

While we come to understand discursive contextual closure incrementally, step by step as with a syllogism, nondiscursive closure strikes us with a sense of immediacy. Eyjólfur Kjalar Emilsson in his book *Plotinus on Intellect* said that Plotinus wrote of the nondiscursive as wisdom communicated in its all-at-once state. In Aristotle it is the immediate grasp of an essence. One can understand this difference in comparing language to vision. The statement "the bird is black" is discursive and propositional. But the image of a black bird is received in its all-at-once state. It is nondiscursive and nonpropositional. We see it in our memory's eye. Emilsson wrote:

A reason for using vision as a metaphor for nondiscursive thought is to convey the idea that the grasp of the conceptual relations between a whole array of concepts may be analogous to the grasp of spatial relations in vision: . . . [the] experience of thinking nondiscursively has about it a clarity and immediacy concerning multiple conceptual relationships that vision has about spatial ones. . . . What Plotinus seems to be suggesting is a vision-like experience of the region of concepts . . . that is not structured in the manner of propositions. . . . Its apprehension of these things is not broken up into separate components. . . . Rather, grasping beauty is a matter of "seeing" a lot of things, all together."[4]

Plotinus insists on our holistic experience of the intelligible world that we can take it in all at once. The fact that a poem, like music, is a sequential art with information coming out of an apparent future would seem to argue against its being "wisdom communicated in its all-at-once state." Indeed, different parts of a poem may be propositional, as in a Shakespearean sonnet. But our ambition in reading the poem is similar to the grasping of beauty, seeing a number of parts altogether, having a sense of an integrated, harmonious whole. This is different from working through a series of propositions to a conclusion. In a poem, we move through the parts sequentially, though our ambition is not to experience the conclusion, but rather to experience the whole structure of which the conclusion forms one element. This is what makes the entire poem a symbol of affective life. Could it be said that the keystone of an arch is the conclusion of the arch? Contextual closure often works like this. There are many individual types of closure in poetry, but if we see the end of the poem as being an equal part of the whole rather than the conclusion of a body of evidence, then we are reading the poem nondiscursively. Collins's "The Dead" comes to us sequentially, syllable by syllable out of the future, but with subsequent rereadings we come to grasp it holistically, and that is how we hold it in our memories.

The discursive ending is often joined to the logic of the syntax, but the apparent shift of focus of the nondiscursive ending can be a result of unexpected juxtaposition, of apparent contrast. We are driven back into the poem to discover the nature, function, and reason for this contrast. Perhaps the simplest form of nondiscursive closure is a simile.

Here is Kenneth Rosen's "The Cold That Owns Us" from *The Origins of Tragedy* (2003):

Why so sore, throat? I did nothing bad to you:
   No kisses or cigars, no second-hand smoke.
Do I detect an up-and-coming disgrace
   With fate? Why is life such a rough
Patch of overexcited chemicals in a bag of skin
   So beautiful and yet so barely adequate

Every piece of the puzzle, ankles, knees, throat,
   Not to mention the heart or core, sooner
Or later in surrender or revolt? In the end we return
   To the stars that made us, and to the cold
That owns us, and irresistibly fall like motes
   From fortune and men's eyes.[5]

This is a deceptive poem. The title is rather menacing, but the first line is comic, relatively. The speaker is addressing his sore throat as alter ego, as other self. The tone is ambiguous. The seemingly comic continues through the third line until we reach "disgrace / With fate." At its furthest extreme, this is a metaphor for approaching death. At its most humble, it is the sore throat. But what is the cause of this sore throat? It might be a cold, it might be cancer, it might be anything in between. And, given what follows, the sore throat suggests sheer physical failure and all the dreary particulars of aging.

So the tone grows more serious, although in entering the long central sentence—a question—to describe a human being as "overexcited chemicals in a bag of skin" is comic in a mordant way. But the question is increasingly serious: death will take us no matter what we do. Then comes the last sentence: three and a half lines without a trace of humor. This, too, is commentary of a sort, a generalized overview of death. So, tonally, the poem seems to end in the opposite place from where it began. It begins with a sore throat; it ends with falling "From fortune and men's eyes."

We may also see that the last line quotes Shakespeare's Sonnet 29. Here is the sonnet's first quatrain: "When, in disgrace with fortune and men's eyes, / I all alone beweep my outcast state / And trouble deaf heaven with my bootless cries / And look upon myself and curse my fate . . ."[6] Once we make this connection, if we do, we may also make a connection between the fourth line of the sonnet and the second sentence of Rosen's poem: "Do I detect an up-and-coming disgrace / With fate?" This may suggest that the words don't refer only to imminent death, but also to the sort of failure that Shakespeare describes in the next quatrain: "Wishing me like to one more rich in hope, / Featured like him, like him with friends possess'd, / Desiring this man's art and that man's scope, / With what I most enjoy contented least . . ."

But Rosen's line "Do I detect an up-and-coming disgrace / With fate?" differs from Shakespeare's "And look upon myself and curse my fate," if only because the former looks forward and the latter looks back. Rosen's disgrace with fate addresses what has not yet happened, flu or cancer or something else, and not something in the past.

But none of this occurs to us in our first reading. It is not until the last line that we realize we might be missing something important. Then, as we keep going through the poem, we may see that the upcoming disgrace with fate is simply a death that occurs after an old age of escalating decrepitude—a process brought to mind by the sore throat. One of the many difficulties with death is its paradoxical aspect: it is completely common and a complete surprise. The speaker in Rosen's poem knows of course that he is going to die, but he dislikes the increasing evidence of it.

Another related element is that the speaker moves from the individual *I* at the beginning of the poem to the all-embracing *we* at the end. We will die and be forgotten by the world and humanity. What softens this, perhaps, is that no one goes alone.

So how do we read the form of this poem, the manner of its telling? The first line seems prose-like, but then we might notice that it is either a headless iambic hexameter line or a trochaic line. And we may decide that the poem's last two lines are basically iambic as well. In addition, we may see that an off-rhyme in each line structures the poem: *throat, smoke, detect, fate, adequate, throat, heart, revolt, that,* and *motes.* These noisy closed syllables that mostly end with a T-sound tie the poem together. Then Rosen drops it. The last line has no such rhyme. "Fortune" makes a halfhearted attempt, but it's not convincing. The dominant rhyming sound is let go just as life is let go, and, in consequence, it becomes a little metaphor for life. We have seen in other poems how poets used an element of rhyme at the end as a way of adding stress. Rosen does the opposite. He established a pattern and then ends it in the penultimate line.

The first half of the last sentence, "stars that made us" and "cold / That owns us," takes on importance by being the spot that gave rise to the title.

That gives this section a lot of emphasis. It also darkens the poem and moves us from the comic element. The sore throat is trivialized by the sheer size of the cold that owns us. But as we continue through the sentence, we come upon the word "irresistibly," which receives emphasis from the caesura earlier in the line. It also receives emphasis from being the poem's longest word apart from "overexcited" in line 4.

So what do we make of "irresistibly"? Its ambiguity comes from meaning that we have no choice but to fall, but also that the act of falling is irresistible, that is, it's desired, if only because we have become so decrepit that death looks good to us. Then we have the simile: in death we become inconsequential and are quickly forgotten; we fall like motes and so on. The ironic comparison to a falling tear suggests not grief but the way we fall from life, and it is set against Shakespeare's second line: "I all alone beweep my outcast state."

Once we go back again to the beginning of the poem, we may see the first line not as comic but as foolish bravado. We also see the poem's quick pace because of the short-duration syllables. Some are a bit longer—*rough* and *beautiful*, although *rough / patch* with its long-duration syllables and enjambment lets us see it as frustration; a nuance that wouldn't exist if *rough / patch* were in the middle of a line. But what stops the momentum of the poem is *irresistibly*. Its five syllables make us pause before we start up again; it makes us focus more directly on the simile.

In addition, the difference between stressed and unstressed syllables in the poem is very strong. Lots of little words are set against the heavily stressed words. This, too, seems to stop at the word "irresistibly." And if you read the poem without "irresistibly," the end changes. It becomes casual and offhand; it seems unfelt. The result is that "irresistibly" becomes the poem's strongest word. It emphasizes our helplessness.

The conceit of Rosen's poem is that of a man addressing his own sore throat. This continues for three sentences, three-fourths of the poem, and then we have the commentary. The sore throat becomes an emblem for increasing dilapidation. It is a metaphor that we accept without thinking it's a metaphor. In that way the whole poem is a nondiscursive description of the late stage of the aging process.

Rosen takes this rather banal subject and makes us see it in a new light. He makes it fresh again. As for the Shakespearean reference, I expect it's meant somewhat ironically. For instance, there is an ironic distance between "sore throat" and "fortune and men's eyes," a shift from the mundane to the vaguely hyperbolic. But it still creates a chill in the reader. We die twice: once in our bodies and then in men's minds.

The surprise of the ending sends us back into the poem: we read and re-read. In this process, the poem's closure stops being closure in the usual sense. It doesn't close the poem, but seems to restart the poem. So we go around and around. The first three sentences are questions, so it is difficult to think they conclude anything. That leaves the last sentence and, more importantly, the word "irresistibly." In trying to understand its ambiguity, we keep returning to it as if it were the keystone of the arch.

Tomas Tranströmer will also often use the nondiscursive through the entire poem in such a way that if the title didn't establish the context, we wouldn't know what he was talking about. Here is his poem "After a Death" (translated by Robin Fulton):

Once there was a shock
that left behind a long pale glimmering comet's tail.
It contains us. It blurs TV images.
It deposits itself as cold drops on the aerials.

You can still shuffle along on skis in the winter sun
among groves where last year's leaves still hang.
They are like pages torn from old telephone directories—
their names are eaten up by the cold.

It is still beautiful to feel your heart throbbing.
But often the shadow feels more real that the body.
The samurai looks insignificant
beside his armor of black dragon scales.[7]

This is a poem that teaches us how to read it as we move along. Because of the title, we understand that the shock in the first line is a death, while the comet's tail is the grief of memory. For a while, we see the world through the filter of this shock: "it contains us." Our grief and memory of the death are like cold drops on the aerials that blur the images on the TV. Of course the details do more than this, but this is the basic information. We don't need to know who died; we don't need to know who is grieving. What is being de-scribed is what the grieving process is like.

Trained as a psychologist, Tranströmer has a keen sense of our subjective vision, how our emotional/psychological state affects how we see the world around us. We are not destroyed by this death, we can still enjoy things, but we can't forget it. So we begin to see last year's leaves like pages from old phone books listing the names of the dead.

In the third stanza, he reiterates the idea that we can still take pleasure in things, and perhaps the memory of the death of someone important to us makes our own lives more precious. Even so, the grief and memory can seem bigger than the body. Then Tranströmer gives a conclusion that is totally surprising. It, too, is a shock, and we scramble to make sense of it. At last, perhaps, we see it as a simile, that our grief dwarfs us in the same way that the samurai is dwarfed by his elaborate armor.

But at first the end seems to make no logical sense. This returns us to the beginning, at which point we begin to see the poem holistically. The poem's information again comes to us sequentially, but we also hold it in our memory as a complete thing. We read it through the lens of its conclusion. The parts come to depend on each other as the stones of an arch depend on each other, with the conclusion forming the keystone.

In trying to understand the poem, I have a conversation with it as I fit its different parts into a whole. At this point, I may or may not be on the right track as I try to shift parts from the descriptive to the metaphoric. What are the cold drops on the aerials, what is the armor of black dragon scales? We come to understand a poem by first identifying possible meanings and then finding sufficient evidence to turn one of those possible meanings into a probable meaning. That probable meaning has to make sense of the whole poem, not just a part. For instance, I could say the first two lines refer to what happens when I put a nail into an electric outlet. This is true, but it doesn't clarify the rest of the poem. That is why it is necessary, in this case, for the title to establish the context. We see that everything in the poem results from that death. Tranströmer is asking what it feels like to grieve; how do you give that vague word substance? And as I come to understand it, I begin to recognize the feeling. I have felt it. And briefly I remember many deaths and how they affected me. And, yes, I can say that the fact of the death rose above me like a samurai's armor rises above the samurai.

If the last line is an act of closure, what does it do? First of all, it's totally surprising. It operates theatrically. Second, it tells me nothing more is needed.

I may not understand it, but the information in the last lines is enough for the poem to form a whole. Third, the voice is filled with authority. These declarative sentences suggest no doubt. But if the poem is a whole, just what sort of whole is it? This takes me back into the poem: twelve lines of uncomplicated language. What is said is both familiar and strange. Yet the concluding statement doesn't close the poem. Because I go back into the poem to make sense of it, I don't reach an end; rather, I continually approach an end. There is no contextual closure, and I remain within the poem continuing to experience it till I turn away.

Here is "Brahma" by Phillip Nast.

We each know the other's moves. You buck
and spin as soon as we leave the chute,
and I hang on, with my free hand high,
not waving, but keeping my balance.

And so it will be in the heart's rodeo,
until the day you leave the arena and say,
Let's skip the drama and have a smooch,
or you pitch me off and the clowns don't show.[8]

The first four lines we assume refers to a bull-riding event. The descriptive language is clear, and we begin to anticipate how the poem will work itself out. But at the beginning of the second stanza, there is a shift. "Heart's rodeo" makes us realize this isn't your usual bull-riding event, though we may not grasp the precise meaning of those words until the end of the seventh line with "smooch." Here we might guess the usual implications of that line will continue: first smooching and then whatever comes after smooching. Instead, there is a reversal. The rider may be pitched from the Brahma, and the absence of clowns practically ensures serious injury or death. But the meaning of that absence isn't immediately clear. It forms a surprise that we need to think about.

We then return to the beginning to put together the poem's two elements: the object and the image, the actual and the conceit, as we see the first four lines do not describe bull-riding, but form a metaphor for lovers going through a difficult time. Then the poem seems to turn with the fifth line. There is a change to future tense and the word "heart" shifts, or clarifies, the subject matter. We may also see that while the first four lines use short-duration syllables, the long-duration syllables in the fifth line slow everything down. Lines 6 and 7 maintain this slower speed, while the last line speeds up again and is more in keeping with the first stanza. And, as we have seen happening in other poems, the next-to-last line could, syntactically, be the end of the poem. It wouldn't be very interesting, but it would serve. This small deception makes the actual ending with its reversal a small surprise.

Once again the ending sends us back into the poem. We reread the poem in order to fully understand the conceit, and we continue going through the poem until we see it holistically. What comes closest to closure is the fifth line right in the middle like the keystone of an arch.

One thing I like about the poem is that the first six lines present the information simply and with great clarity, while the change at the end makes the poem expand as we grasp the conceit and what it represents. This mild complexity stands against the poem's simplicity, giving a sense of space within eight short lines.

Bill Knott's sonnet, "An Obsolescent and His Deity (Polyptych)," presents us with another kind of nondiscursive closure, where the closure is at first obscured by the oddness around it, an oddness seemingly made up of disparate parts. Yet when it is at last understood, the oddness joins the poem into an understandable whole. In addition, while the poem in several places seems ready to dissolve into confusion and mystery, the fact that it is a sonnet (complete with a rhyming couplet at the close) assures us that nothing can get too crazy, as if the sonnet form were a corral confining a number of wild horses.

Bending over like this to get my hands empty
Rummaging through the white trashcans out back
Of the Patent Office, I find a kind of peace
Here, in this warm-lit alley where no one comes.

For even the lowest know that nothing new
Is going to be thrown out now—no formula,
Never not one blueprint will show up in these
Bright bins, their futures are huge, pristine.

Old alleymouth grabbags my attention at times
I see the world flash by out there, furtive as

The doors of decontamination chambers—

I return to my dull, boring search, foraging
For the feel it gives me of the thing which has
Invented me: that void whose sole idea I was.[9]

We might at first think the poem's oddness makes it what we like to call
surreal, but then, reading closely, we understand that the entire poem may be
seen as a realistic description and only the language is odd: "Old alleymouth
grabbags."

The short narrative appears to be about a man searching through the
trashcans behind the Patent Office for evidence of his beginnings. But there is
a peculiarity: instead of seeking something to put into his hands, he is trying to
empty them. Another peculiarity is that the alley is warm, almost cozy, while
the world that passes the entrance of the alley is unpleasant in a confusing
way, or at least we can't paraphrase the metaphor that describes it: "furtive as
/ The doors of decontamination chambers." I don't know why those doors are
furtive, but there is nothing nice about them.

We also see at the end that the speaker isn't searching as much as touch-
ing. He's seeking the feel of nothing. Besides being a surprise, this and the
paradox that serves as closure pose a riddle: How can someone be something
that doesn't exist? But the answer isn't so difficult. Knott often puns on his
name as I discussed in Chapter 3. To be Knott is to be not. Consequently, only
a void could invent a not.

This returns us to the beginning, where see an accumulation of negatives
and nothing new being invented. Soon the trashcans will be empty and pristine: only within emptiness can a void invent a Knott. Success exists in not
being; success is in no success. Going further, we see the lyric as celebrating
what doesn't exist, which is the speaker, or author, celebrating an existential
self, which doesn't, in fact, exist, except perhaps in the word "lowest" in
line 5.

This nonexistence creates in Knott a mildly cheerful pessimism. After all,
how can one be responsible, blamed or accused of failure if one is a not? In
this description, success lies in not being; that if one is a not, then all negatives
are removed and not being becomes the only being. Going through the poem
again and again, the poem's paradox only becomes more complicated, less

open to paraphrase as we see non-being as the only evidence of being, which, for the poet, becomes both self-judgment and praise. We reach some understanding of the poem by grasping it holistically, by trying to see the whole thing at the same time, by seeing nothing. If you find this complicated, that's the point: the paradox that nothing contains the possibility of everything and vice versa.

The last line, though informative and strange, doesn't conclude the poem; rather, we see in our rereadings that the future lies in the emptiness of these white and bright trashcans in line 8: "Bright bins, their futures are huge, pristine." And this seems to be the future the speaker desires. To continue with the metaphor of the arch, line 8 would seem to be its keystone that holds the rest together, but we see this only when we begin to see the poem holistically.

But a nondiscursive ending can also be quite simple, as in Kay Ryan's "Blunt" from her book *Say Uncle* (2000).

> If we could love
> the blunt
> and not
> the point
>
> we would
> almost constantly
> have what we want.
>
> What is the
> blunt of this
> I would ask you,
>
> our conversation
> weeding up
> like the Sargasso.[10]

The structure is discursive: if this, then that, with these consequences. But the turn at the end is a simile arguing that our talk would become like the seaweed-packed Sargasso Sea as a consequence of loving the blunt. As in other discursive poems we have seen, Ryan intensifies the ending with rhyme: "ask you," "Sargasso." But the conditions of the poem, the *blunt* and the *point,* are also metaphors, although they refer to abstractions.

Syntactically, the poem could close with the third stanza. That would satisfy the logic, but would be unremarkable. The last stanza represents a shift in focus, a shift to the visual. Rereading the poem, we find it dominated by that visual image. Our rereading also highlights another part of the poem: if we could love the blunt, we would *almost constantly have what we want.* So is the motivation disappointment, a condition that won't look half so bad once we've turned our conversation into a morass? By evading contextual closure, the poem keeps us within it. We interact with it and experience it holistically, until we stop reading.

Here is another metaphor for the holistic, "The Altar" by Charles Simic:

The plastic statue of the Virgin
On top of a bedroom dresser
With a blackened mirror
From a bad-dream grooming salon.

Two pebbles from the grave of a rock star,
A small, grinning windup monkey,
A bronze Egyptian coin
And a red movie-ticket stub.

A splotch of sunlight on the framed
Communion photograph of a boy
With the eyes of someone
Who will drown in a lake real soon.

An altar dignifying the god of chance.
What is beautiful, it cautions,
Is found accidentally and not sought after.
What is beautiful is easily lost.[11]

We have here a metaphor of Simic's method: a number of disparate elements joined through juxtaposition. Our job as readers is to ask what links them together. Through our rereadings, we come to see these elements holisti-cally: common objects joined by chance on the surface of a dresser as if before an altar. We see them all at once. Or, as Plotinus argued, "Grasping beauty is a matter of 'seeing' a lot of things, 'all together.'" The conclusion is discursive; it is propositional, but it is a conclusion drawn from nondiscursive material. What remains of the rock star is two pebbles. What remains of the circus is a windup monkey. What remains of Egypt is a coin. What remains of the movie is a ticket stub. What remains of the drowned boy is a communion picture. All describe the transient and fragile. Our sense of the rose's beauty is heightened by its fading. Reading the last line, we are surprised by its statement. We had not realized we were reading about loss, and so we reread the poem to learn about it. Once again the poem doesn't end; it continues to give back meaning.

More importantly, by reentering the poem, the reader becomes a partici-pant, by engaging with the language and asking why. It is this process that allows the reader to link with the poem as a symbol of affective life, to see that the symbol is applicable not simply to the poet but also to the reader. The reader discovers his or her life through the process of attempting to discover the poem's contextual closure.

In sum: every lyric poem has four types of closure: visual, syntactic, narra-tive, and contextual. Syntactic closure may be divided into discursive and nondiscursive. Both seek to create a surprise or shift of focus at the end of the poem, which leads us to reread the poem to understand the apparent change of direction, to discover the contextual closure. By rereading and investigat-ing the relation between sense data and abstraction, we begin to perceive the poem holistically. In addition, we, ideally, begin to experience it as a symbol of affective life.

Edgar Allan Poe wrote that there was no such thing as the long poem. Charles Baudelaire quoted this seeming axiom, adding that the limit is about one hundred lines. At first glance, the remark seems frivolous, but what they are pointing to is the need to hold the lyric poem in the mind—not word by word, but the experience of the poem and the need to see the poem through the lens of its conclusion: to experience it holistically.

Through the promise of contextual closure, the poem undertakes to an-chor the ineffable, but it is a false promise. As Merwin writes in "Going," each word communicates and fails to communicate at the same time, and the more we study the word, the more we grow aware of that failure. This is reminiscent of the human condition: our grasp is always partial.

But the very nondiscursiveness of the image promises that more will be revealed. Indeed, the single image and entire symbol of the poem become, holistically, objects of contemplation, which we may meditate upon over a long time. They remain dynamic. Some of these poems I first read twenty or more years ago, and, when I read them now, they are not the same poems. But, unfortunately, it is not the poems that have changed. I see many things in a poem, but I also see my subjective self, and it, too, is fragile, transient, and easily lost. It is the poem's false promise of contextual closure that leads me repeatedly back into the poem. And I learn from that; I see more and more. But I don't see all.

Contextual closure is a contradiction of terms. It is closure that defies the nature of closure. Through that process the world of the poem, or the illusion of that world, takes on a reality far greater for me than that other world, the one we like to call real.

nine

revision

When I was much younger, I would write a poem in the morning, work on it through the day, and then go to bed with a sense of accomplishment. The poem seemed finished. However, when I looked at it the next morning, all was changed. What had seemed graceful now looked clumsy; what seemed intelligent was now vague, while the formal qualities I had admired were a mishmash of inexact barrowings. My first sense, though I knew it wasn't true, was that someone had entered my apartment in the night and wrecked my poem. Then, for much of the day, I would trail around under a gloomy cloud flinging rude remarks at myself. But in the evening, I would again work on the poem, rewriting it until its seeming brilliance once more shone on the page. Again I would go to bed with a feeling of accomplishment.

But the next morning the poem would seem terrible. Sentences and images had alternative meanings I had never suspected. The rhythm of many lines no longer rattled along as nicely as I had thought. Worst of all, it didn't make any sense. I would look at various lines and wonder how I had been so stupid to write such a thing. However, and this gave me hope, the poem was a little better than it had been the previous morning.

This went on for many years, and I learned that the first axiom for being a writer is to forgive yourself for writing badly. I learned that no matter how badly I had written, I could make it better. What I needed were marks on a page, a beginning, a few rudimentary ideas and emotions, and an image or two, and the fact that it seemed to have been written by a mentally challenged third-grader didn't matter.

In high school I never revised anything. I always got a C or B and so revision didn't matter. I disliked school, and getting mediocre grades was one of the many little ways I rebelled. It took quite a few years to see the foolishness of this. In college I revised a little more, but not much. I still got adequate grades. Then, later, as a writer, the only person grading me was myself, and I hated everything I wrote. But I found out something that made me keep going: the poem exists not in that first burst of creativity, but in revision.

The shift between composition and revision is the shift from the imaginative to the analytic, the nondiscursive to the discursive, the expansive to the controlled, from freedom to restraint, license to judgment. But exactly where it occurs is an uncertain line, different with every poem. If revision begins too soon, the poem may be spoiled. Or if it consists of only a cursory tidying, the poem will probably remain unfinished.

Over the years I've acquired a number of tricks to help me write a poem. "Tricks" may sound like the wrong word, but they have helped me see the poem more objectively. My subjective self is being tricked. Some of the tools I describe here will make a better poem, while others are shortcuts, meaning that I spent a lot of time fussing around trying to learn them, and maybe, if you hear them, your way won't be as long. None will make a good poem, however, unless that seed is already emerging from your rough draft. A few of these suggestions I've written about in other places, but I thought it might be useful to put them all together.

Writing a poem is mostly the process of mining one's unconscious; or, if you prefer, the left brain mining the right brain. It begins in various ways, but mostly it starts when the poet hits upon something that can be used as a metaphor, although at times even this is too precise; rather, there is a sudden alertness and one begins writing to discover why one is writing. After all, writing in both poetry and prose is a form of thought *about things that can only be reached through writing.*

Yeats (as described in Chapter 7) often began with a prose description, and at times the crucial metaphor appeared within it. Whitman, too, put down notes for a poem, which might include its subject matter and a few details. But he seemed to put down so few notes that critics are still arguing about how he managed to write what he wrote. Some people begin by freewriting or automatic writing, just putting down words quickly and without apparent thought to see what turns up. This is a process of trolling one's unconscious, and, again, it might reveal a useful metaphor. Nadezhda Mandelstam described how her husband would get a certain rhythm in his head and would walk around, sometimes for days, repeating that rhythm until words joined it. He called this process *remembering* the poem. Often he then recited the poem to his wife and she wrote it down. But in this process, too, one can imagine metaphor. Some poets collect stray lines in a notebook and then try to link several together. Roethke often did this. Rilke, for a while, went to the Paris zoo and wrote about animals, until an idea or metaphor emerged that he could use. His poem "The Panther" started like that. Then there is the rare "gift" when the poem rolls out almost complete. Or sometimes the poet will hit on a particular paradigm that can lead to a large number of poems. Berryman's *Dream Songs* are like this. So is Ellen Bryant Voigt's *Kyrie,* as well as a number of books by Louise Glück and, of course, by Rilke. Sometimes the poem starts with a specific subject and specific intention—a wedding poem or an elegy for Aunt Kate—but here, too, there is the discovery of metaphor. If a poem is a symbol of affective life, then the subject of an elegy is part of that symbol.

One has at any one time a number of concerns: lifetime concerns and temporary concerns, which I discussed at some length in Chapter 2. The metaphor one is seeking consciously or unconsciously links these concerns in some meaningful way, and the poet begins to write, as I say, to discover why he or she is writing. In that writing process anything should be possible. Indeed, it is possibility itself that one is pursuing. This should be a period of pure inventiveness as one idea or image or emotion bangs off another with as little judgment as possible. In letters Rilke condemned his early poetry, meaning poetry he wrote before 1900, saying the poems didn't have enough patience in them. Instead of waiting when he felt stuck, he forced the poem in a certain direction with his intellect, while the language for the most part was a result of default moves; that is, language or ideas he had used in other poems.

Rilke's impatience sprang from a worry about how the poem would end. Most of us do the same. I've got it rolling, I think, but where is it going? This is where Rilke said he didn't wait long enough. He would force an ending that sounded good, but it didn't resolve the poem. Many poets do this. At times I read a poem by an inexperienced poet, and the poem stops right where it should begin. The poet has hit upon an evocative something (an image, perhaps), hopes that it is relevant, and decides this is enough of an ending. It is possible to imagine such endings. One might be "And the geese fly north into memory." A line like that can be slapped onto the bottom of many poems. Another might be "And who am I but the shadow the sun seeks in setting?" Both lines are complete nonsense, but some writers keep notebooks of such lines. They have a certain poetic tone and the appearance of meaning, but nothing is resolved. The poems are muddy. A common revision tool is to rewrite the poem using that last line as the first line to see what might happen.

It is easier to write too much and then cut back, than to write too little and have to add; the period of inventiveness and exploring possibility should be expansive. It takes great patience during this period not to turn to judgment. After all, one is engaged in allowing rather than forcing, and one must put off judgment as long as possible. But the left side of the brain, being uncertain of the direction of the poem, wants to take control, and so the inner critic may shove aside the inner poet and impose an ending that works logically rather than poetically. It stops the poem, but doesn't *conclude* the poem. Don't let the critical mind interfere with the creative; make it wait.

Unfortunately, the conscious, rational mind has an agenda and many constraints. It wants to be liked; it wants approval; it wants success. And so bad choices are made and the poem is bent in a particular direction. Such constraints, even for the sake of political correctness, amount to self-censorship, and the poet may not know it is happening. What is the line between being self-governed and being governed by outside forces? Where we were brought up, our education, our sex, our time in history, ethnic background, prejudices, compulsions, genetics, sexual preferences, physiology—all these factors and more affect how and what we write. In addition, most writers come out of a middle class that often taught them as children to mute their voices, to be nice, to fit in, and this is truer with women than men. These social pressures, too, often result in self-censorship. Because of these and other considerations, it is necessary to go over one's nouns and verbs to see if any have been softened, and to replace slack verbs with descriptive verbs.

Determinists, literary theorists, and some neuroscientists will argue that is a useless activity, that there is no such thing as authorial intention. What you write and how you write are outside of the province of free will. Their causes, or many of them, were put in motion before you were born. Set against determinism are theories of compatibilism or soft determinism, which argue that free will and determinism are compatible, although it would be different in each person. This view, I think, is the best we can hope for if we are to believe in the freedom of our choices, to believe that our work, as well as ourselves, can change and get better.

The beginning writer must question his or her influences and constraints, must develop a necessary degree of self-knowledge in order to estimate to what extent his or her choices are determined. All our choices are determined to some extent, and so they will interfere with or influence the mining of the unconscious. Discovering all of one's influences and constraints is impossible, yet the efforts toward self-understanding, sustained step by step over a lifetime, bring parts of one's unconscious into one's conscious and so increase self-knowledge. This, in turn, can improve your work.

After the poet has spent a fair amount of time with the poem, things begin to seem obvious that perhaps would not be obvious to the reader, or things may seem strident that are really only in the middle range of emotion. This sort of distortion is common. But the result is that the poet may cut out necessary links and information. All poets hate to be called "too obvious," and so they may erase necessary material. The poet may also begin to mute his or her voice. This is usually destructive. Try to read from the reader's point of view to see whether you are muting your voice or you've cut out necessary bits and pieces. The language needs to be interesting or at least have that chance instead of being confined to the bland and inoffensive.

A wide variety of interior forces also affect one's writing, such as emotions, physical well-being or the lack of it, and the complicated effects of the unconscious. All can diminish free will. At times I think my best revision tool is my attempt to work against my propensity for self-deception, which means questioning each element of the poem to determine if its presence is due to anything more than an aesthetic choice. I have to ask why I'm doing what I'm doing, and I have to realize my answers may be incomplete or untruthful. The left side of the brain (the rational, logical side) can block information coming from the right. It can be too scary, too risky, too revealing, too strange. A lot of revision consists of identifying and then getting around that sort of self-censorship.

But after a period of writing the poet usually has a page of something. At this point it is necessary to forgive oneself for any bad writing, for any surprising revelations and interior nastiness, for any political incorrectness. You must write out of your totality, and that totality needs to be reflected on the page no matter how much it might disturb your left brain or superego, your preferred self-image. So it is necessary to be patient with the parts you don't like or that make you feel uncomfortable instead of cutting them out. One has to understand their purpose before deciding to remove them.

Ideally the poet now knows what the poem is about and why he or she wrote it. Perhaps it's a dead grandmother poem, but neither death nor grandmother are mentioned. If there is a discrepancy between what one wants and what is on the page, it can be helpful to write out a prose description of one's intention and then compare the results to the draft of the poem. But after working on that first draft, one hopes the writer has more or less all the necessary information in an order that suggests a beginning, middle, and end. The poem appears full of promise. Then the left brain gradually takes control as the writer tries to make the poem better. This can be a difficult period, as both left and right sides of the brain make an effort to work as one. The danger is in cutting parts that seem rough or don't make sense instead of investigating them and perhaps adding to them. Again, you can't let the critical mind interfere with the creative. One needs to trust one's intuition; if something is on the page, it is often there for a reason. To cut something out before discovering its originating cause can be a mistake, and is usually a result of impatience. The notion that we can be objective about what we have written is an illusion, but we can at least work to be less subjective.

As discussed, a reader comes to understand a poem by asking questions of it, and one question is: "Why does this poem have this shape rather than another?" Long lines, short lines, a mixture of both, no stanzas, stanzas of equal length, stanzas of unequal length—all give information to the reader as well as indicating a sense of the effort lying ahead. Stanzas of equal length can create a sense of orderliness; stanzas of unequal length can create a sense of an organic development; one long unbroken stanza can create a sense of unrelenting thought and/or narrative. The shape of the poem creates certain expectations that are useful to its understanding. The poet needs to make use of this, or at least give the poem a shape that doesn't detract. In this sense, the iambic pentameter line was a useful tool. It was the default position of most formal poetry. But if one chooses something, there must be a reason. If you use stanzas, make it clear why. If you use open stanzas, be careful about how far you extend the sentence or meaning into the next stanza. It could raise the question why you are using stanzas in the first place. If something appears gratuitous, or accidental, the writer loses credibility.

Next the reader looks at the title. It can be simply "poem," or it can be a label that gives a sense of the context, or it can do some work. For instance, if the title is several words drawn from an important part of the poem, then, when the reader reaches that part of the poem, those words take on special emphasis. Or the title can be the effect of the causes presented in the poem. Any of these types of title can be useful, but the writer has to decide which will be most effective. To have the title "poem" or no title at all forces the reader to enter the poem without a title's guidance and puts more emphasis on the first line. This can be something that is wanted, or it can be an evasion. Labels are often the weakest titles because they don't do enough work. At times they are useful because they might establish a context, but mostly they suggest laziness.

"I'm terrible at titles," I hear students say. One can't title a poem until one knows what it is about. One reason a reader reads is to discover the purpose of the title. After all, the reader wants to know why the poem was written. The reader's uncertainty about the meaning of the title is often a source of energy that can encourage the reader to move down the page. But if, after a number of readings, nothing is clarified by the title, then the reader will be frustrated, not to say irritated.

Revision partly consists in challenging one's choices, so in looking at the beginning of one's poem one has to ask why it starts where it starts. What if it began with the third line, or the tenth, or the last? Sometimes the first few lines serve as a runway into the important part of the poem. They were useful once, but are useful no more. Or the poem can begin by detailing an event chronologically, with the first part of the poem being important only because it leads to the second part. You need to question your use of a chronological sequence. Start with the action, start with something that takes the reader's attention. Editors are swamped with submissions, and when they read, they mostly are looking for a reason to stop reading. If the first line is simply introductory—"After lunch, I walked to my car."—an editor might not even make it through the line. You need to take this into account.

One is also still dealing with those constraints and influences mentioned above. To revise successfully, a writer must look at the poem from a different perspective. Replacing the opening line can help bring this about. It makes one rethink the poem's progression and argument. The writer need not keep it like that, but it can be helpful in clarifying one's intention. Rilke said in a letter, during the writing of *New Poems*, that subject matter is always pretext. This may or may not be true, but you need to investigate your ostensible subject to see what lies beneath. It is extremely common in a workshop to come upon sexual meanings that the writer is unaware of. Aside from livening up the class, they show that the writer hasn't learned enough about his or her poem.

A different sort of change of perspective is to write in other forms, especially sonnets, but also villanelles. Or one can make up one's own form. The rigors of form might require different word choices than exist in free verse. And in one's reading, one should also seek out different perspectives, and read for contrast: contemporary, modern, nineteenth-century poems and before, and poems in translation from any language. To read only contemporary American poetry limits one's sense of possibility.

Another mode of revision is to change the point of view from first person to second or third person, and so on. When one changes from first to third, it puts emphasis on details that might have gotten short shrift when the poem was in first person. After all, where the poem is taking place is usually important. Or the poem may have a vague *you* who might be lover, mother, father, or friend. Such a usage only confuses to the reader. Putting the poem in third person can clarify the nature of that *you* and help to show where necessary information is missing.

The writer may have a sense that his or her choices are correct, but one needs to be suspicious of one's own partiality. To change the first line and to change the person challenges this. They can always be changed back. If the original choices can't be defended, perhaps they were the wrong choices. The Belgian novelist Georges Simenon once described his revision process as going through the manuscript and cutting out everything he thought beautiful, by which he meant anything self-indulgent. Be suspicious of what you consider the most successful parts of the poem. Just because a line is well written doesn't mean it's necessary.

A good fiction writer in writing and rewriting will automatically run through certain questions: Where is the light coming from? What is the hour of the day? What is the season? What is the weather? What is the space that the characters inhabit? How are the characters positioned within that space? Are the characters in motion or stationary, inside or outside? What makes the space different from other spaces? And there are other questions. Each carries emotional/psychological nuance—a rainy evening in late fall or a bright spring morning—that may entirely change the mood of the poem. Many of these questions may be unimportant, but one must ask them until they are automatic.

What is the language of the first few lines, what is the diction? The assumption is that the poet wrote because he or she was unable to remain silent. The reader expects that compulsion to energize the language. If the language about some large event—a death or a divorce—is flat, the poem loses credibility. The poem, among other things, is a piece of theater. That, too, needs to be reflected in the writing. Lines should have interesting words. That doesn't seem too much to ask. One's use of small words—conjunctions, prepositions, articles, pronouns, and so on—may be necessary to form unaccented syllables to set against accented syllables, but a line made up mostly of small uninteresting words saps the poem's energy. In addition, each line has to contain within it a reason to read the next line. This can be done with enjambment, syntax, narrative, surprise, and the speed and energy of the line. And presumably the poem's emotional and intellectual content also gives the reader some reason to keep reading. All of this has to affect the reader's interest. You have to engage the reader with the questions of what is going to happen and why it matters.

Most words carry with them sexual/psychological/emotional nuance in their connotative forms, just as colors and sounds can carry such nuance. How we use words and which words we use is deeply affected by sexual, psychological, emotional, cultural, or historical considerations. This is simply a fact. One must constantly go over one's word choices to see if they connote or suggest a meaning one doesn't intend. The poet can have such a clear idea of what he or she means that he or she doesn't bother to look for possible alternative meanings. Make a practice of going over those words in revision. Read the poem aloud. If a word or sentence suggests another meaning, you may want it or not want it, but you have to be aware of its connotations.

The writer needs to question the syntax of his or her sentences. Are there too many repetitions of subject, predicate, direct object? In a classical sentence the most important words are the final words. This also creates energy as we try to anticipate what will happen. Are important words revealed too early in the sentence? It is useful to change the syntax, if only temporarily, to see what effect it will have. Likewise, the writer should restate his or her sentence in its simplest form—*See Spot run.*—and then compare it to the original. Are those extra words necessary? At times we imagine our words and sentences as set in stone. Perhaps they are, but we must challenge our choices.

The tone of the poem should be established at the beginning. If it changes later, it must be by design. Likewise, the range of diction—the word choice, or vocabulary—used in the poem must be established at the beginning. If some other sort of diction appears later, it can change the tone. At the beginning of the poem, the reader is more accepting, and the writer can use language or details that might not work later. The writer always works to make the reader accept the writing or just to make it credible. Jarring tone changes can weaken this. Generally, what we get in the first lines is the poem's range in diction and tone. Any poem teaches us how to read it. This is how that teaching begins.

The first sentence obviously begins at the head of the first line. Where do others begin? The line and the sentence can have a slightly different rhythm. The contrasting sound of both together is called counterpoint. Where the sentence begins on the line affects this rhythm. Some writers, such as Charles Simic, begin most of their sentences at the head of the line, which creates a sense of control. Many inexperienced writers begin their sentences at any available point, which creates a sense of the gratuitous.

The positions of greatest emphasis in a line are at the beginning and the end. If the line is enjambed, that puts even more emphasis of the first word of the next line. It is necessary to arrange the information to put important words in the places of greatest emphasis, unless there is a specific reason not to do so. To bury an important word in the middle of a line weakens the sentence. Emphasizing an unimportant word at the beginning or end of a line does likewise. Nuance in a poem is partly controlled by this sort of positioning. Rewrite your poems to see the effects of different words at the beginning, middle, and end of the lines.

You write the poem on two different levels at the same time: sound and sense. As a result, a line may sound right to your ear, but may detract from the sense. And of course the opposite is also true. When you get either sound or sense working in the way you want, you can mistakenly think both are working. This is a common error. The line gives you a sense of success, but one part of it, either sound or sense, still isn't right.

At times your right brain (the creative, visionary side) may start a pattern without the left brain perceiving it. This may consist of partial rhymes, degrees of consonance and assonance, different degrees of stress; or it may be a metaphor. In revision it's tempting to remove these rhymes or inflections because they don't seem to fit, but the right brain must have had a reason for them. Try to identify the reason and learn its purpose before you do any cutting. Once understood, you can heighten, flatten, or change them according to the poem's needs. At times it is useful to prolong one of these patterns through to the last line.

It is impossible to visualize any unspecified plural form. At times it won't matter—a stand of trees or a group of people—but at other times it is important: three trees on a hill, two men under a streetlight. The specific number allows a reader to have a visual response; an unspecified number doesn't. Make sure the pronouns are clear and uncluttered. Pronouns in particular may be mistakenly used where the writer has no doubt about the referent while the reader remains confused as to who "she" or "you" is supposed to be.

A poem uses its initial energy to move forward through patterns of tension and rest. This can be obvious, as might be the case with rhyme and meter, or it can be so subtle as to appear nonexistent. An enjambed line creates tension; an end-stopped line creates rest. A long sentence creates tension; a short sentence creates rest. Obscurity creates tension; clarity creates rest. These are obvious instances. But even a repeated off-rhyme within the body of the poem can create the expectation that it will happen again. This adds a bit of tension. In fact, any sound or rhythm within the poem can be repeated to create the expectation of a reappearance. The poet can take advantage of this or not, but when it occurs accidentally, it might emphasize a word or phrase that isn't worthy of emphasis. As these patterns continue and then disappear and reappear, more tension is created, which translates into the energy necessary to read and take pleasure from the poem. If tension keeps building without a rest—for instance, using one enjambed line after another—the reader may grow weary and turn away from the page. If there is no attempt to create tension, then the poem will be rather dull.

Something needs to energize the reading, and these small patterns create small unexpected jolts of energy. John Berryman's *Dream Songs* are a brilliant example of this. A comic or ironic element can also create such a jolt. They are unexpected and can affect the tone, which may energize that part of the poem.

Patterns of tension and rest are often easier in metered poems. Using a succession of iambic lines without a substitution is incredibly dull, just as using a sequence of exact rhymes bores the reader. Substitutions and off-rhymes form other ways to create nuance and something mildly startling. Very mildly, perhaps.

Syntax and diction can also use tension and rest. These words coming to us out of the future, if we find nothing we expected, we may grow frustrated. If we find just what we expected, we may become bored.

Poems are noises of various durations, and much revision is focused on adjusting that noise. The noise can be complicated and loud, or it can be a mild drone, as in Yeats's "Her Praise" discussed in Chapter 7. Even if the poet does nothing, that noise will exist, so it makes sense to employ it judiciously instead of creating unintended affects. Ideally, the poem is all of a piece, with everything working together so that unexpected sounds or transitions create emphasis, and details have some metaphoric reverberation with the whole. This is how we read. If we come upon a double stress or a spondee, we assume the writer is trying to tell us something. Otherwise why would he or she insert the emphasis? The same is true with a trochaic substitution. In fact any departure from the rhythmic norm can be used to create nuance.

The sound of the poem is not simply a vehicle for the meaning, but can be equal to the meaning in importance, and often the sound has a metaphoric relation to the meaning. This is more easily achieved in a formal poem, but it can also be done in free verse. Yet a common problem occurs, as I mentioned earlier in this chapter, when the poem is finished in terms of sense, but not in terms of sound, or when it's finished in terms of sound, but not in terms of sense. The writer reads the poem and feels it is finished, but it's an illusion because only one aspect of the poem is completed. The writer must read the poem out loud to hear the effect of the sounds and rhythms. This should be done with an uninflected voice with as little expression as possible—I like to think of it as "the robot voice"—since it is easy to create nuance and emphasis in the voice when there is none on the page.

The rhythm and speed of the line is created in part by the nature of the syllables and by the relation between stressed and unstressed syllables, as I discuss in Chapter 4. This is true whether the poem is in formal or free verse. If a majority of the syllables are unstressed, the line can sound flaccid; if a majority are stressed the line can sound clotted. The reason why polysyllabic words are less common in poetry is because most have one stressed and three or four unstressed syllables. A number of these together may make the line flaccid and turn it to prose. The speed of the line isn't necessarily affected by its length, but rather by the duration of the syllables and the particular sound of the consonants. A line made up of long-duration syllables and soft consonants will move slowly and seem long even if it is short.

The poet is constantly juggling synonyms to create a particular rhythm, exchanging a two-syllable word for a one-syllable word, or a one-syllable word for a two-syllable word. Many synonyms of small words have the same meaning: *someone, somebody; just, only; start, begin; seem, appear; out of, from; another, each other,* etc. These words are interchangeable, as are many others, and the addition or subtraction of a single syllable or noise can affect the rhythm.

The writer wants to convince the reader of the truth of the utterance—not whether something actually happened; that is unimportant—but the truth of the *meaning* or act of witness. It was to tell this truth that the writer broke silence in the first place. The poem exists to present evidence of this truth both in form and in content. And of course the poem is written and the evidence is chosen and arranged to convince the reader. Because of this the poem is like an argument. The evidence comes in various ways, but a major way is in the poem's use of detail. Each detail can push the reader further toward understanding. If two very different and excellent details present the same idea, then they become chaff and one must be removed. In addition, details should move from the weaker to the stronger, as Keats does in "On First Looking into Chapman's Homer."

The specificity of the details acts on the reader's memory, which either authenticates the detail from experience and/or imagination, or finds the detail too incredible, inappropriate, or commonplace. An important aspect of the detail is its sense data, which the reader reexperiences: seeing what is to be seen, hearing what is to be heard, and so on. This links the reader to the poem through a creative act.

Here is Kenneth Rosen's "Apple Tree":

Cold weather came. In a yard by the playground
Some boys with sticks climbed an old apple tree,
A fat bag lady of a tree loaded with strings
Of big ones dangling like an old dog's balls
Or tits, and they climbed up its twisted trunk, went out

On a limb to knock loose some fruit, and the tree

Gave itself a shake of its green skirts as if

It didn't mind missing a few, even blushing

Through its tangled hair as the boys slashed with their sticks

And shouted to each other, and laughed,

But when one of them cracked a branch

It whispered, "Ding dong, you son-of-a-bitch, ding dong."

That house belonged to a murderer, a humble,

Hobbling little guy who served his time in Thomaston,

Got out and got old with a yard by the playground,

Checked into a nursing home and then

The great penitentiary of the sky,

And today, as if it cursed itself, that tree is gone.

No snake, no paradise, *finis*, gone.[1]

One enters this poem through its details, which, in this case, have a commonness to them. Nothing at the start is unusual. Reading the poem slowly, we reexperience each detail by checking it with our memories. The poem uses details of touch, of hearing, but mostly the sense of sight. The place is familiar and unfamiliar, but it doesn't matter. But by line 3 Rosen begins to stretch our imaginations: the tree resembles a fat old bag lady; the apples resemble an old dog's balls. Then the description returns to the realistic, but not quite. There's that pun of going out on a limb. In line 7 the bag lady is given skirts; in line 9 she is given hair; in line 12 she curses. Because we are grounded at the beginning and then move step by step, we most likely accept the fantastic elements, which allow us to imagine the tree and suspend our disbelief. The scene is completely common and completely unique. What we may forget is the use of the past tense of the poem's first three words. Then, in the next-to-last line, the poem shifts to the present; we learn the tree is gone, which is when we realize this is a memory. But before we can consider it, we are given the odd last line: "No snake, no paradise, *finis*, gone." Rosen has shifted from the denotative to the connotative. The poem isn't about apple picking. Instead, it's a meditation on the passage of time and then a statement about the absence of heaven and hell. This is surprising, and we reenter the poem to make sense of it, though this time we see the tree both denotatively and connotatively, and realize it can symbolize the apple tree in the Garden of Eden, while the snake is the snake from the Garden. The tree and the boys, the season and the place become symbols of a larger world, but what allows us to make this journey is the sense data that is there from the start.

Above I referred to how a writer may use a pattern of off-rhymes to create a pattern and texture. In this poem, Rosen uses a pattern of closed-syllable 'k' sounds and 't' sounds from lines 2 through 11, which he then drops. But those sounds energize the first half of the poem, while the lack of them softens the second half.

In going through a poem, the poet asks, "What do I know, what do I not know, what do I need to know?" And the poet should also ask, "Why am I saying this, do I need to say it, do I need to say it here?" Again, one is trying to get around one's prejudices and become conscious of one's choices.

The poet charts the arc of the poem: its beginning, middle, and end. The poem works on an emotional level, an intellectual level, and a physical level. Each has its little arcs, and the poet checks to see if the different parts are proportionate to one another. One doesn't want the beginning twice as long as the middle. Perhaps the three parts don't need to be exactly proportionate, but one needs to be conscious of the differences. What is the emotional center of the poem, and why is it important? The poet then goes over the poem to remove unnecessary words and/or intensifiers. They can be useful in the first reading, but become chaff by the second. Most adjectives are relative and communicate little information. If they can't be cut, the poet tries to replace them with an image.

These suggestions won't create a great poem, but they will make a better poem. There are no rules in poetry, just advice and a list of options. However, the writer's main loyalty is to the poem. To worry about what people might think is just another constraint. The poem must be clear enough so that readers—plural—have a growing understanding of one's meaning and intention, as well as understanding the relationship between form and content—but that, perhaps, is all the poet needs to consider in terms of the reader's perspective. The poem, for the most part, is a private conversation that the reader is allowed to overhear with the hope that it might touch his or her life. Consequently, the poet needs to make room for the reader's presence, to help the reader overhear and to make understanding possible.

moral inquiry

a poem or piece of fiction is, among other things, an instrument of moral inquiry. That is not to say that by itself it is moral or immoral, but it presents material about which moral judgments may be made. In consequence, the writer isn't just making aesthetic choices; he or she is making ethical choices.

"Ethical thought," as defined by Sir Isaiah Berlin, "consists of the systematic examination of the relations of human beings to each other, the conceptions, interests and ideals from which human ways of treating one another springs, and the systems of value on which such ends of life are based."[1] In addition, the writer is making ethical choices not only by what he or she puts on the page, but also by what he or she chooses not to put on the page. What one doesn't say can be as significant as what one says.

The art of any historical period is a microcosm of that period. It reflects that period's self-definitions and aspirations, its frustrations and failures. It reflects its range of ethical thought. I write about this in my essay "Notes on Free Verse" (collected in *Best Words, Best Order*), but it bears repeating. There I argue that it's not just the content of a poem that reflects the age in which it was written, but also the form. The heroic couplet reflects the ideas and values of the age of Enlightenment. And, in such a way, free verse reflects the twentieth century, its rush and contradictions and emphasis on self-expression. Whitman said his free verse was fashioned by the events leading up to the Civil War and by the war itself. Those events, for Whitman, were a period of violence and political corruption in New York in the 1850s, as well as the war's ferocity, carnage, and rupture with the past. Only through his own free or fractured verse, he felt, was it possible to write about it.

Baudelaire touches upon something like this in his essay "The Painter of Modern Life," where he wrote that "beauty is made up of an element that is eternal and invariable . . . and, on the other, of a relative, circumstantial element," which reflects its contemporary aspect.[2] Without that circumstantial element, which might be only its form, our entry to the work would be limited. We wouldn't feel that it spoke to our own lives. Though we read work from other periods that does speak to our lives, we read it through a compensatory filter. We focus on human emotion, psychology, and interaction, while registering the author's differences in viewpoint as being due to the time in which he or she lived.

Isaiah Berlin traces this emphasis on differing viewpoints to the eighteenth-century Italian philosopher Giambattista Vico, whom Baudelaire certainly hadn't read. Vico, wrote Berlin, argued, "That every society had . . . its own vision of reality, of the world in which it lived, and of itself and of its relation to its own past, to nature, to what it strove for. . . . For Vico there is a plurality of civilizations . . . each with its own unique pattern."[3] These ideas were developed by eighteenth-century German philosophers, specifically Johann Gottfried von Herder and Johann Gottlieb Fichte, and became basic tenets of Romanticism.

Consequently, the art of any particular society at any particular moment is unique to it. We may not like it, we may think it is terrible, but it is unique to the society from which it arose. In addition, we can no more write in the voice and manner of another age than we could take on the fashion and habits of another age. If we accept that a poem is, among other things, an instrument of moral inquiry, this is in part dependent on its relationship to the world that gave rise to it, that it is a microcosm of that world. The choreographer Martha Graham once said: "No artist is ahead of his time. He *is* his time."[4]

This is what Baudelaire called "a relative circumstantial element." And if in style and subject matter the poem tries to identify with another world—say, the world of the 1890s—then we find it difficult to suspend our disbelief, unless the poem is meant to be ironic or a satire or parody. We also understand that art, unlike technology and scientific discovery, does not improve generation by generation. We may think that societies of certain periods have better art than societies of other periods, but this is not due to artistic advancement, but is rather a matter of taste or affinity.

It seems important to keep these ideas in mind when we look at critical writing. How is the playing field for good and bad art established? First of all, it would seem necessary to separate the concept from the practice; that is, how well the poem is written. The concept may be how the poet chooses to treat his or her subject, and it reflects the poet's particular aesthetic. When Charles Bukowski is dismissed as simplistic and crude, the judgment derives from the concept that drove his poetry in general and drove a specific poem in particular. But was the poem written badly? It was written exactly as Bukowski wanted. So if I say it was written badly, I refer not to how he wrote it, but to how he *chose* to write it: the poem's motivating concept. So if I criticize Bukowski's ability and intelligence, I have no basis for my criticism. All I can say is I disagree with his concept.

Implicit in my argument is that poetry has certain requirements: that a poem to be a poem must have X, Y, and Z. Unfortunately, these ideas have been under attack ever since the advent of Romanticism, which argued that expressiveness was more important than obeying a number of preexisting rules. The Romantic poets didn't follow rules, or, so it could be argued, the Romantic poet invented his or her own rules, and the poem arose organically from the poet's psychology, ego, and emotional need, as well as from the poet's often idiosyncratic ideas about form and how a poem should be written. Free verse is one of those idiosyncratic ideas. What is honored in particular is sincerity and emotional force, while the form of the poem is an aspect of the poet's expressiveness. It grows organically from the content.

This, from a critic's standpoint, is a perilous position. It opens the door to rampant relativism. It suggests something is a poem only because its author calls it a poem. It suggests that poetry has no real value, that its only requirement be that it is a microcosm of the time in which it was made, and it is hard for the poet to avoid that. Even if the poet chooses to write a poem in the style of the 1890s, he is in part reacting against the time in which he or she lives, meaning that, paradoxically, the poet's specific period of history exists in the poem even by *not* being in the poem. But for a critic, who seeks to control the terms by which we suspend our disbelief, this is a potential nightmare.

Relativism is a false issue, however, because certainly some poems are better than others. It is often necessary to identify the aesthetic of the critic who is doing the judging. Charles-Augustin Sainte-Beuve was the greatest nineteenth-century French critic, an early champion of Romanticism, and a friend of Baudelaire's, yet he refused to write an article about Baudelaire's *Les Fleurs du Mal* or his volume of translations of Poe's short stories, despite Baudelaire's requests. In addition, he would not publicly support Baudelaire against the government's successful prosecution of him and his publishers for creating an offense against public morals, nor would he support Baudelaire's admission to the French Academy. Indeed, he asked Baudelaire to withdraw his application. Sainte-Beuve's only public mention of *Les Fleurs du Mal* was in an article on the various candidates up for election to the Academy. He referred to Baudelaire's masterwork as "this little lodge, which the poet has built himself on the tip of the Kamchatka Peninsula of literature, I call it 'the Baudelaire Folly.'"[5] He closed by saying that, despite what might have been heard, Baudelaire was a person who "improves on acquaintance, so that those who were expecting some strange eccentric to come in, found themselves meeting an exemplary candidate, polite, deferential, a nice fellow, refined of speech and with perfectly correct manners."[6]

Marcel Proust, appalled by Sainte-Beuve's words, suggested that the critic had given way "to the sort of verbal hysteria which from time to time made him find an irresistible pleasure in talking like an illiterate grocer."[7]

Sainte-Beuve thought the poems distasteful. He disliked reading them and he didn't want to write about him. In a letter to Baudelaire, thanking him for a copy of the book, he said little more than, "You must have suffered much, my poor lad."[8]

We read a poem through a filter made up of our previous reading experience, psychology, and history, and by asking questions of it, while the filter informs the nature and complexity of our questions. What then happens is that an interaction or dialogue occurs between the poem and the reader on the levels of intellect and emotion. For instance, the intellect can tell us the poem is badly written or simplistically realized, even when the poem is emotionally powerful. (This is the basis of some of the criticism against Bukowski.) Or we can feel that the poem is intellectually brilliant and emotionally flat, which may be the criticism against some obscure and inaccessible poets. In both cases, something limits the degree of interaction between reader and poem, although the poem will still be a microcosm of the time that gave rise to it, with one poem perhaps being called populist or descended from Whitman and the other possibly called postmodernist. In such cases, our reading filter may judge the populist poem to be overly accessible and crude, while the postmodern poem may be intellectually stimulating yet remain abstruse. We have many ways of talking about it, while still being unable to describe what it says. Yet even that way of non-saying, we may argue, is a form of saying.

The question is whether this intellectual complexity makes up for the poem's being emotionally flat in its presentation. Or we may argue that a refusal to emote is itself a form of emotion: (paradoxically) by denying its emotion the poem expresses its emotion. And it should be clear that when our "reading filter" is shallow or inexperienced, we are more likely to be impressed by poems that we later regard as superficial or too much like other poems. What we once saw as mysterious, we now see as vague. What we once saw as evocative, we now see as a rhetorical device. So, as is the case with Sainte-Beuve, our judgments might arise from our own shortcomings rather than the writer's.

As our reading experience grows, our pleasures become more complicated and our frustrations more easily aroused. This is one reason why we demand that a poem be more than the sum of its parts, that it resist paraphrase while still being a rewarding object of contemplation. We demand entry, or the possibility of entry, to the poem's dominating symbol.

These demands concern both how the poem is told and what is told. As our sense of a poem's complexity increases, so our demands increase. Ideally, however, we continue to see that the simplicity of language and presentation in a poem by Bukowski or Frank O'Hara is part of the concept: that the choice of such simplicity constitutes an argument about the nature of the poet's aesthetic, and the apparently uncomplicated language may be informed by tone, such as irony and/or emotion. With such poems, no matter how simple, no matter how apparently paraphrasable and easy to encompass, we still have a sense that it contains more. The poem continues to function as metaphor, as symbol.

Look at James Wright's poem "Small Frogs Killed on the Highway":

Still,
I would leap too
Into the light,

If I had the chance.
It is everything, the wet green stalk of the field
On the other side of the road.
They crouch there, too, faltering in terror
And take strange wing. Many
Of the dead never moved, but many
Of the dead are alive forever in the split second
Auto headlights more sudden
Than their drivers know.
The drivers burrow backward into dank pools
Where nothing begets
Nothing.

Across the road, tadpoles are dancing
On the quarter thumbnail
Of the moon. They can't see,
Not yet.

This is a simple poem with odd complexities. On first reading we take in the narrative about which we may have a few questions. But the slight surprise of the last line creates a larger question, and we go back into the poem to find an answer. In most of Wright's free verse poems, we don't so much read from line to line as fall from line to line. Rhythmically it feels as if we are descending a flight of stairs. This is partly because each line withholds meaning; so we read a line not only to discover its meaning, but also to discover the meaning of the previous line. Nearly every line contains a question about what comes next and an answer about what just came before. The first line, "Still," doesn't give us a sense of its meaning until the next line, "I would leap too." This clarifies "Still" while it raises a question about where the speaker "would leap" and the meaning of "too." This we learn in the next line: "I would leap . . . into the light." And why? "If I had the chance"—but this doesn't give the reason but the intensity of the desire.

Another element that affects this falling quality is that the word in the line that receives the most stress is the last word, and the word that takes the least stress is the first. There are exceptions, but for the large majority of lines this holds true. And the majority of the syllables are of short duration, which makes the lines move more quickly.

A paraphrase is quite simple: I, too, would like to die in a flash of light with the sense that I would live forever. What the frogs are leaping toward across the road is paradise—"It is everything, the wet green stalk of the field." What they are leaving is the world where tadpoles grow, tadpoles that will soon duplicate the actions of the frogs. But for me the oddest thing is the last three lines of the first stanza—"The drivers burrow backward into dank pools / Where nothing begets / Nothing." What sort of judgment is this? The drivers are nothing and can beget nothing, while the frogs beget passionate tadpoles? Also the pond of the drivers is dank; the pond of the tadpoles is lit by the moon.

Most poems begin with a question and end with an answer. This poem does just the opposite; or, rather, under its narrative a mystery is constructed. I have read this poem many times, but the drivers and their relationship to the frogs remain mysterious. In addition, the light, the green field across the road, the last three lines of the first stanza, and the poem's last three lines approach the level of symbol, a symbol to which I draw near, but can't embrace. The images continue to resonate.

So when I say that our reading experience over time makes the filter through which we read poetry more sophisticated, it doesn't mean the poems we respond to become more intricate and difficult. That may be the case, but it doesn't have to be. Complexity is a quality, but it's not a necessity, and many seemingly simple poems continue to resonate and give back.

Recently I read in Walter Benjamin's essay "The Paris of the Second Empire in Baudelaire" the following sentence: "What Baudelaire expressed could thus be called the metaphysics of the *provocateur.*"[9] What struck me most was the fact that I was struck at all. Baudelaire often sought to provoke. When *Les Fleurs du Mal* appeared in 1857, it created a public scandal. In the court trial, Baudelaire, his publisher, and the printer were fortunate to stay out of jail. Instead, they were fined and six of the poems were banned. They weren't published again in France until 1949. The publisher soon went bankrupt.

The very first poem, "Au Lecteur," begins by berating the reader: "Folly, error, vice and avarice / fills our souls and belabors our bodies . . ." It was the ambition of Baudelaire and the so-called decadent poets of the time to "épater le bourgeois," to shock the middle classes, the conventional. The concepts dominating his poems reflected an ethical choice. Even Baudelaire's three poems on cats have disturbing qualities.

Yes, Baudelaire could provoke, but to say he expressed the metaphysics of the provocateur is to suggest this desire existed in him not necessarily psychologically, but philosophically. The event that might cause him to act out was pretext. His wish to shock was a symptom of it—not a cause. In the French Revolution of February 1848 that ended the reign of Louis-Philippe, Baudelaire was seen on a street corner waving a shotgun and shouting, "Down with General Aupick!" This was Baudelaire's hated stepfather, Jacques Aupick. The world, for Baudelaire, began with the personal and then spread out in ever-expanding circles.

Still, when Baudelaire was lecturing about poetry in Brussels in 1864–66, the Belgian police were certain he was a French police spy. He was a shady character. He moved about in a mysterious manner. It was later thought that Baudelaire himself had started this rumor, which would have been characteristic. In a note from this time, quoted by Benjamin, Baudelaire wrote: "I would be happy not only as a victim; it would not displease me to play the hangman as well—so as to feel the revolution from both sides! All of us have the revolution in our blood as we have syphilis in our bones; we have a democratic and syphilitic infection."[10] This was shortly before Baudelaire's syphilis at last struck him down, leaving him aphasic for the final seventeen months of his life. What is interesting about Baudelaire's desire to be both victim and hangman is his yearning to embrace such a range of human experience. It is also, obviously, a provocative statement.

When one reads about Baudelaire's life and the history of his times, as well as about the history of Romanticism, one sees nothing terribly original about his position. The models who influenced him were many and well known. He dedicated *Les Fleurs du Mal* to another controversial and provocative writer, Théophile Gautier, who promulgated the idea of art for art's sake. Paris was full of eccentric Romantic poets when Baudelaire was growing up. What separated him from the rest was his incredible tenacity in terms of his work, making him an island of discipline in a sea of rampant irresponsibility. The extreme fastidiousness that led him to spend several hours each day at his toilet (shaving, grooming himself, dressing, adjusting his tie, etc.) was a meticulousness he directed also at his poems. What also separated Baudelaire from the others was his aesthetic isolation. Walter Benjamin wrote, "Baudelaire was not based on any style, and he had no school. This greatly impeded his reception."[11] The same could be said of Whitman, whose work at the beginning was rejected for both its form and its content. *Leaves of Grass,* too, was seen as an offense against public morals.

So it's Benjamin's use of the word "metaphysics" that sticks in my mind, that Baudelaire expressed the *metaphysics* of the *provocateur*. It was this attitude that disturbed Sainte-Beuve. Much of the subject matter, Sainte-Beuve thought, was inappropriate for poetry. He praised the practice, but hated the concept. The same may be said in our day of the poet Bill Knott, who also exhibits a desire to shock the bourgeois. It is not that he is a provocateur, though he can be, but he expresses the metaphysics of the provocateur. For me, that means the poem has a confrontational quality; it often seeks to jar the reader's complacency and exhibits a willingness to express human totality, the uncensored self. What this means is that to express human totality requires that *absolutely anything* in human thought and experience becomes available as subject matter, no matter how unattractive. The alternative means that some censorship, some softening occurs. The conscious mind seeks to please or not to displease; it seeks to be successful and liked. And it might have other agendas, such as getting even with one's parents or ex-wife. Sainte-Beuve had a sense of decorum concerning subject matter, and Baudelaire violated it. Not only did Baudelaire embrace his human totality in the first poem, "Au Lecteur" ("To the Reader"), but he said his and the readers' totality were the same. He denied the reader his or her moral platform.

But Baudelaire was no lyric poet confining himself to a life of solitude. His poems, like Whitman's, were directed outward. He was an urban poet, and many of his poems concerned people he had seen on the street. Benjamin wrote, "The masses were an agitated veil, and Baudelaire views Paris through this veil."[12] He was a dandy and a flaneur, a wanderer of the streets, an idler-about-town, especially in the 1840s. In this he was again like Whitman in 1840s New York. Whitman wasn't quite a dandy, but he was certainly dapper in a conservative sort of way. He called himself a "loafer," which is one of the synonyms of a flaneur. This was nearly a political stance. It was a slap in the face of the petite bourgeoisie; it made a mockery of their pursuit of money and success. The flaneur who walked a turtle on a string through the Arcades, or Nerval walking a lobster on a ribbon, was rejecting the essential middle-class aphorism "time is money."

Both Baudelaire and Whitman were very aware of their public personas and dressed accordingly. After 1850, Whitman began wearing colorful shirts

open at the neck, a red kerchief, a slouch hat, and baggy pants tucked into his
brown leather boots. He liked to attract attention, at least until about 1863
(during the Civil War) when he changed to a black suit with a white shirt.
Both men carefully oversaw the printing of their books and calculated their effect. Benjamin wrote, "[T]hrough [Baudelaire's] deep experience of the nature
of the commodity, he was enabled, or compelled, to recognize the market as
an objective court of appeals. . . . Through his negotiations with editors, he
was continuously in contact with the market. . . . Baudelaire was perhaps the
first to conceive of a market-ordered originality, which for that very reason
was more original in its day than any other. . . . This *creation* entailed a certain
intolerance. Baudelaire wanted to make room for his poems, and to this end
he had to push aside others."[13] The same could be said of Whitman, who, like
Baudelaire, saw a number of his poems as using sensational material to pander
to an audience. He also dismissed formal poetry as being European, rather
than American. Here is a rare confrontational poem by Whitman; he gave it
several titles, but it is mostly known as "Respondez." I will give the beginning
and some later lines.

Respondez! Respondez!

Let everyone answer! let those who sleep be waked! let none evade!

Must we still go on with our affectations and sneaking?

Let me bring this to a close—I pronounce openly for a new distribution of
        roles.

Let that which stood in front go behind! And let that which was behind
        advance to the front and speak.

Let murderers, thieves, bigots, fools, unclean persons, offer new
        propositions! . . .

Let men and women be mocked with bodies and mocked with souls! . . .

Let contradictions prevail! let one thing contradict another! and let one line
        of my poems contradict another! . . .

Let the people sprawl with yearning aimless hands! let their tongues be
        broken! let their eyes be discouraged! let none descend into their
        heart with the fresh lusciousness of love! . . .

Let the crust of hell be neared and trod on! let the days be darker then the
        nights! let slumber bring less slumber than waking-time brings . . .

Let him who is without my poems be assassinated.[14]

This is a sixty-line poem with 104 exclamation marks. It first appeared in the 1856 edition of *Leaves of Grass* and in every edition through 1876. Then he removed it because he worried it might tarnish his image as "the good, gray poet." This is surely Whitman's most cynical poem, and it was brought on by his hatred of the bourgeoisie, by what he saw as the corruption and hypocrisy of his times, and by his disenchantment with American life. It was also brought on by his disappointment that the 1855 edition of *Leaves of Grass* wasn't embraced with the fervor that he had expected. Here is one more line from "Respondez": "Let there be wealthy and immense cities—but still through any of them, not a single poet, savior, knower, lover." This is how Whitman saw himself: poet, savior, knower, lover. His description is neither dispassionate nor objective. He scorns those who rejected him. But in this one place he sounds like a modernist, and it is the one poem in which he stands side by side with Baudelaire.

Here is Baudelaire's poem "L'Héautontimorouménos," which is Greek for "the one who tortures himself." The translation is mine.

I shall strike you without anger
And without hate, like a butcher,
Just as Moses struck the rock!
And from your eyes I shall make

The waters of suffering break forth
To irrigate the sands of my Sahara.
Filled with hope at last, my desire
Will float upon your salt tears

Like a ship putting out to sea,
And in my heart, drunk with brine,
Your beloved sobs will ring out
Like a drum beating the charge!

Am I not a discordant note
In the heavenly symphony,
Thanks to voracious Irony
Who shakes me and bites me?

. . .

She's in my voice, the shrill shrew!
All my blood is her black poison!
I am the menacing mirror
Into which the Megara gapes.

I am the wound and the dagger!
I am the blow and the cheek!
I am the limbs and the rack,
Victim and executioner!

I am the vampire of my heart
—One of those premier derelicts
Condemned to eternal laughter,
But who can smile no longer![15]

In French these are rhymed eight-syllable lines. Though this was long seen to be a sexual sadomasochistic poem, it is now generally accepted that the poem is about writing poetry, with the first three stanzas being the poet addressing himself. They describe the poet's practice. The fourth stanza gives the reason for this: the only discordant element in God's universe is man, who, because of his divided nature, torn between appetite and his moral sense, torments himself with a "voracious Irony." He is, after all, conscious of this divided nature. (*Ironie* with a capital *I* was a late revision.) Baudelaire's "A Voyage to Cythera" ends with the lines, "Ah, Lord! give me the power and courage / To contemplate my body and soul without disgust." This is the poet's task, and what is described in the first three stanzas of "L'Héautontimorouménos." The action is dispassionate and, ideally, objective. The "she" beginning the fifth stanza is his muse, his poet self "who shakes me and bites me" and transforms his blood into the black ink with which the poems are written. The second half of the poem, as one critic has pointed out, describes the poet's moral and metaphysical dilemma.[16]

The laughter in the last stanza is a reference to Melmoth, in Charles Maturin's 1820 novel *Melmoth the Wanderer*, who sold his soul for knowledge and wanders the earth trying to get it back. Maturin wrote, "A mirth which is not riot gaiety is often the mask which hides the convulsed and distorted features of agony—and laughter, which never yet was the expression of rapture, has often been the only intelligible language of madness and misery. Ecstasy only smiles—despair laughs."[17] And Baudelaire wrote in his essay "On the Essence of Laughter": "And this laughter is the perpetual explosion of [Melmoth's] wrath and his suffering. It is—be sure and understand me—the necessary product of his dual and contradictory nature, which is infinitely great in relation to man, infinitely vile and base in relation to absolute truth and righteousness."[18] In the Garden of Eden, both tears and laughter were unknown, since what was there to complain about or mock?

"L'Héautontimorouménos" expresses what it is to have the metaphysics of the *provocateur*. Clearly it is romanticized—Melmoth was one of the great icons of the Romantic age—but it makes an uncomplicated statement: the writing of a poem requires the dispassionate dissection of self. For Baudelaire this is moral inquiry, and it is propelled by and further reveals what he saw as his divided nature, and ideally the creation of the poem will help him transcend that nature. What it required of the poet was a willingness to reveal a nature, which he saw not as idiosyncratic but as representative. After all, in the final line of "Au Lecteur" he calls the reader his double, his brother: "Hypocrite lecteur,—mon semblable,—mon frère!" He also saw this moral inquiry as being destructive to the poet.

Freud removed much of the onus from human complexity, the psychiatrist's couch replaced the confessional, but the poet in analyzing his or her nature is still engaged in moral inquiry, and any inquiry that skirts or modifies human totality is considered bogus. So to be a provocateur is not necessarily to provoke, in its simplest sense (though it may be), but rather to define exactly and to offer up a mirror to mankind, just as Baudelaire's "Au Lecteur" offers up a mirror. It is necessary not for the poet to shock but to be available to whatever the unconscious turns up and to analyze it dispassionately. This is to be neither confessional nor autobiographical, since those strategies may have agendas to show off the poet in a particular manner. In such cases the poet holds up a mirror to the self and is solipsistic. He or she is invested rather than dispassionate.

"I know why you only half love Baudelaire," wrote Proust. "In his letters . . . you have come on merciless passages about his relations. And he is merciless in his poetry, merciless with the utmost sensibility, his ruthlessness the more startling since one feels that he had felt to his nerves' ends the sufferings he makes a mock of and describes with such composure."[19] But to write dispassionately and to be dispassionate are not the same, and Proust proceeds to discuss Baudelaire's poem "The Little Old Women," in which "no item of the old women's sufferings escape him." What Baudelaire displays in this poem, and others, is a great empathy heightened and perhaps enabled by what Proust calls his composure, his knowledge of the divided self and its resultant suffering.

Baudelaire's task is to bear witness to his representative nature, to perhaps rub the reader's nose in it, and to give testimony free of the entanglements of the ego. This last is of course impossible, but in his testimony he struggles to do this. There are many things he hates, and much of what he despised he found in the rising bourgeoisie: bad taste, superficiality, materialism, and cruelty. Visiting Paris in June 1848, the Russian writer Alexander Herzen wrote in his memoirs: "Under the influence of *petit bourgeoisie* everything was changed in Europe. Chivalrous honor was replaced by the honesty of the book-keeper, elegant manners by propriety, courtesy by affectation, pride by a readiness to take offense, parks by kitchen gardens, palaces by hotels open to *all* (that is all who have money)."[20]

In addition, Baudelaire romanticized the role of the poet, that prince of clouds, as a seer engaged on a spiritual journey. He was fiercely proud, despite his poverty. He was theatrical and confrontational. The details of his poems are often gruesome, precise, and witty. After all, if one wants to give testimony, one must get the reader's attention.

Sainte-Beuve didn't believe poetry should be confrontational. The rising bourgeoisie placed high value on decorum and manners. They were the new aristocracy and wanted to show they were more civilized than the old aristocracy. But decorousness, as a major value, weakens poetry as an instrument of moral inquiry. Decorousness imagines that it ennobles poetry. Moral inquiry, among other things, asks why decorousness is important. Baudelaire saw the emphasis on decorousness as hypocritical. By bearing witness to man's divided nature, he meant to reveal that hypocrisy; by dissecting the self, he was engaged in moral inquiry. However, that wasn't the purpose of the poem. The only purpose was to make something beautiful. That it was also disturbing comes out of his particular metaphysic. It is also part of the poem's concept.

Almost any good poem seeks to disturb the reader's complacency by showing us something we haven't seen or haven't seen in exactly that way. An image of the world is held up against our own idea of the world. It may offer a challenge, as is often the case with Baudelaire, or it may be a contrast between frogs and drivers as in Wright's poem. Whichever it does, it can lead us to reconsider that world, to recognize and reinvestigate it. Baudelaire offered a challenge, which the critic Sainte-Beuve chose not to pick up. But even Wright's poem offers a kind of challenge to the reader to recognize the world he has created. I may see myself in Wright's world, which is something he thought a poem should do: to offer points of contact between one life and another. I may prefer not to see myself in Baudelaire's world, though it is hard not to. This point of comparison is what heightens a poem as instrument of moral inquiry. As for Whitman, he seeks to drag me into his embrace. Except for "Respondez," he doesn't so much hold up a mirror to the reader as he appropriates the reader. His work is more than a moral inquiry; he wants to change us, to improve us.

Decorousness is not a poetic attribute. At best it might be a tool; it might offer a strategy. The need is to create a world that the reader can use to investigate his or her own world. That comes under Isaiah Berlin's definition of ethical thought. Not only is the writer making ethical choices, but one of the functions of the piece of writing is to expand the reader's empathy and moral experience by depicting how other people live and interact at different times and places. Wright's poem challenges me to accept the truth of his narrative, and certainly I do, with reservations. Those reservations are the differences between his world and mine. Or, in Baudelaire's case, those reservations can be points of similarity that I don't wish to admit to. Whitman, on the other hand, sought to bring us into a great family. He saw the 1855 edition of his book as the new Bible that would lead to the purification of the United States.

Peter Gay in his book *Modernism: The Lure of Heresy: From Baudelaire to Beckett and Beyond* wrote that modernists had two defining attributes: "first, the lure of heresy that impelled their actions as they confronted conventional sensibilities; and, second, a commitment to a principled self-scrutiny."[21] This was true of Baudelaire and partly true of Whitman. After all, it was Baudelaire's heresy that Sainte-Beuve was protesting.

These attributes are not quite so common in poetry today. Self-scrutiny has been replaced by people telling the story of their lives. The decorous has replaced the lure of heresy, partly from political correctness and because so much of poetry comes out of a middle-class university environment. Sainte-Beuve, or his descendants, are again in favor. This has produced many boring poems, and is one more reason why critics dismiss Bukowski (and others, in reaction to the polite and decorous, like him).

To tell the difference between taste and aesthetic judgment it's necessary to define what constitutes a "successful poem" in such a way that some elements belong and some do not. Critics and reviewers attempt to control the definition of that X. If X is not present, says the critic, then it is not a successful poem. Half a dozen years ago, a reviewer in *Poetry* magazine lambasted an anthology edited by Garrison Keillor entitled *Good Poems*. The reviewer found the poems simplistic; to his mind they offered no complexity in either form or content. Dozens of contemporary poets were represented, as well as Dickinson, Yeats, Frost, Hopkins, Blake, and other poets belonging to what used to be called the canon.

The reviewer tried to present his personal taste as aesthetic judgment and failed. The poems in the anthology were all immediately accessible, had strong narrative elements, and reflected Keillor's taste. What Keillor saw as qualities, the reviewer saw as shortcomings. He saw the poems as middlebrow and pointed out that many great poems are not immediately accessible and are formally more interesting. What he wasn't willing to admit was that the field of poetry is vast enough to encompass both types, and what he was complaining about was their motivating concept, rather than how they were written, because, after all, they were written exactly as the poets wanted.

A number of years ago, I had dinner with a well-known critic and well-known poet. At one point, the critic said that she disliked narrative poems. Narrative wasn't a poetic quality, she said, but belonged to prose. The poet answered by asking: "What about *The Divine Comedy?* Isn't Dante's poem narrative?" The critic replied, "I've always thought Dante was an overrated poet."

The poet Joseph Brodsky denied that free verse was a workable medium for poetry. It only produced bad poems. A poem without meter simply wasn't a poem. Like many refugees from totalitarianism, he was something of a totalitarian himself.

But what is to be done with the thousands of free verse poems, and those that use narrative, that successfully give testimony to a strong emotional experience? This, according to the reviewer of *Good Poems,* as well as Brodsky and others, is only due to their ignorance and perhaps perversity. These poems lacked X. Only real poems have X. Consequently these are not poems, but pseudo-poems. But the argument can't be sustained. One can't dismiss those who disagree as being ignorant and/or perverse. This was Sainte-Beuve's argument against Baudelaire: that Baudelaire chose to remain unenlightened. Instead it is the concept of the poems they object to.

A poem is a form of communication and must be capable of communicating. For me that is an axiom. What we see in Baudelaire and Whitman is that there is no limit to the range of that communication, and that to be disturbed can be as valuable an aesthetic experience as to be pleased. What is necessary—another axiom—is that nothing is off limits, that one draws one's work from the uncensored self. It is this in particular that makes the poem valuable as an instrument of moral inquiry. In addition, if a poem fulfills these axioms and is a symbol of affective life, then to condemn it because of its motivating concept is simplistic and an error. It is not prejudice that distinguishes between good and bad poems, but how well the poem does its job.

eleven

bearing witness

everything within the poem heightens the poem's symbol and partici-
pates within it. All the poem's elements are directed to this end, which,
traditionally, is to recreate a set of emotions the writer has experienced that
will also be experienced by the reader, though to a lesser degree. Wordsworth's
Sonnet XVIII (also known as "Surprised by Joy"), for instance, begins in the
midst of a simple event. The speaker is surprised by something that creates a
feeling of delight, which, for a moment, distracts him from himself, and in his
pleasure he briefly forgets the larger moment. He turns to share the occasion
with his daughter, his "heart's best treasure," only to remember she is dead.
The poem is addressed to the daughter and forms an apology for having forgotten her death even for an instant. Indeed, when he remembers her death, it
is as if she had died once again. In writing he is bearing witness to an aspect of
the world, and, as we read the sonnet, our own sense of the world increases.

> Surprised by joy—impatient as the Wind
> I turned to share the transport—Oh! with whom
> But thee, deep buried in the silent tomb,
> That spot which no vicissitude can find?
> Love, faithful love, recalled thee to my mind—
> But how could I forget thee? Through what power,
> Even for the least division of an hour,

Have I been so beguiled as to be blind

To my most grievous loss!—That thought's return

Was the worst pang that sorrow ever bore,

Save one, one only, when I stood forlorn,

Knowing my heart's best treasure was no more;

That neither present time, nor years unborn

Could to my sight that heavenly face restore.[1]

The joy that begins the poem is replaced by horror that he could have allowed himself to feel joy, a horror signified on the page by a simple exclamation, "Oh!," while the disjointed syntax, the persistent rhyme of the nasal consonants, the enjambment and breaking of the sentence across the line all stand in metaphoric relation to the anguish felt by the speaker. To read the poem carefully is to experience, in a diminished way, what Wordsworth felt. We recognize the feeling; we can imagine it.

No single word can convey Wordsworth's experience. The word "grief" doesn't describe it; it is only a sign. Only through art do we come to appreciate his emotional state as we engage in an act of imagination that makes the poet's experience our own. The social function of this within the society is that it forges links between us. Art uses metaphor to prove to us that we are not alone; other human beings share our most private feelings. It creates community and a sense of joint responsibility by increasing our sense of empathy.

A metaphor, like the poem itself, is an example of nondiscursive thought. We seem to move spontaneously from a state of ignorance to a state of knowing. Consider these two epigrams: "Gets a free bowl of soup; demands a cloth napkin," and, "Dips his words in honey, you still taste the salt." We take in the words with the left brain, which then asks for corroboration from the right. The exchange continues until some sense is discovered. This exchange can occur in a nanosecond. Our two kinds of thought—discursive and non-discursive—tend to work in conjunction to give us information, but the logic of a metaphor, its discursive underpinning, comes after we have first grasped it nondiscursively.

We approach the writing of a poem as a search for a metaphor that encapsulates the emotion we wish to communicate. Language develops in much the same way. Both are bearing witness. A word is coined which is physically descriptive and which acts as a metaphor for what it is trying to communicate.

For instance, "supercilious" comes from the Latin for "above the eyelid," indicating the raised eyebrow, an expression of haughtiness. "Coward," also from Latin, describes a frightened animal with its tail between its legs.

English is a joining of two languages. As noted previously in Chapter 4, Old English, a Germanic language, was rudely intruded upon in 1066 by the Norman Conquest, which imposed upon it the French language of the conquerors. In addition, Latin, both before and after the Conquest, was the language of learning. Not only was it the language of the church and universities, but also legal and government documents were written in Latin. So, for three centuries after 1066, England could be considered trilingual. By the fourteenth century, however, Old English and French had begun to merge, while the Statute of Pleading in 1362 required that court proceedings be conducted in English, rather than Latin. Around this time, in the 1380s, the English theologian and reformer John Wycliffe initiated the first translation of the Bible from Latin into English. But it wasn't until the beginning of the sixteenth century that we find a literature written in a language easily read by a modern reader.

The Conquest gave us a French vocabulary to put beside the Old English, with the result that modern English has more synonyms than any other Western language. There was also a class difference between the languages, which stays with us still. The upper classes have occupations, the lower classes have jobs; the upper classes perspire, the lower classes sweat. In many cases, the Old English word was replaced altogether. The word "conscience" first appears in manuscripts in the fourteenth century. In the early 1380s, Wycliffe wrote, "The worschippers clensid oonys, hadden no conscience of synne fer-thermore." It derived from the Latin "to know with oneself only, to know within one's own mind," and it replaced the Middle English word "inwit." "Wit" was derived from the word "to know," and "inwit" meant to know within oneself. In 1393, Langland wrote, "Hus wyf and hys inwit edwited hym of hus synne."

English words, according to the *Encyclopedia Britannica,* tend to be more human and concrete; French words are more intellectual and abstract. Consider these English and French parings: freedom and liberty, friendship and amity, hatred and enmity, love and affection, likelihood and probability, truth and veracity, lying and mendacity. "Craftsmen," says the *Britannica,* "bear names of English origin: baker, builder, fisherman, hedger, miller, shepherd, shoemaker, wainwright and weaver; but names of skilled artisans are French: carpenter, draper, haberdasher, joiner, mason, painter, plumber and tailor."

The Germanic and Latinate languages are Indo-European languages derived from peoples who inhabited the Russian steppes north of the Black and Caspian seas. Indo-European or Proto-Indo-European (PIE) developed between 4500 and 2500 BCE. "Steppe" is the Russian word for grasslands. It was here that the wheel came to be joined to the capabilities of the horse and people began to travel more rapidly. The first three divisions of Proto-Indo-European were into Anatolian, Greek, and Indo-Iranian. Most of our words can be traced back to Proto-Indo-European, but we also find many borrowings from other language groups. The word "skunk," for instance, is from the Algonquin Indian language.

When we look at the etymology of a word, we often find the descriptive action or metaphor that gave rise to it. To return to Wordsworth's sonnet and the word "grief," we now hear the word as an abstraction. It takes a poem like Wordsworth's to give it sufficient specificity and to enable us to experience it. The word, however, derives from a Latin word—*gravis*—for heavy, coming from a PIE base—*gwer*—meaning heavy but also mill, as in heavy as a millstone. To grieve is to carry the weight of a millstone. Long ago to utter the abstraction was to experience the specificity of the metaphor.

Consider "vicissitude" from Wordsworth's fourth line, where he describes the tomb as "that spot which no vicissitude can find." It derives from the Latin *vix* (genitive *vices*), meaning a change or alternation. The word "vicarious" has the same root, as does "vicar," a person who acts in the place of someone else. The Latin word derives from the PIE word *weik*, meaning to bend or change. This is the source of the word "weak," lacking in strength—but also of "week," meaning a period of change. But the PIE word first meant a plant with thin, flexible branches. The word "wicker" has the same source, as does "willow," so the word "weak" meant to bend as a reed bends. The condition of constant change, which is found in "vicissitude," is, again, to bend as the reed bends. The original coining of the word formed a metaphor for weakness and changeability, and its source came from the environment of those who used the word.

So, to coin a word often meant hitting upon something that stood in metaphoric relation to whatever one was attempting to verbalize. To speak, for instance, was to scatter sounds in front of one's audience as one might scatter sparks or straw. It was once supposed that one could not think unless one had language—Aristotle said, "Speech is the representation of the experiences of the mind"—and while that is no longer believed true, it is still argued that the greater one's command of language, the greater one's quality of thought. We live, however, in a period of late language when the simple expression of the word no longer conjures up the metaphor that lies hidden within it. Clearly, language evolves, and new words, which may be metaphoric coinings, come into use—such as "bottom line" and "loose cannon"—but the main way we regain a precise sense of a word is through poetry, as we have seen in Wordsworth's sonnet.

In earlier periods, poetry was mostly epic and narrative, which bore witness to an idealized world, presented codes of behavior, and praised gods and famous men. The *Odyssey* is about many things, and one of them is the laws of hospitality. As a language aged, epics and heroic narrative poetry were increasingly replaced by lyric poetry, until in nineteenth-century English verse, lyric poetry predominated, as it does still. The subject of a lyric is our emotional life, and the best lyrics work to bear witness to who we are and to define for us and engage with specific emotions, providing us with something missing from the language—the metaphor hidden within the word. Now, poetry does many things. It is entertainment, sound, idea, and so on, but it also educates our understanding of our emotional life. As language flattens out and its emotional and descriptive underpinnings become invisible, we increasingly use the lyric to supply that physical sense of the world and our common emotional life.

Other changes within the society in the past 250 years have also affected the lyric. The advent of Romanticism placed new emphasis on the individual and stressed the subjective over the objective. The rise of psychology as a serious study in the nineteenth century again emphasized the individual, while in the early twentieth century Freud changed forever how we see one another and ourselves, as well as challenging whether objective vision is even possible.

From the 1830s to about 1910 education in the United States was standardized through the use of McGuffey Readers. Their influence continued into the 1930s. Herbert Hoover, for instance, was brought up on the Readers. Their emphasis on religion, patriotism, the importance of the family, and what came to be thought of as traditional values shaped American thinking over a hundred years. Such values were also exemplified by the examples of literature, poems like "The Boy Stood on the Burning Deck" and "Barbara Fritchie," where we find a tetrameter couplet directed to an abashed Stonewall Jackson: "Shoot if you must this old gray head, / but spare our nation's flag, she said."

The McGuffey Readers gave a sense of national community. They sought to implant specific principles in American children, and they taught history as being American history; that is, the history of the white, Anglo-Saxon, male-dominated majority. Other than English history, European and world history were hardly noted.

In his six-volume history *Our Times,* published between 1925 and 1935, Mark Sullivan wrote, "This teaching, that America was 'God's Country,' may have accounted for a certain air of condescension, not always tolerant, which American doughboys carried with them through the Great War, to the puzzlement of some of their Allies who had not learned relative values of nations from the same schoolbooks. The same cause may lie behind America's attitude of self-sufficiency in international relations, its unwillingness to join the League of Nations, the readiness with which American politicians can stir the American people into insistence upon isolationism."[2] The geography section of one Reader stated: "Half-civilized peoples, like the Chinese and Mexicans, have towns and cities, cultivate the soil, and exchange products; but have few arts and little intelligence."[3]

The effect of the McGuffey Readers was to create an illusion of unanimity among Americans that began to break down after World War II. The talk about the loss of "traditional values" in recent decades does not so much demonstrate the existence of those values, but shows that McGuffey Readers hammered them home. My grandparents were taught from those books, and what they absorbed deeply affected how my parents saw the world. One thinks of the existential angst that began to appear after the war: the questions of who am I and where did I come from were hardly an issue in an America instructed and formed by McGuffey Readers. We find in the 1950s a growing nostalgia for a lost identity that to a great degree was a fiction promulgated by the schoolbooks of previous generations.

Many factors, of course, contributed to existential angst: growing urbanization, the effects of World War II and the Cold War, French existentialism, the increasing restlessness of minorities and the disenfranchised, and increased suspicion of the government. But there was also a growing need among Americans to identify themselves: Who am I, where did I come from, and where am I going?

These concerns helped effect a change in art and, obviously, in poetry. The speaker of the poem became less representative and more idiosyncratic. One can see such a change in two books of Robert Lowell's: *The Mills of the Kavanaughs,* published in 1951, and *Life Studies,* published in 1959. The first contains mostly dramatic monologues; the second has mostly autobiographical poems. Lowell moved from formal poems, using a strong iambic pentameter line and rhymed couplets, to free verse poems. A poem from the first book, "Mother Maria Therese," is spoken by a Canadian nun in New Brunswick and begins:

Old sisters at our Maris Stella House
Remember how the Mother's strangled grouse
And snow-shoe rabbits matched the royal glint
Of Pio-Nono's vestments in the print
That used to face us, while our aching ring
Of stationary rockets saw her bring
Our cake . . . [4]

In contrast, the fifth stanza from "Skunk Hour" in *Life Studies* begins:

One dark night,
my Tudor Ford climbed the hill's skull;
I watched for love-cars. Lights turned down,
they lay together, hull to hull,
where the graveyard shelves on the town. . . .
My mind's not right.[5]

Lowell's purpose in *Life Studies* was self-definition with the good and bad mixed together, though in the landscape of dysfunction the good was rarely visible. *Life Studies* went on to influence a whole generation of poets—James Wright, Galway Kinnell, W. S. Merwin, Phillip Levine, Adrienne Rich, Sylvia Plath, and others—who not only changed from formal verse to free verse poems, but also changed their subject matter, focusing more on the self.

A second change during this period can be traced to Adrienne Rich's book, *Diving into the Wreck*. In effect, her poems gave female poets permission to speak, to take material from their own lives, to understand they had been silenced by the male hegemony, and to write about whatever they wanted. Clearly, many feminist writers wrote on similar topics, but Rich did it through poetry, while her book also opened the way to a wide variety of minority and ethnic writers to follow her example.

The result over fifty years has been a great upsurge in poetry which has led to many wonderful books, but the shift from the representative to the idiosyncratic or marginal has also produced books where the autobiographical or memoiristic narrative took precedence over the poetry. In many cases what poets wanted from their audiences changed as well: approval or praise for what they said about their lives. They wanted their identities, or what they saw as their identities, authenticated, validated.

In his short essay on the poet in the 1993 edition of the *Princeton Encyclopedia of Poetry and Poetics,* T. V. F. Brogan wrote:

> The first thing to say is that the poet is a maker of poems, and that the maker is not the same as the person. The quality of the maker's productions is not diminished by his or her personal shortcomings or failings in life, and conversely, the successes or social privilege of the person do not improve mediocre poetic production: all that is *ad hominem*. The person, in the course of coming into and passing through adulthood, forms a self out of life's experiences, but the maker is formed specifically out of a decision to write poetry, to practice . . . , to learn technique, and to continue to write. . . . Thus the poet develops a second self, emergent from the first yet supersessive to it; from such augmentation comes enhanced opportunities for complex psychic relations. The maker is able to quarry the person (i.e., memory and sensibility) for experiences, reflections, insights, sensations, ambiguities, ambivalences, feelings, and thoughts—all potential threads to be woven into the emergent fabric of the poem. Most importantly, the maker can take advantage of these complex psychic interactions by creating a speaker for the poem, a persona that is quite distinct from the person. One may reasonably wonder if it is even possible to say when one is the one self and when the other. The person is a person ever, obviously, but the maker is only a maker in the act of composing verse.[6]

The person and the maker may have separate agendas. The maker's intention is purely the making of the poem, to quarry the person and to create a persona; but the person's agenda may concern how he or she is seen by the reader. We see the world and our participation within it through a subjective lens, just as we see ourselves through a subjective lens. When the poet manipulates the agenda of the poem, it is often to claim objectivity for that subjective vision, to present arguments that one's subjective vision is in fact true, and to affect the reader's response to it. This is dangerous for the poem, and it has little to do with poetry. The poem becomes propaganda meant convince the reader of the validity of the person's argument.

John Stuart Mill in his 1833 essay "What Is Poetry?" wrote, "Poetry is feeling confessing itself in moments of solitude." When what is said "is not itself the end, but a means to an end . . . of making an impression on another mind, then it ceases to be poetry, and becomes eloquence."[7] When the poem's agenda is controlled by the person, and not the maker, this is in danger of happening. It may also happen when the poet stresses the idiosyncratic over the representative. I'm not saying that the poet can't be eccentric. Philip Larkin was quite eccentric, but he was also representative. It has to do with the poet's intention, not what he or she actually is as an individual.

If all perception is subjective and truth is relative, then what is left to the poet if we rule out self-justification and self-aggrandizement? I think it goes back to what one discovers in the history of the language and how language is created: one bears witness. One observes the world and creates metaphors from what one sees. That act, certainly, is also subjective, but that's not important. As a human being one collects these acts of witness. One looks to see what others are doing in order to define one's own actions. For instance, I look at Wordsworth's expression of grief to see if it is similar to my own. If Wordsworth were the only poet and his sonnet the only artistic expression of grief, that would be a problem, but there are thousands. My view of the world comes from direct experience and a mass of secondary experience—movies, television, newspapers, novels, poetry, and a whole lot more. None of this do I necessarily accept as true, and so I adjust my examination of this experience with a mass of corroborative information. How do I know whether my perception of the world is valid; how do I know whether my feelings are idiosyncratic or shared by others?

I look for many things within a poem, but one thing I look for is corroboration of human experience. If the poet's purpose is to point to his or her own idiosyncrasy in order to affect how I see the poet as a human being, that doesn't interest me much, though what is written may be stylistically beautiful. In addition, if the poem is not meant to communicate—if, for instance, it strings together non sequiturs that are not intended to "mean" in the conventional sense—then that doesn't interest me either, though again the writing might be stylistically beautiful. Such poems are ultimately decorative, as wallpaper is decorative; they please by their surface, not by their content.

The word "despair" comes from the Latin *desperare,* meaning to be without hope, from the word *spes,* "hope." The Proto-Indo-European base, *spei,* means to prosper, expand, succeed, and seems to go back to the idea of sowing seeds, growing crops. If your crops grow, you prosper and have hope. If your crops fail, you don't prosper—you despair. The word was coined as a metaphor—that hopeless feeling experienced when one's crops fail. The person who coined the word was defining a feeling within himself or herself, and drew a construction from a not uncommon experience. The word entered the language because other people recognized the experience and felt this word expressed the feeling better than something else. If the experience had been idiosyncratic to the coiner, then it most likely wouldn't have been embraced. The coiner was bearing witness to the world, and other people identified with his experience. They were able to empathize with it.

Now I want to make a somewhat radical shift to the Greek poet Homer.

The *Iliad* and the *Odyssey* were composed in the eighth or ninth century BCE and then seemingly modified by the various singers or rhapsodes who presented them until they were written down in the six or fifth century BCE. Both were intended for an aristocratic audience. According to the classicist Werner Jaeger, they presented the "ideal of heroism devoted to the community" and "a combination of proud and courtly morality with warlike valor."[8] In the *Iliad* these codes of behavior are seen on the battlefield; in the *Odyssey* they are mostly seen in peace and domestic settings. What are the rules governing the host and the guest?

In the *Odyssey* we don't meet Odysseus until Book 5, after we have learned he has been missing from Ithaca for twenty years and his house is full of suitors seeking the hand of his wife, Penelope. They behave abominably, violating the laws of hospitality and insulting Telemachus, Odysseus's son. We then turn to Odysseus, who has been living with the goddess Calypso on her island for the past seven years, but now he has to leave. He sails off on a

raft, but is soon shipwrecked and lands on another island where he meets the
Princess Nausicaa and her maidens washing clothes on the shore. He is led to
her father, King Alcinous, to whom Odysseus presents himself as a humble
petitioner, and eventually he tells the story of his travels. And it is a good
story. The king and his retinue listen enthralled. Also, as a good host, the king
understands the laws of hospitality. Eventually Odysseus is given great gifts
and is sent on his way.

But there is a subtext, which we find in the relation between the real-life
singer, whom we may call Homer, and his aristocratic audience. Homer, like
Odysseus, has come from nowhere and is probably dressed badly. He, too, is
dependent on the hospitality of the lord to whom he sings his tale—the Greek
word *homeros* means a pledge, hostage, one who is led and hence is blind.
And Homer's tale, like Odysseus's, is a great tale. Among other things, it is
the tale of lords who showed respect and kindness for the ragged singer who
came to their house; who obeyed the laws of hospitality and achieved great
honor and lasting fame by being bound up within the poem. It is also the tale
of lords who violated the laws of hospitality and were punished. For when
Odysseus at last returns home, he kills the suitors and those who had served
them. But there are exceptions. In Book 22 of Alexander Pope's Latinized
translation we read:

> Phemius alone the hand of vengeance spared,
> Phemius the sweet, the heaven-instructed bard.
> Beside the gate the reverend minstrel stands;
> The lyre now silent trembling in his hands;
> Dubious to supplicate the chief, or fly
> To Jove's inviolable altar nigh . . .
> His honor'd harp with care he first set down,
> Between the laver and the silver throne.
> Then prostrate stretch'd before the dreadful man,
> Persuasive thus, with accent soft began:
> "O king! to mercy be thy soul inclined,
> And spare the poet's ever-gentle kind.
> A deed like this thy future fame would wrong,
> For dear to gods and men is sacred song.
> Self-taught I sing; by Heaven, and Heaven alone,

The genuine seeds of poesy are sown:

And (what the gods bestow) the lofty lay

To gods alone and godlike worth we pay.

Save then the poet, and thy self reward;

'Tis thine to merit, mine is too record.[9]

And so Phemius as well as the herald, Medon, were spared.

The name Phemius means "the one who spreads report." Our word "fame" derives from it, and its Proto-Indo-European root, *bha,* is one of the words for "speak." The poet wasn't spared because he had behaved particularly well; he was spared because he could spread report. "A deed like this thy future fame would wrong, / For dear to gods and men is sacred song." It was Odysseus who would suffer if Phemius were killed: he would be forgotten. None of this was lost on the audience who listened to Homer. So far there are three singers: Odysseus, Phemius, and Homer. Through Odysseus and Phemius, Homer entwined himself with the events of which he sang, and if his listeners did not treat him well, his story showed what dishonor might befall them. But there is also a fourth singer: Demodocus, whose name means "received by the common people." Here is how he is introduced at the banquet for Odysseus in the court of Alcinous in Richmond Lattimore's translation:

The herald came near, bringing with him the excellent singer

Whom the muse had loved greatly, and gave him both good and evil.

She reft him of his eyes, but she gave him the sweet singing

Art. Pontonoos set a silver-studded chair out for him

In the middle of the feasters, propping it against a tall column

And the herald hung the clear lyre on a peg placed over

His head, and showed him how to reach up with his hand and take it

Down, and set beside him a table and a fine basket,

And beside him a cup to drink whenever he desired it.[10]

The description is so detailed it suggests it was made either by someone who had witnessed it or someone who experienced it, and, indeed, it has also been suggested that this is meant to be Homer. Demodocus sings three songs: a quarrel between Odysseus and Achilles, a story about the love of Ares and

Aphrodite, and the story of the Trojan Horse. During the first and last songs Odysseus weeps uncontrollably.

But before Demodocus begins his last song, Odysseus gives the singer a succulent slice from a loin of pork, saying in Pope's translation:

> This, let the master of the lyre receive,
> A pledge of love! 'tis all a wretch can give.
> Lives there a man beneath the spacious skies
> Whose sacred honors to the bard denies?
> The Muse the bard inspires, exalts his mind;
> The Muse indulgent loves th' harmonious kind.[11]

And a few lines later, Odysseus says to the poet, again in Pope's translation:

> O more than man! thy soul the Muse inspires.
> Or Phoebus animates with all his fires;
> For who, by Phoebus uninformed, could know
> The woe of Greece, and sing so well the woe?
> Just to the tale, as present at the fray,
> Or taught the labors of the dreadful day:
> The song recalls past horrors to my eyes,
> And bids proud Ilion from her ashes rise.[12]

If you think of Homer, or another bard, singing these lines in the courts of the wealthy and powerful, then you can see it as shameless self-advertisement. Homer is thinking of his fee. Secondly, he is stressing the fact that without the poet the Trojan War and even the court of Alcinous would disappear into oblivion. The poet keeps alive the deeds of god and men. And so there is no possibility that Odysseus will kill Phemius. It would be like killing himself, for where would Odysseus be without the one who spreads report?

Bearing witness, spreading report was the poet's job, and his or her value was in being representative. We are, first of all, concerned with our own lives. When I read someone's poem, I am seeking myself, by which I mean I seek out experience that is meaningful to me. For a poem to do this, the poet has to see himself or herself engaged in an act of communication. Even if obscure, the poem must be capable of being understood. In his essay

"On Obscure Writing," which discusses the poetry of Paul Celan, Primo Levi wrote, "Talking to one's fellowman in a language that he cannot understand may be the bad habit of some revolutionaries, but it is not at all a revolutionary instrument: it is on the contrary an ancient repressive artifice, known to all churches, the typical vice of our political class, the foundation of all colonial empires. It is a subtle way of imposing one's rank."[13] This is rather harsh on Celan, but it still contains its element of truth.

The poets I have discussed are all descendants of Phemius; they attempt to bear witness to the world. They define what it is to be a human being. Like Phemius, their poetry arose from the craft, which had to be learned, and from some undefined thing deep within them. Whatever it was, it left them with no alternative. They were unable to remain silent. About their impulse to write, they would say, like Phemius, "That here I sung, was force, and not desire: / This hand reluctant touch'd the warbling wire."[14]

counterpoint

n prosody, the term "counterpoint" describes several linguistic occurrences. One refers to the relation between the metrical frame of the line and the syntactic frame of the sentence. Because they may be of different lengths, each can have its own rhythm, and the disparity between them can create a sort of counterpoint. I say "sort of" because the term derives from music, referring to the simultaneous sound of two or more melodies. So the word's usage in poetry is metaphoric, more descriptive than analytic.

Counterpoint is also used to describe what occurs when we read a line of metrical verse. Set against the actual line, we may also hear the ideal metrical pattern. So in the first quatrain of Shakespeare's Sonnet 76, we read,

> Why is my verse so barren of new pride,
> So far from variation or quick change?
> Why with the time do I not glance aside
> To new-found methods and to compounds strange?[1]

The first line begins with a trochee and ends with a pyrrhic and spondee; the second ends with a pyrrhic and spondee; the third begins with a trochee; and the fourth has a pyrrhic and two spondees. So instead of a quatrain of twenty iambs, Shakespeare uses eleven, while having a little fun in responding to the hypothetical allegation: Why is your verse so conventional? In the second line, the concluding pyrrhic and spondee give us an example of the "quick change" to which he refers; while the metrical complexity of the fourth line heightens our sense of "new-found methods" and "compounds strange." In addition, the nouns and modifiers in the quatrain describe abstractions and generalities, but the metrical substitutions particularize them by giving them descriptive emphasis.

If we didn't read these lines with a sense of the ideal metrical pattern, we would not realize that Shakespeare meant to spoof his supposed convention-ality. The question is often raised whether we really hear both meters at the same time: the actual and the ideal. Perhaps we don't. But our mental aware-ness of the ideal, which is an abstraction, is a controlling factor in how we hear the actual line.

Our sense of how the meter *should* be, is of a subjective "should." If all lines were exactly iambic, they would grow tedious. In any case, the wide variety of sounds within the English language makes our metrical ideal impos-sible to imagine.

Plato posits the idea of the ideal form versus the actual form. The differ-ence between the two is the difference between an actual chair and its shadow. I have a sense of how my life is and how it should be. By analyzing the dif-ference, I may be able to fix what I feel needs to be fixed. In all things the substantive reality reflects a higher abstraction. We may be unable to describe that abstraction, but we know that between it and the actual the difference is huge. We do this all the time, and it is one of the main elements of literature. Our sense of an ideal metrical pattern is the only way we can investigate the actual. Literature would be impossible without this. How else could we judge a bad piece of writing if we couldn't measure it against an ideal?

Affecting our sense of what exists and what should exist is our psychol-ogy, our belief system, our history, and even comparatively superficial factors such as whether we got a good night's sleep. Each of us has this multiple perception of reality, which may mean slight variations in our belief system and how we feel day to day—hung over/not hung over—and our sense of how things should be is measured by the discrepancy between the actual and the ideal. Though people may be in approximate agreement about the substantive reality of something, the fact that each person sees it through the window of his or her own subjectivity makes total agreement impossible. A Red Sox fan and a Yankees fan watching a game between those teams will see two completely different games.

We also notice this when looking at the range of human behavior. We all understand the emotions of envy, jealousy, love, desire, greed, spite, and so on, but because we are never freed from our subjectivity, we all understand these emotions a bit differently. Yet these emotions are part of what it is to be human. When Agamemnon appropriates Achilles' slave girl and Achilles in anger withdraws from the battle to sit in his tent, we understand his feelings, even though we may have little understanding of Achaean culture. This is true of all the characters in the *Iliad*. We have a clear understanding of the emotions driving them, because we have experienced similar emotions. So even though it is impossible for any two people to be in complete agreement, we have degrees of agreement, sometimes close, sometimes not. But the agreement is always close enough so that two people discussing the nature of pride, for instance, can believe they are talking about an emotion that each has experienced in ways that are not too dissimilar.

But it isn't a matter of just two realities: the actual and the ideal. The hamburger on the plate may be the actual hamburger, but my notion of a better hamburger is a composite of a variety of empirical evidence. So I might imagine the hamburger needs a little ketchup, a slice of tomato, a bit of cheese. The more my memory becomes involved, the more my imagination is activated and the more the hamburger expands, not just on a concrete level, but also on an abstract level. For instance, when I was sixteen, living outside of Detroit, my friends and I would drive up and down Woodward Avenue, visiting one drive-in restaurant after another. We would get our hamburgers, chat with the carhops, smoke cigarettes, and discuss the world. The hamburger, I can say, was emblematic of that time.

Our memory and imagination permit the objects to multiply. Any object in our present can open a door to our past, while the longer we look at a thing, the more likely it is that it will reproduce, not simply giving us a sense of the actual and ideal, but how it might be with a whole variety of changes, what it summons up from the past, what associations it has, what Rorschach-like resemblances. These transformations are also affected by our mental or emotional state at any given moment. So any object, even the most mundane, is a potential source of mystery.

It is one of the functions of art to explore this mystery. My subject here is sense data and the governing context in a piece of literature. What checks do we have on our own solipsism, or self-centeredness? How do we know that the actual and ideal worlds we imagine are in any way similar to the worlds that other people imagine? Let me step away from this subject for a bit.

In her essay "The Nature and Aim of Fiction," Flannery O'Connor describes what she calls "anagogical vision," which is "the kind of vision that is able to see different levels of reality in one image or in one situation."[2] This, she says, is one of a writer's most important tools. In fact, he or she can't write without it.

When a philosopher, scientist, or psychologist discusses the discrepancy between the actual and the ideal, he or she attempts to convince us with the tools of discursive thought: logic, reason, and analysis. We in turn analyze the evidence, test the logic, and then either agree or disagree.

An artist does it differently. A literary artist takes on the discrepancy between the actual and ideal with the imagination. He or she uses the tools of nondiscursive thought: metaphor, simile, analogy, symbol, and so on. This is not to say that the philosopher or scientist doesn't use the imagination and the artist doesn't use reason; rather, their primary approach is different, even though both groups, if you will, are investigating the actual, the ideal, and the discrepancy in between.

Flannery O'Connor describes fiction as being "an incarnational art" that works by appealing to the reader through the senses and says that "fiction has to be largely presented rather than reported." The story is the *experience* of the story, and the reader accepts the illusion that the story is "unfolding around him" by suspending disbelief.[3] A paraphrase or a synopsis is no more the actual story than a map of New Jersey is the actual state, though both have their uses. O'Connor asserts that a writer of fiction is "speaking *with* character and action, not *about* character and action."[4]

The fiction writer begins to write by putting specific characters and events into motion in a way that he or she thinks is significant, just as a philosopher might begin by putting specific abstract thoughts into motion. Neither might have a specific destination in mind, but the process itself is a form of thinking that leads the mind through structures of cause and effect. Within this process evidence is accumulated, discoveries are made and conclusions drawn. Many writers, including O'Connor, have said that the practice of writing—whether fiction or poetry—leads to ideas that could not have been reached in any other manner. O'Connor attributes this to what Jacques Maritain called "the habit of art," habit in this sense being "a certain quality or virtue of mind."[5] She discusses this further in her essay "Writing Short Stories," where she says that "fiction writing is something in which the whole personality takes part—the conscious as well as the unconscious mind. Art is the habit of the artist; and habits have to be rooted deep in the whole personality."[6]

As an example, O'Connor discusses her story "Good Country People," in which, in her description, "a lady Ph.D. has her wooden leg stolen by a Bible salesman whom she has tried to seduce."[7] She continues:

> When I started writing that story, I didn't know there was going to be a Ph.D. with a wooden leg in it. I merely found myself one morning writing a description of two women I knew something about, and before I realized it, I had equipped one of them with a daughter with a wooden leg. As the story progressed, I brought in the Bible salesman, but I had no idea what I was going to do with him. I didn't know he was going to steal that wooden leg until ten or twelve lines before he did it, but when I found out that this was what was going to happen, I realized that it was inevitable. This is a story that produces a shock for the reader, and I think one reason for this is that it produced a shock for the writer.[8]

What O'Connor describes is a process of thought with the abstract ideas located within the characters, events, and objects of the story, and that process is also a process of discovery. The wooden leg becomes a symbol of spiritual affliction, but first of all it is a wooden leg. She says, "before I realized it, I had equipped one of them with a daughter with a wooden leg." What does she mean by "before I realized it"? How was it done? It's very simple. She gave herself permission. She writes, "The writer has to judge himself with a stranger's eye and a stranger's severity. The prophet in him has to see the freak. No art is sunk in the self, but rather, in art the self becomes self-forgetful in order to meet the demands of the thing seen and the things being made."[9] To give oneself permission is to set aside the ego and open oneself up to all possibilities, no matter how unpleasant, while also having the humility to subject the results to the scrutiny of revision. In addition, these discoveries will not be made, O'Connor says, unless the writer commits himself or herself to seeing, to using the five senses in the creation of sense detail.

In "The Nature and Aim of Fiction," O'Connor discusses two sentences of Flaubert's in *Madame Bovary* as an example of the precision that can be attained through sense detail. O'Connor gives the last half of a four-sentence paragraph, and I'm prefacing it with the first half. The paragraph occurs about one-tenth of the way into the book. Charles is Emma Bovary's husband, and they are recently married.

> Sometimes she would draw; and it was great amusement to Charles to stand there bolt upright and watch her bend over her cardboard, with eyes half-closed the better to see her work, or rolling between her fingers little bread-pellets. As to the piano, the more quickly her fingers glided over it the more he wondered. She struck the notes with aplomb and ran from top to bottom of the keyboard without a break. Thus shaken up, the old instrument, whose strings buzzed, could be heard at the other end of the village when the window was open, and often the bailiff's clerk, passing along the highroad, bareheaded and in list slippers, stopped to listen, his sheet of paper in his hand.

O'Connor writes, "It's always necessary to remember that the fiction writer is much less *immediately* concerned with grand ideas and bristling emotions than he is with putting list slippers on clerks."[10] This is nondiscursive thought at work.

O'Connor's reason for the existence of the clerk is analytical; "Flaubert had to create a believable village to put Emma in."[11] But that is only part of the answer.

Emma Bovary felt trapped by her marriage, trapped by the small town in which she lived, and trapped by bourgeois convention. Under the possessive eye of her boring husband, she is not playing the piano in the sense of playing music; she is running her fingers from the top to the bottom of the keyboard. The old instrument protests by buzzing, and the noise is heard by the bailiff's clerk passing along the highroad. The scene, while not necessarily metaphoric, has metaphoric resonance. Emma Bovary is testing the limits of the instrument by striking the notes from top to bottom without a break. How does it change our response if she strikes the notes from the bottom to the top? This is a novel about a woman's downfall, and the movement of the notes from the top to the bottom is in keeping with that. And presumably many people could have heard the notes, yet Flaubert chooses a bailiff's clerk (like a police officer or a sheriff's deputy), but there is a slackness to him, a bourgeois complacency that is true of the entire town. He is bareheaded and wears cheap slippers. Then we learn that the clerk "often" stopped to listen, that Madame Bovary often tested the limits of the instrument. This is a regular event. And what does the clerk think as he stands with the sheet of paper in his hand? We don't know, but it paves the way for the general censure that eventually will cause Emma Bovary to take her life. We come to see the piano itself as being a metaphor for bourgeois convention, and she is shaking it up. The metaphoric resonance of this passage allows us to read it on several levels, while it also foreshadows Emma's eventual destruction. Charles watches with condescension and wonder, as he might watch a child, but her action is passionate and in no way childlike. We can't read this description without realizing that trouble lies ahead.

Did Flaubert intend all this? Perhaps. But he also had the habit of art, in Maritain's phrase. Every paragraph of the novel reflects Flaubert's anagogic vision. Emma Bovary is an exuberant spirit confined to a small space. If you were to describe how the piston in the combustion chamber of an engine squeezes the gasoline vapor, you would describe it analytically. Flaubert describes a similar process occurring to a woman in a small town using the tools of nondiscursive thought. Both describe a very similar phenomenon.

Here is another example of detail working as idea. It's from Chekhov's story "A Journey by Cart," about a rural schoolteacher, Marya Vasilyevna, who is required to travel regularly to the city by cart to get her salary, a two-day trip. She has taught for thirty years, the area is poor, and her life is full of hardship. It is early spring; the roads are muddy and sometimes flooded. Semyon, an elderly peasant with a fund of ignorant gossip, drives the cart. Here is a section describing their arrival at an inn where Marya will have a cup of tea.

> To find a dryer, shorter road, Semyon sometimes struck across a meadow or drove through a back yard, but in some places the peasants would not let him pass, in others the land belonged to a priest; here the road was blocked, there Ivan Ionov had bought a piece of land from his master and surrounded it with a ditch. In such cases they had to turn back.

They arrived at Nizhni Gorodishe. In the snowy, grimy yard around the tavern stood rows of wagons laden with huge flasks of sulphuric acid. A great crowd of carriers had assembled in the tavern, and the air reeked of vodka, tobacco, and sheepskin coats. Loud talk filled the room, and the door with its weight and pulley banged incessantly. In the tap-room behind a partition someone was playing on the concertina without a moment's pause. Marya Vasilyevna sat down to her tea, while at a nearby table a group of peasants saturated with tea and the heat of the room were drinking vodka and beer.

A confused babel filled the room. . . .

The door banged, men came and went. Marya Vasilyevna sat absorbed in the same thoughts that had occupied her before, and the concertina behind the partition never ceased making music for an instant. Patches of sunlight that had lain on the floor when she had come in had moved up to the counter, then to the walls, and had finally disappeared. So it was afternoon.[12]

We find here the same metaphoric resonance we saw in Flaubert, as well as a more obvious use of symbol, for the road in the first paragraph functions as a symbol for the path of Marya Vasilyevna's tortured life.

The description of the inn engages our five senses, and also presents a spatial and temporal sense. Each detail has metaphoric resonance. Chekhov didn't need to include wagons, or, if he did, he could have filled them with tomatoes or cabbages. The presence of the sulfuric acid sets the tone for everything that follows. We are asked to understand the effect of the scene on the schoolteacher, to accept it as a piece of evidence showing how she has been crushed. Her own thoughts constantly revolve around the subjects of money, the fear of losing her position, and her despair of ever escaping. As Chekhov says elsewhere, "She was afraid of everything, and never dared to sit down in the presence of the warden or a member of the school board." The slamming door, the concertina, the confused babel—it is as if we are seeing the interior of Marya's mind. This functions as what T. S. Eliot called an objective correlative: "a set of objects, a situation, a chain of events which shall be the formula of that *particular* emotion; such that when the external facts, which must terminate in sensory experience, are given, the emotion is immediately evoked."[13] The need is for the details to include specific sensory experience; in this paragraph all of the five senses are engaged. The patches of sunlight moving across the floor, up the counter and walls to at last disappear, creates a vivid sense of time, while forming an image of the transience of Marya's life. "So it was afternoon," Chekhov concludes. Earlier we have learned she is in her late forties: the afternoon of her life. The description of specific sense details constitutes the formula for specific emotions.

Here is example from a more recent story, Yuri Trifonov's "The Exchange," published in 1969. The main character, Dmitriev, lives in a room in Moscow with his wife and daughter. They have recently learned that Dmitriev's mother is terminally ill with cancer. Dmitriev's wife, who is stronger than her husband, has begun to scheme to get the mother's room, which is nicer than their own.

> Dmitriev had turned thirty-seven in August. Sometimes it seemed to him that everything was still ahead. Such surges of optimism came in the mornings when he suddenly awoke fresh, with inadvertent cheerfulness—the weather had a lot to do with it—and, opening the vent window he would begin to wave his arms in rhythm and bend and straighten at the waist. . . . [O]n those mornings when Dmitriev awoke, gripped by incomprehensible optimism, nothing irritated him. From the height of the fifth floor he looked out onto the square with the fountain, the street, the column holding the trolley schedule, and a dense crowd around it, and further on, the park, the multi-storied building against the horizon and sky. On a balcony of the next building, very close by, twenty meters away, a young unattractive woman in glasses appeared in a short, carelessly tied robe. She squatted down and did something with the flowers which stood in pots on the balcony. She touched and stroked them, checked under their leaves, lifted up some of the leaves and sniffed them. Because she was squatting, her robe opened and her large bluish-white knees became visible. The woman's face was the same shade as her knees, bluish-white. Dmitriev watched the woman as he did his exercises. He watched her from behind the curtain. Why was inconceivable—he didn't like the woman at all—but his secret observation of her inspired him. He thought about how all was not yet lost, thirty-seven—that's not forty-seven or fifty-seven, and that he still could achieve something.[14]

We have one initial fact—Dmitriev turned thirty-seven in August—and a place, a fifth-floor room. The description occurs about one-tenth of the way into a long short story. Because of our empirical knowledge of the world, we understand how Dmitriev is placed on the arc of life and can guess something about his expectations and memories. Were he twenty-seven or forty-seven, our sense of him would be different. Once we are given his age and location, everything can be read anagogically (that is, as Flannery O'Connor wrote, seeing "different levels of reality in one image or in one situation"). That is not to turn everything into a symbol, but to open it to the possibility of metaphor. They may not be metaphors we can paraphrase, but they give information about Dmitriev's condition. Even the prospective from a fifth-floor window gives a sense of him. How would his thoughts be changed by a second-floor window or a tenth-floor window? After we learn that Dmitriev is gripped by incomprehensible optimism and that nothing irritated him, Trifonov could have written that Dmitriev felt powerful and capable of dealing with any conflict. Instead, Trifonov writes, "From the height of the fifth floor he looked out on the square." This is his sense of power, his sense being able to cope—he is looking out on the world from a significant height. After we learn what Dmitriev sees, he thinks, "He could still achieve something." The specific location becomes part of the formula for a specific emotion.

Our growing impression of Dmitriev is that he is ineffectual and incapable of getting anything more than he already has. He feels superior to the unattractive woman, on the balcony of the opposite building as he does his optimistic exercises, but we wouldn't reach this level of awareness without those bluish-white knees. "He watched her from behind the curtain. Why was inconceivable—he didn't like the woman at all—but his secret observation of her inspired him." The complexity and mystery of any human being is suggested in those two sentences.

The locations and actions in these three examples are perfectly familiar to us despite our limited experience with mid-nineteenth-century life in a French village, late nineteenth-century life in rural Russia, and Moscow in the 1960s. That is because we are given the tools to imagine what is being described and because human behavior is universal. The sense details particularize the abstractions of loneliness, fear, pride, and so on, which allow our imaginations to carry them directly into the intellect. To say that the drama of the story doesn't require "large bluish-white knees" is to miss the point. As O'Connor said, the writer's job is to put list slippers on clerks.

The precision of detail in these examples not only lets us understand the emotion; it lets us experience the scene, which we wouldn't be able to do if the sense data were absent. Because it has metaphoric resonance, the sense data is able to carry concepts and abstractions directly into our intellect. The scene that Dmitriev observes from his window is idea and emotion conveyed in terms of things. The window he is looking through is the window of his own optimism and inadvertent cheerfulness. What he is looking at is himself; that is, his mood determines what is significant. Trifonov doesn't have to say this; he only has to say exactly what Dmitriev sees. Likewise with Chekhov, when Marya Vasilyevna is driven into the yard by the tavern, she sees not only the exterior world but her interior world: "In the snowy, grimy yard around the tavern stood rows of wagons laden with huge flasks of sulphuric acid." This reflects her mood and inner torment. It's not a place nice.

The purpose of the imagination is to be able to perceive systems of cause and effect, to perceive possibility. It is a survival mechanism. Our reason and gathering of empirical evidence tells us a saber-toothed tiger might be lurking in the forest. Our imagination lets us visualize it. This is both parts of the mind working together. A poet or fiction writer tries to engage the reader's imagination to let the reader experience the poem or story. This is done by presenting a governing context, which is often a narrative context, with details of sufficient precision or specificity to stimulate the reader's memory. It is the memory, that great body of empirical evidence, that feeds the imagination and lets the reader experience the scene. And it doesn't matter if the reader has never personally experienced the scene. Chekhov's description—"In the snowy, grimy yard around the tavern stood rows of wagons laden with huge flasks of sulphuric acid."—is outside of my experience in its totality, but I have had experience, either direct or indirect, with its different parts. And I have the governing context—this is late nineteenth-century rural Russia—which further enables me to visualize the scene. If the governing context included Milwaukee in 1935, I would visualize something different.

Any poem or piece of fiction is a metaphor for a specific arrangement of ideas and emotions that could not be presented in any other way. That arrangement enters our intellect through our imagination. The sense data constitutes evidence, and because we read anagogically, any character or object or event can take on metaphoric resonance. The wooden leg in "Good Country People" is not just a wooden leg; it is an idea. What makes a story convincing is the logic of its details and the logic of how those details connect with one another. We are convinced by the story or poem as it unfolds around us, because its many parts form a logical structure in the way that a compelling discursive argument has a logical structure. Indeed, any good story or poem works like an argument. The writer tries to convince us with a body of evidence. Every detail, word, or iamb is part of that evidence. We test the evidence with our imaginations, and if satisfied we suspend our disbelief, and this leads us to becoming a participant. We don't just understand that the tavern in Nizhni Gorodishe is a chaotic place; we experience it.

In addition, it doesn't matter if the evidence is realistic or surrealistic. But it has to be credible; that is, we must be able to imagine it, and we must be able to test it with some sort of system of cause and effect. This can be very loose. At the beginning of Nikolai Gogol's short story "The Nose," we are told that a man wakes in the morning to find that his nose has vanished. Then we are told that the nose is getting into a carriage disguised as a German ambassador. Gogol has given us a narrative platform that posits a world where this can happen, but which violates our sense of reality. But we have surely experienced this world in dreams or folktales or children's songs and poems. We can imagine it. That creates the paradox behind all literature: that something is impossible, yet credible.

The successful poem or piece of fiction gives us a convincing world, and this too is metaphor. That world can be as complicated as Tolstoy's *War and Peace*, as seemingly simple as Beckett's *Waiting for Godot*, or as bizarre as Kafka's *The Castle*. How do we make sense of it; how do we grasp the writer's intention?

We have our sense of an actual world and our sense of an ideal world. What we can never know for certain is how close another person's actual and ideal worlds are to our own. The poem or story or novel gives us a metaphor for a third world, as it were, to set against our sense of the actual and ideal. Just as we see a discrepancy between our actual and ideal worlds, so we see a discrepancy between those worlds and the world of Kafka's *The Castle*. We understand the novel and Kafka's intention by analyzing this discrepancy, by measuring it against our actual and ideal worlds and trying to make sense of the differences. But to do this, we must experience the novel. For a short time we must enter its world and make it our own. Our analysis of the discrepancy can be simple and nearly unconscious, meaning no more than we are able to suspend our disbelief, or we can make ourselves conscious of it by asking ourselves about it. The significance of any poem, story, or novel lies in its discrepancy between our sense of our personal world and what we think the world should be.

Isaiah Berlin describes something like this in *The Roots of Romanticism* when he describes how Sir Walter Scott's historical novels made him a Romantic writer.

> The point is that by painting these very attractive and delightful and hypnotic pictures of these ages he placed alongside our values—by which I mean the values of 1810, the values of 1820, the values of his own contemporary Scotland, or his own contemporary England or France, which were what they were, the values of the early nineteenth century—by the side of those values, whatever they may have been, Protestant, unromantic, industrial, at any rate not medieval, he placed another set of values, equally good if not better, in competition with them. This shattered the monopoly, shattered the possibility that every age is as good as it can be, and is indeed advancing to an ever better one.[15]

When we take in this fictional world, we measure our feelings, ideas, and experiences against those of the fictional characters. This can be the speaker of a poem or any character in a story or novel. Setting the experience of our lives against their lives, we may come to realize that, despite the differences between the worlds in which we live, our most private feelings are in fact shared by others. The underlying subject of any literary work is the question: how does one live?—which arises out of comparing one's daily world and ideal world and measuring them against a fictional world. By experiencing the life or an aspect of the life of a fictional character, I gather another bit of information that helps me in the process of formulating an answer to that question. Of course the literary experience is all sorts of things, but in the balancing and weighing of these three worlds I learn not only about the poem or piece of fiction, but about myself.

Consider this poem, "Mother," by Zbigniew Herbert (translated by John and Bogdana Carpenter):

He fell from her knees like a ball of yarn.
He unwound in a hurry and ran blindly away.
She held the beginning of life. She would wind it
on her finger like a ring, she wanted to preserve him.

He was rolling down steep slopes, sometimes

he was climbing up. He would come back tangled, and be silent.

Never will he return to the sweet throne of her knees.

The stretched-out hands are alight in the darkness

like an old town.[16]

The title, "Mother," provides a governing context, and then each of the
next six lines gives specific information relating to that context through metaphor or simile derived from precise sense data. We can visualize it. The first
stanza presents a complete action with a beginning, middle, and end. The
second stanza presents us with something that at first seems outside of this
structure, but then we realize it is the memory controlling the information that
appears in the first stanza. The first stanza is in past tense; the second stanza
is in present tense. The bridge between them is the future tense of last line of
the first stanza—"Never will he return to the sweet throne of her knees." This
holds true of the past and present, as well as the future.

We measure the world of the poem against our own experience and our
sense of an ideal. The poignancy of the poem derives from our understanding
that the conflict Herbert presents offers no solution. Even if he could "return to
the sweet throne of her knees," it would make nothing better. All he has is memory: "The stretched-out hands are alight in the darkness / like an old town."

The ideas of the poem are presented as sense detail functioning as metaphor. Our imagination carries them to the intellect, which either finds them
credible or doesn't. But the simplicity of the first image—"He fell from her
knees like a ball of yarn."—is hard to fault, and it forms the narrative platform. Herbert then gradually makes the images more complicated—he teaches
us how to read his poem—until he arrives at the last image, which is the most
complicated. Along the way certain words take on extra metaphoric meaning.
For instance, we may realize that "tangled" in line 6 also identifies the boy's
confusion and ambivalence.

In reading the poem, we not only experience it; we also become the character of the boy. The poem becomes about us and our relationship with a parent. Even if we couldn't get away from those maternal knees fast enough, we
still have a sense of how things should have been. The discrepancy between
our actual world and the world of the poem will be comprehensible only if

we also imagine an ideal world, because even if the mother-son relationship is the best possible, the son won't be able to live happily forever after on his mother's knees. We reach this conclusion because the sense data has engaged our memory and allows us to experience the event in our imagination. We come away understanding not just something about Herbert or Life with a capital L, but also something about ourselves.

Here is an eight-line poem, "Biscuit," by Jane Kenyon, which appeared in her book *Constance* (1993):

> The dog has cleaned his bowl
> and his reward is a biscuit,
> which I put in his mouth
> like a priest offering the host.
>
> I can't bear that trusting face!
> He asks for bread, expects
> bread, and I in my power
> might have given him a stone.

The poem, we come to see, is about power and the speaker's conflicted nature, which is also our conflicted nature. The dog's trust leads the speaker to imagine how that trust could be abused, which leads her to a sense of her duality. Her anger in the fifth line isn't at the dog but at herself; while the image of the priest offering the host raises the ante, takes the mundane event of the first three lines, and boosts its potential for meaning. The event of the poem is enacted—it isn't simply referred to—and the scene can be easily visualized. Indeed, most of us have been in similar situations. Because of the precision of detail, we don't merely read the poem, we experience it, though each of us might imagine a different breed of dog. The details of the poem, in their totality, engage the imagination and carry the subject's abstract material directly into the intellect. This is exactly what Eliot was calling an objective correlative: "a set of objects, a situation, a chain of events" is the blueprint for a "*particular* emotion; such that when the external facts, which must terminate in sensory experience, are given, the emotion is immediately evoked."

We wouldn't have a sense of our duality if we couldn't imagine an ideal state where we would exist without it. The reference to the priest offering communion brings that ideal state to mind. Thinking about the poem, we weigh the actual against the ideal in our own lives and then against the world existing in the poem. Most of us, I expect, will hear that voice shouting, "I can't bear that trusting face!" and hear it as our own.

I originally titled this essay "Metaphysical Counterpoint," perhaps with some irony, in order to describe the simultaneous interplay of multiple conceptions of reality, different perceptions of being. The potential for this exists in all that we read. The greater irony is that this most abstract of subjects is communicated in the literary arts through concrete objects, situations, chains of events presented through precise detail and basic sense data, for instance, a bailiff's clerk in list slippers, a puppy nibbling his biscuit.

thirteen

the nature of metaphor

In *De doctrina Christiana,* begun in the year 396, St. Augustine wrote that when Adam and Eve were expelled from the Garden of Eden, the sense of unity and oneness they had experienced with God, with one another, and with everything around them was stripped away, and they could only communicate by gesture. In the words of one writer, they had suffered "a dislocation of consciousness [which] produced the distance between the inquiring intellect and the object of its search. The word of God was veiled, in order to exercise the seeker."[1]

So there they stood outside the gate, as they wondered what to do next. It was then, we read in another story, that Satan appeared and offered them language, not as a gift but as one more torment. "This veil, the language of sign and symbol, was both the distance of the mind from God and the avenue by which the philosophic might reach him."[2] But reaching that goal was impossible, and the farther one advanced, the more the seeker would be aware of the distance between his chattering and the consciousness of God. This inadequacy of language, in Satan's view, would always remind the speaker of what had been lost. Whatever its benefits, language would be a punishment. It could never recapture the subtlety of thought that had once existed in the mind, nor recreate the sense of total unity that Adam and Eve had experienced in the Garden. Or to put it more simply, as Ludwig Wittgenstein is supposed to have said, "Language is a net."

In this essay I wish to look at the development of language to show how the coining of words was often the search for a word to describe what something was like or what something did. These words used sense detail to indicate the thing being defined. Historically, the coining of these words, often miniature metaphors, was the job of poets.

What is striking is how important it has been for the human race to discover the reasons and origins of languages and why they differ. In Genesis the descendants of Noah spoke one language until they went to Babylon to help construct the famous tower. "And the Lord came down to see the city and the tower, which the children built." Unfortunately, they built the tower not in praise of God, but in praise of man. And so they were punished: "And the Lord said, Behold, the people is one, and they have all one language; and this they begin to do; and now nothing will be restrained from them, which they have imagined to do. Go to, let us go down, and there confound their language, that they may not understand one another's speech . . . and from thence did the Lord scatter them abroad upon the face of all the earth."[3] Tradition has it that seventy-two languages were created at this time. Other cultures have similar stories. In Greek mythology it is Hermes who scatters the languages; in Hindu belief it is Brahma.

For our purposes the story begins with Sir William Jones, chief justice of India, orientalist, and linguist who knew twenty-eight languages. In 1786 in Calcutta he delivered a speech to the Asiatic Society of Bengal on Indian culture in which he said:

> The Sanskrit language, whatever may be its antiquity, is of wonderful structure; more perfect than Greek, more copious than the Latin, and more exquisitely refined than either; yet bearing to both of them a stronger affinity, both in the roots of verbs and in the forms of grammar, than could have been produced by accident; so strong that no philologer could examine all the three without believing them to have sprung from some common source, which, perhaps, no longer exists. There is a similar reason, though not quite so forcible, for supposing that both the Gothic and Celtic, though blended with a different medium, had the same origin with the Sanskrit; and the old Persian might be added to the same family.[4]

Even though these similarities had been described before, Jones's speech is seen as the start of comparative linguistics, but Jones, like other eighteenth-

and seventeenth-century linguists, traced languages back to the sons of Noah—Shem, Ham, and Japhet—labeling the languages he had just described as Japhetic languages. In the next forty years further studies in Denmark and Germany separated linguistics from the Book of Genesis, while in 1813 the term "Indo-European" was coined by the English polymath Thomas Young, sometimes called "the last person who knew everything."[5] His entry "Languages" in the *Encyclopaedia Britannica* compared the vocabulary and grammar of four hundred languages.

Eventually, after a great deal of work by a great number of people, it was decided that 449 languages located between Iceland and the Tarim Basin in western China were descended from something called Proto-Indo-European, which is not so much a language as an educated inference. By tracing back these languages to their earliest roots, it could be shown that they evolved from a tribe living on the Pontic-Caspian Steppe in the Ukraine and southern Russia between 4500 and 2500 BCE, whose expansion began when they domesticated the horse. The Proto-Indo-European root *demə*, meaning "to force," referred to breaking horses and is the source of our word "tame."

In his book *The Horse, the Wheel and Language*, David Anthony wrote, "The speakers of Proto-Indo-European were tribal farmers who cultivated grain, herded cattle and sheep, collected honey from honeybees, drove wagons, made wool or felt textiles, plowed fields at least occasionally or knew people who did, sacrificed sheep, cattle and horses to a troublesome array of sky gods, and fully expected the gods to reciprocate the favor."[6]

During those two thousand years, Proto-Indo-European moved from Pre-Proto-Indo-European to Mature-Proto-Indo-European to Late-Proto-Indo-European, then to being just another dead language. Its early speakers became a wealthy tribe or group of tribes through the trading of horses, and they covered a lot of territory riding horseback and later traveling with their wagons. They buried their dead in kurgans, earthen burial mounds, some of which are as wide as a football field. Hundreds have been dug up with the richest containing pottery, gold, jewelry, ornate weapons, wagons, and domesticated animals including horses and cows. Over time these people separated into three main groups: western, north-central, and eastern. Then parts of these groups split off to try their luck elsewhere, the first being the Anatolian group around the middle of the fourth millennium that eventually settled in Anatolia (roughly corresponding to present-day Turkey), developed the Hittite civilization, and was well-established by 2000 BCE. Their capital city, Hattusa, reached a population of about 50,000 and then was destroyed around 1200 BCE, apparently by the Sea Peoples, who came from somewhere in the West and also destroyed a great deal of Anatolia, Syria, and Palestine before being driven back by the Egyptians. Hattusa was abandoned and the language forgotten, only to reappear in the early twentieth century when archeologists uncovered about 30,000 cuneiform clay tablets that made up part of the royal archives. More tablets were found in other Hittite cities. Their contents range from letters and contracts to prophesies and myths gathered from neighboring non-Indo-European speakers. A great many Hittite words indicate that Hittite is descended from Proto-Indo-European (PIE). In consequence, the date when the Anatolians left the steppes can be fixed by the arrival of the wheel around 3500 BCE. The Anatolian word for wheel is different from the word used in all other Indo-European languages, a word meaning "the thing that turns."

Over the next thousand years other groups split off from the Indo-Europeans, going as far as Ireland to the west, the Tarim basin in Chinese Turkestan to the east, and Iran and India to the southeast. Those going westward left their distinctive burial mounds with wagons as far west as Brittany. They were wealthier than the many villages they came across, and their horses made them very difficult to defeat in battle. They became the dominant culture, and eventually most people in Western Europe were speaking Proto-Indo-European.

The speakers of the language that became Greek arrived in Greece around 2300 BCE, making their way south from Romania or eastern Hungary. How slowly everything occurred, yet how amazing were their discoveries and inventions in a world without precedents. The spoked wheel was invented around 2000 BCE somewhere in western Siberia and the west Asiatic Steppe. This led quickly to the invention of the two-wheeled chariot. Stone fragments of projectile points dating back to 60,000 BCE have been found in Africa, but the first bow fragments in Europe were found north of Hamburg and dated around 8000 BCE. These early bows and arrows were rickety affairs of no standard size, with flint points wedged or tied into the split tip of the stick, which easily broke off if they hit anything substantial. The composite recurve bow—the kind Odysseus used when he killed the suitors—was invented toward the end of the second millennium, and standardized arrowheads with a cupped socket for the end of the arrow were cast from copper.

The date when these people left Africa and how many groups left Africa at how many different times have been the subject of fierce disputes for nearly two hundred years. Then came an article published in the magazine *Science* on May, 13, 2005, by a team of geneticists led by Dr. Vincent Macaulay of the University of Glasgow. The authors had studied mitochondrial DNA variation in isolated "relict" populations in southeast Asia, specifically the Orang Asli, a term meaning "original people," of the Semang tribe, a group of pygmy-sized Negritos "who live (or lived until recently) in small, nomadic hunter-gatherer groups in the lowland rainforests of Malaysia. . . . There is a well-documented archaeological record of continuous occupation by hunter-gatherers throughout the Holocene, and an essentially continuous hunter-gatherer record from at least 40,000 (perhaps 70,000) years ago."[7]

Mitochondrial DNA is a genetic material inherited through the female line and has been used to prove that all non-Africans descend from one woman—called the Mitochondrial Eve, who lived in eastern Africa between 150,000 and 200,000 years ago. She is our most recent common ancestor. Of course, other women lived at that time who also have living descendants, but only the Mitochondrial Eve is connected to all non-African humans alive today.[8] In addition, a large number of Africans can be traced back to this woman, but not all.

Dr. Macaulay and his associates revealed by analysis of complete mitochondrial genomes that only one successful dispersal of *Homo sapiens* occurred from Africa—not two or more, as had been thought—and it occurred between 60,000 and 75,000 years ago. According to the study, "This most likely involved the exodus of a founding group of several hundred individuals from East Africa" that moved along the coast of India and Malaysia to Australia at a time when the sea level was 200 feet lower than it is today. "This evidence suggests that this coast trail was likely the only route taken during the Pleistocene settlement of Eurasia by the ancestors of modern humans, and that the primary dispersal process, at least from India to Australasia, was very rapid . . . 66,000 years ago in India to 63,000 years ago in Australasia."[9] Also "the colonization of western Eurasia . . . was most likely the result of an early offshoot of colonization along the southern route, followed by a lengthy pause until the climate improved and the ancestors of western Eurasians were able to enter the Levant and Europe" between 55,000 and 45,000 years ago.[10]

Some archeologists dispute Dr. Macaulay's theories, saying that no archeological evidence exists to show humans outside of Africa before 60,000 years ago. Macaulay suggests that evidence "may have been lost to sea level rises," which occurred with the melting of the glaciers. Further genetic studies have supported Macaulay's theories.

So here we have evidence that everyone outside of Africa is descended from this single group who made their way to India about 65,000 years ago. When these people got to where they were going, they found the land occupied by Neanderthals who had arrived in Europe as long as 350,000 years ago and were bigger and stronger than the *Homo sapiens,* but not smarter. Neanderthals used stone tools and hunted in groups of men and women together. Their skeletons often show a large number of fractures, which, studies show, are like those sustained by modern rodeo clowns, suggesting the Neanderthals leapt on their prey and either stabbed it or brought it down by brute force. There is some evidence, often disputed, that they engaged in grave rituals, and what appears to be a flute, also disputed, was found in western Slovenia. Another matter of dispute is whether or not they had language.

The arriving *Homo sapiens* had developed projectile weapons—slings, spears, and perhaps bows and arrows—and had a division of labor between men and women. They practiced grave rituals, body ornamentation, music, and painting and "had already mastered the skills of speech, art and symbolic representation long before leaving Africa."[11] These people replaced the Neanderthals, who disappeared from Asia 50,000 years ago and from Europe 33,000 to 15,000 years ago. As to why they disappeared, the *Homo sapiens* probably killed them, and while this too is disputed, it is supported by evidence that the last pockets of Neanderthals lived in rather inaccessible places in southern Spain, Croatia, and the Crimea, hiding out, as it were.

Incidentally, an article in the *Proceedings of the National Academy of Sciences,* December 2006, entitled "Paleobiology and comparative morphology of a late Neandertal sample from El Sidrón, Asturias, Spain" focused on an extended family of twelve Neanderthals (six adults, three adolescents, and three children) found in a huge cave complex, El Sidrón, near the northeast coast of Spain. All twelve had been cannibalized at more or less the same time about 40,000 years ago. According to the article, "Anthropic activity is evinced by the presence of cut marks, flakes, percussion pitting, conchoidal scars, and adhering flakes. Immature skull bones . . . show a higher frequency of cut marks, possibly indicating skinning activities. Long bones . . . show short and deep cut marks related to disarticulation processes. . . . [T]he clear evidence of bone breaking . . . is presumably related to processing for marrow and brains, which strongly suggest a nutritional exploitation. Given the high level of developmental stress in the sample, some level of survival cannibalism would be reasonable."[12] There is no evidence who cannibalized these people, whether Neanderthals ate other Neanderthals or whether they were eaten by *Homo sapiens,* who might have reached that area 5,000 years before.

There is also DNA evidence of interbreeding between the two groups, though it seems to have been extremely rare. Neanderthals and *Homo sapiens* share from 99.5 percent to 99.9 percent of the same DNA.

Throughout the world primitive societies display many similarities, and while it doesn't prove these similarities all arose from that single group that left Africa, the Orang Asli of Malaysia remained relatively unchanged for perhaps 60,000 years. Grave goods and grave rituals have been found all over the world, while very similar dolmens have been found in Europe, the Middle East, India, and Asia. Korea has 30,000, and many look like dolmens in Ireland. Each stood over at least a single chamber grave, and many had more than one chamber, in which the corpse was buried with grave gifts. Native American tribes also disposed of their dead with grave gifts.

As for language, a theory of the origin of language advanced by the great linguist Otto Jespersen in the 1890s argued that modern languages should be traced as far back in history as possible: "If by this process, we finally arrive at uttered sounds of such a description that they can no longer be called a real language, but something antecedent to language—why then the problem will have been solved."[13]

But resulting studies have shown that languages spoken by the earliest people are as complicated and sophisticated as any in modern Europe, that among the world's nearly 7,000 living languages none are crude or undeveloped. The American ethnologist Horatio Hale published a study in 1887 on the creation of a spontaneous, individual language that occasionally occurs between very young siblings or friends, a language both complicated and unrelated to the parents' language. He felt this pointed to "what may be termed the language making instinct of very young children."[14] This anticipated Noam Chomsky's theory that knowledge of the structure of language is innate and that all languages follow the same set of rules, though the effects of these rules will differ, and this has led to many languages. But a baby is born with the information about linguistic structure already in place "and need only actually learn the idiosyncratic features of the language(s) it is exposed to."[15]

In *An Essay on Man* Ernst Cassirer wrote that in the early stages of human culture the relation between language and myth "is so close and their cooperation so obvious that it is almost impossible to separate one from the other. . . . Whenever we find man, we find him in possession of the faculty of speech and under the influence of the myth-making function."[16] Elsewhere he wrote that no matter how different language and myth might be from one another, "the same form of conceptual thinking is operative in both."[17] Cassirer called this metaphorical thinking, the idea being that metaphor is the intellectual link between language and myth. Nor is it a matter of one preceding the other. "Language and myth stand in an original and indissoluble correlation to one another, from which they both emerge but gradually as independent elements."[18]

Not long ago the ability to make metaphor was seen as a somewhat trifling matter. Metaphors were exaggerations, fictions. It is now argued that the ability to make metaphor not only was necessary to the survival of the human race, but is necessary for our survival today. What makes it necessary we will get to later.

Again in *An Essay on Man* Cassirer wrote that just as a child "demands by more or less articulate sounds" the presence of its mother and learns she will come in response, so "primitive man transfers this first elementary social experience to the totality of nature. To him nature and society are not only interconnected by the closest bonds, they form a coherent and indistinguishable whole. . . . [From this] we can easily understand the use and specific function of the magic word. The belief in magic is based upon a deep conviction of the solidarity of life. To the primitive mind the social power of the word, experienced in innumerable cases, becomes a natural and even supernatural force. Primitive man feels himself surrounded by all sorts of visible and invisible dangers. He cannot hope to overcome these dangers by merely physical means. To him the world is not a dead or mute thing; it can hear and understand. Hence if the powers of nature are called upon in the right way they cannot refuse their aid. Nothing resists the magic word."[19]

In using the word "primitive" I mean it in its original sense of "first" or "earliest," from the Latin *primus*, "first," and deriving from a Proto-Indo-European word meaning "beyond." It was never meant to be pejorative. Presumably Cassirer uses it the same way.

Cassirer expanded upon primitive man and nature in another chapter, writing that while modern man habitually divides his life into "the two spheres of practical and theoretical activity," primitive man's view of nature is primarily *sympathetic*.

> Myth is an offspring of emotion and its emotional background imbues all its productions with its own specific color. Primitive man by no means lacks the ability to grasp the empirical differences of things. But in his conception of nature and life all these differences are obliterated by a stronger feeling, the deep conviction of a fundamental and indelible *solidarity of life* that bridges over the multiplicity and variety of its single forms.[20]

Primitive man's nature doesn't display a hierarchy; rather, everything is equal and exists on the same level. This led to totemism, which is a belief system that gives spiritual significance to a natural object or animal that is accepted by a group as its emblem. Primitive man didn't think of himself as merely descended from and symbolized by a totemic animal or plant. "A bond that is present and actual as well as genetic connects his whole physical and social existence with his totemistic ancestors. In many cases this connection is felt and expressed as identity."[21]

One function of these beliefs was to eradicate death. The sense of the solidarity of life was not simply a spatial awareness, unity with all living things; it was also a temporal awareness. Through beliefs in reincarnation and ancestor worship the clear division between past, present, and future ceased to exist. Cassirer wrote:

> In primitive thought death is never regarded as a natural phenomenon that obeys general laws. It always depends upon individual and fortuitous causes. It is the work of witchcraft or magic or some other personal inimical influence. . . . The conception that man is mortal, by his nature and essence, seems to be entirely alien to mythical and primitive religious thought. . . . In a certain sense the whole of mythical thought may be interpreted as a constant and obstinate negation of the phenomenon of death. . . . In his individual and social feeling primitive man is filled with this assurance [that the dead live]. The life of man has no definite limits in space or time. It extends over the whole realm of nature and over the whole of men's history.[22]

This belief system is found in the earliest pyramid texts; found in nearly every Indian tribe from Alaska to Patagonia; found among the Romans and in the hundreds of Neolithic and Bronze Age kurgan burial mounds of the Proto-Indo-Europeans; found in the burial practices of the early *Homo sapiens* and among the Aborigines of Australia. Excavations in Gua Cha, a large limestone rock shelter in the center of West Malaysia, have identified graves with rudimentary grave goods 12,000 years old. Neolithic graves, between 3,000 and 8,000 years old, contain jewelry, pots, chisels, weapons, axes, animals, wagons, and even ships to help the deceased in the next world. It seems certain that such practices also existed among that first group of hunter-gatherers who left Africa.

But this community of all living beings couldn't exist by itself. Cassirer wrote that it had to be "preserved and reinforced by the constant efforts of man, by the strict performance of magical rites and religious observances."[23] These efforts are located in a taboo system found in every known primitive society. In many, "the only known offense was taboo breaking."[24] Yet taboo systems weren't logical. "The essence of taboo is that without consulting experience it pronounces a priori certain things to be dangerous. . . . In its original and literal sense taboo seems to mean only a thing that is marked off—that is, not on the same level as other usual, profane, harmless things. This danger has often been described as a supernatural one, but it is by no means a moral one. . . . [It] does not mean moral discrimination and it does not imply moral judgment."[25]

A taboo could be broken by chance or accident without personal responsibility, but once a man breaks a taboo, "his family, his friends, his whole tribe bears the same mark. They are stigmatized; they partake in the same miasma."[26] Nor is there a limit to the possible damage created by breaking the taboo. "'A single thing taboo,' it has been said, 'might infect the whole universe.'"[27] Nor is any special type of thing deemed taboo. "It may be taboo by its superiority or its inferiority, by its virtue or vice, by its excellence or depravity."[28] The only constant in the taboo system is that all taboos are negative. "Some things have to be avoided; some things have to be abstained from," Cassirer wrote. "For it is fear that dominates the taboo system; and fear knows only how to forbid, not how to direct. It warns against the danger, but it cannot arouse a new or moral energy in man. The more the taboo system develops the more it threatens to congeal the life of man to a complete passivity."[29]

Set against the taboo system is mana, a Polynesian word, first written about in R. H. Codrington's *The Melanesians* (1891). Most simply, mana is luck or respect or strength, and it leads to a belief in charms, talismans, and amulets. Codrington's research in Melanesia showed while mana itself is impersonal, it is "always connected with some person who directs it; all spirits have it, ghosts generally, some men." When a man has it, he becomes chief. It is the cause of all success, whether in battle, growing a large crop, or making poetry. It is "what works to effect everything which is beyond the ordinary power of men, outside the common processes of nature; it is present in the atmosphere of life . . . and is manifested by results which can only be ascribed to its operation."[30] This is similar to the so-called function gods of the early Greeks. Anything occurring outside of the narrowest norm was ascribed to the intervention of one of these minor deities.

Mana can work for good or evil, may be stolen or transferred to someone else. Cassirer saw it as a primitive form of the Stoic doctrine of the breath that is "diffused throughout the universe which imparts to all things the tension by which they are held together."[31] Owing to the incidence of mana in every early culture, "the 'Taboo-Mana Formula' has been regarded as 'the minimum definition of religion,' i.e., as the expression of a distinction which constitutes the essential, indispensable conditions of religious life as such, and represents the lowest level of it that we know."[32]

In his chapter on language, Cassirer wrote of the close relationship between myth and language. Elsewhere he described how myth "combines a theoretical element and an element of artistic creation. What strikes us is its close kinship with poetry."[33] He then quoted from F. C. Prescott's *Poetry and Myth:* "Ancient myth is the 'mass' from which modern poetry has slowly grown by the processes which evolutionists call differentiation and specialization. The myth-maker's mind is the prototype; and the mind of the poet . . . is still essentially mythopoeic." "Myth, language and art begin as a concrete, undivided unity," wrote Cassirer, "which is only gradually resolved into a triad of independent modes of spiritual creativity."[34] A picture of the king had the power of the king; a voodoo doll could control the person it represented. "Especially in the magical realm, word magic is everywhere accompanied by picture magic."[35]

Much has been written about the role of the poet in primitive and not-so-primitive societies: the poet as shaman, as tribal leader, as teacher, as historian.

The Greek oracles spoke in dactylic hexameters; many of the Hebrew prophets spoke their prophecies in poetry; the Vedas, said to be dictated by the (Hindu) gods, were poetry, as were ancient writings of Mesopotamia and Egypt. The pre-Muslim Arab soothsayers delivered their messages in poetry. Among the Celts existed half a dozen degrees of bardship, from Penerwydd the chief bard to Mabinog, a student or apprentice. Bards also had areas of specialization. The Gwyddon was skilled as a physician and an expert on land and cattle. This rigid formalization of roles was thought to go back for centuries. Other groups had similar divisions.

The Greek historian Diodorus Siculus in the first century BCE wrote that the Gauls had lyric poets called Bards.

> These men sing to the accompaniment of instruments which are like lyres, and their songs may be either of praise or of obloquy. Philosophers, as we may call them, and men learned in religious affairs are unusually honored among them and are called by them Druids. . . . Nor is it only in the exigencies of peace, but in their wars as well, that [the Gauls] obey, before all others, these men and their chanting poets, and such obedience is observed not only by their friends but also by their enemies; many times, for instance, when two armies approach each other in battle with swords drawn and spears thrust forward, these men step forth between them and cause them to cease, as though having cast a spell over certain kinds of wild beasts.[36]

Strabo, a younger contemporary of Diodorus, also wrote about the poets of the Gauls in his *Geography*:

> Among all the Gallic peoples, generally speaking, there are three sets of men who are held in exceptional honor; the Bards, the Vates and the Druids. The Bards are singers and poets; the Vates, diviners and natural philosophers; while the Druids, in addition to natural philosophy, study also moral philosophy. The Druids are considered the most just of men, and on this account they are entrusted with the decision, not only of the private disputes, but of the public disputes as well; so that, in former times, they even arbitrated cases of war and made the opponents stop when they were about to line up for battle, and the murder cases, in particular, had been turned over to them for decision.[37]

According to Diodorus, the poets have been given this power by men "experienced in the nature of the divine, and who speak, as it were, the language of the gods."[38]

The poets of the Gauls also recorded the history of the tribe. Without them the past didn't exist. They froze moments in time, just as poets have always done. Poets recited the laws, the taboos; they mapped the known world. They also had the responsibility of creating words and names, as well as creating words to protect against various taboos.

Among the Gauls or Celts a single word for poet didn't exist. Instead, there were specialists with a number of different functions, and words exist for those functions. M. L. West paraphrases the remarks by Posidonous, Diodorus, and Strabo, and adds, "According to Caesar [the Druids] educated many of the young men and made them learn a large quantity of oral verse."[39]

These various words, according to M. L. West, also exist in insular Celtic along with several other languages and go back to Proto-Indo-European. The root of "bard" is a PIE compound word meaning "praise-maker," which is also found in the Vedic. "Vates" is linked to a number of Proto-Germanic words that describe poetry and possession. It is also linked to an Old English word for "mad," "frenzied." Parenthetically, I should add that cannabis seeds have been found in kurgan burial mounds, so altered states of consciousness were clearly known to the Proto-Indo-Europeans.

Comparing the different words for poet, West concludes that two primary roles of poets can be identified in East and West. "They functioned on one hand as bestowers of praise, whether on men or gods, and on the other as prophets and seers, gifted with special knowledge, perhaps through an altered state of consciousness."[40]

Being a poet held high status. West says in Ireland the highest grade of *fili*, the priest-poet, "had a standing in law equivalent to a king or bishop."[41] In both Ireland and India "poetry was a hereditary profession that ran in certain families, passing from father to son. . . . This meant a long period of rigorous training. Caesar says that the Druidic syllabus might occupy up to twenty years. The *fili*, according to Irish texts, trained for seven years, attaining successive grades. He had to learn by heart a very large number of narratives and genealogies in addition to other lore."[42]

For this work the poet was well paid, attaching himself to a court or a successive number of courts of a powerful family. Indian and Celtic poets received gifts of horses and cattle. Vedic and Welsh poets "gratefully record their patrons' gifts of quantities of horses, chariots, cattle, and women . . . the rewards for different *fili* grades ranged from one calf to ten cows, which was the equivalent of five horses, a chariot, or a slave woman."[43]

Looking at the roots of many words for poet or linked to poetry, West shows their connection to a wide number of Indo-European languages: Vedic-Sanskrit, Avestan (a dead Iranian language now found only in the Avesta, a collection of Zoroastrian sacred texts), Tocharian, Greek, Slavonic, Lithuanian, the Germanic and Italic languages, and others. Equally similar are the ways of talking about poetry: poetry as construction, as weaving, as carpentry; the ship of song, the chariot of song, the bird of song, the song "that moves forward and follows a course."[44] In addition, West analyzes poetic idioms, similes, and figures found in Indo-European languages that point to a common ancestor in PIE.

West also compares different metrical forms and finds the greatest similarities between Vedic and Greek, of which he says "the governing principles of prosody and versification are essentially identical."[45] "The sum of correspondences, not only in the structure of individual lines but also in their relationship to one another and in the patterns in which they are combined, is sufficient to show the persistence both in the Rigveda and in Greek poetry of forms already established, at any rate, by the Graeco-Aryan period."[46]

What he finds surprising is that the languages had separated by 2300 BCE. The earliest Vedic text, the Rigveda (also Rig Veda), is dated between 1600 and 1100 BCE, and the oldest has many similarities with Avestan. Its ten sections or mandalas contain over 1,000 hymns, which were composed over several hundred years. This is a tremendous amount of material to be passed on orally for two millennia before being written down, and the Rigveda is only one of four Vedic texts. There were also Sanskrit epics that were memorized, a process that continues even today. The Wikipedia entry for Vedic Chant states that memorization of the Vedas used eleven forms of recitation of the same text. The simplest, called in English "mesh recitation," required every two words to be recited in their adjacent order, then repeated in their reverse order, and then repeated in their adjacent order. (The example given goes like this: "word1word2, word2word1, word1word2; word2word3, word3word2, word2word3; . . .") The next pair was made up of the second and third words; the next used the third and fourth. After all eleven forms had been mastered, the result was compared to different recited versions. No wonder they could take twenty years to learn.

A number of the composers, or rishis, of the Rigveda are known, or at least ten names have come down. The names of more than fifty other rishis who composed other Vedas are also known. These are mostly family members going on for generations. One can see why the root of the Proto-Indo-European word for recall or "call to mind" is found in most Indo-European languages. Recall was one of the poet's most necessary tools. In the nineteenth century, thirty manuscripts of the Rigveda were collected, the oldest being written down in 1464, and the differences between them were minimal.

The Sanskrit also uses the words "measure" and "foot" to describe prosody as, of course, did the Greeks. In Sanskrit, however, the word "foot," or *pada,* refers to a line.

After discussing the metrical similarities in Graeco-Aryan languages, West looks at metrics in other Indo-European languages. He concludes: "If the Tocharian, Baltic, and Germanic evidence is inconclusive, the Italic, Celtic, and Slavonic traditions provide positive encouragement to think that the metrical principles extrapolated from Vedic and Greek were not valid only for Graeco-Aryan but, by and large, also for the rest of Europe."[47] And we can assume that these meters and other aspects of poetry didn't begin in that 2,000-year period that saw the rise and disappearance of Proto-Indo-European, but developed long before.

Among primitive groups a word was not simply a symbol but had an almost three-dimensional reality. Written down, it could be used as a talisman or curse. A Norseman of the tenth century could be cursed by having a single rune written on a piece of bark and put under his pillow at night. The early Germans seemingly had a taboo against using the PIE words for *blood* and instead used a word that meant to bloom or flower. In the Scandinavian languages as well as Anglo-Saxon, Germanic, Celtic, and Latin, kennings were used not only in poetry, but to avoid taboo words, especially in the pre-Christian period. One might be protected by avoiding words that referred to a future action, and so "bait-gallows" would be used instead of *hook,* "battle sweat" refers to blood, "blood ember" to axe, "blood worm" to sword, "brow-stars" to eyes, "feeder of ravens" to warrior, "flame-farewelled" to an honorable death. Diodorus wrote of the Gauls, "The Gauls are terrifying in aspect and their voices are deep and altogether harsh; when they meet together they converse with few words and in riddles, hinting darkly at things for the most part and using one word when they mean another; and they like to talk in superlatives, to the end that they may extol themselves and depreciate all other men."[48] The riddles and circumlocutions were used, presumably, to avoid saying certain words. A number of words that came down to us as originating in metaphors may have first been coined to avoid an earlier taboo word. For instance, the Latin word for ghosts, *manes*, means the "good ones."

In Hebrew and Aramaic the same word meant both "word" and "thing." In the Book of Genesis, God separates light and darkness with the Word and makes the heavens and earth, while Adam was given the power to name all that lived upon the earth. "And whatsoever Adam called every living creature, that was the name thereof."[49] To name them was to have power over them. The name of God is also taboo (sometimes it is seen in English spelled "G-d").

In 1938, Robert Gordis, a Jewish rabbi and scholar, published an essay titled "Some Effects of Primitive Thought on Language" in which he sought to explain "the existence of a large number of roots that possess mutually opposed meanings either within the same language or in different members of the same group."[50] This was especially true of the Semitic group of languages. The word *berech* meant both "to curse" and "to bless"; the word *hesed* meant "disgrace" and "kindness." Roots with opposing meanings were even more common in Arabic. "At times," Gordis wrote, "the opposite meaning develops in different languages. The root *aban* means 'to be willing' in Hebrew, 'to refuse' in Ethiopic; *alam* means 'to be hidden,' 'unknown' in Hebrew, 'to know' in Arabic."[51] Many more examples occurred in Egyptian, as well as a lesser number in German, French, English, and Latin. For instance, the Latin adverb *clam* means "secretly," and the verb *clamare* means "to shout."

Gordis looked for the answer to the puzzle in primitive Semitic societies. He wrote that while language is probably the oldest human invention, it has undergone relatively little basic alteration. "Modern languages have increased their vocabularies tremendously and have sloughed off and modified their inflections, but the basic structure, the linguistic 'drift,' has scarcely changed. Above all, the habitual forms of discourse that constitute the field of syntax have endured. Since 'language [here he takes a phrase from Edward Sapir] does not exist apart from culture, that is, from the socially inherited assemblage of practices and beliefs of the group,' it is in primitive society that we must seek the key to many phenomena in language."[52]

Gordis followed with a discussion of taboo and mana as related to primitive man's belief that a mysterious, nonmaterial force adhered to nearly all parts of human experience. "Mana is thus the positive side of this supernatural power; taboo its negative aspect."[53] Though mana was found everywhere, it clustered "most thickly about the exceptional elements of life, the extremes of power and weakness, and the great occasions, like birth, puberty, marriage and death."[54] This was also true of taboo.

In primitive thought there was "a particularly intimate connection between a thing and its name, a relation bordering on identity."[55] One could control persons and things by manipulating their names, so people kept their true names hidden and instead used a public name. In addition, taboos existed against speaking the names of the dead or chiefs or gods. The pantheon of Proto-Indo-European gods was headed by *dyeu-peter,* "god-father," which became *Zeu pater* in Greek, and *Iupeter* in Latin. The same name appears in Germanic and Norse mythology. We don't know Zeus's true name; it is taboo. When a man became king or chief, he would get a new name, a throne-name, to purify him from the ill fortune that might have accrued to his former name. For instance, King Solomon's earlier name was Jedidiah ("beloved of the Lord"). A sick person would be given an additional name for the same reason so that his or her health might be regained.

But these taboos didn't just concern names. In Java smallpox is known as "pretty girl," while "Arabs call leprosy 'the blessed disease,' and a person bitten by a serpent is described as 'the sound one.'"[56] Often the healthy, beautiful, and valuable are shielded from ill fortune by being described in negative terms. The Arabs described a beautiful mare as "ugly." Shout for joy in Hebrew also meant "moan"; the word for revelry also meant "lamentation." Among the Yiddish speakers of Frankfurt, beautiful girls would be called ugly, and good girls called bad just to protect them. "The Talmud will often replace *Israel* by 'the enemies of Israel' in a passage describing suffering or trouble."[57] In Hebrew death will be called "life" and a cemetery "the house of life." But in time the figurative meaning came to mean what it was meant to replace, so the roots of many words carried opposite meanings. In what Gordis called a "[by] no means exhaustive list," he gave twenty-eight

words: blind for seer, disgrace for praise, curse for bless, cry for laugh, ca-
lamity for healing, folly for wisdom, excrement for food, and so on.

Gordis's examples came from all over the world. A king or chief would
call himself "we two," meaning himself and his mana. From this, he argues,
came the "plural of majesty," the royal we. Language developed polite and
familiar forms of address—you and thou in English—to avoid the taboo of
addressing a powerful person directly. Many times metaphors would be used
as verbal displacements that resemble kennings. Members of an African tribe
would tell children not to speak of men on a hunting expedition by saying,
"Don't talk of birds who are in heaven." Valuable or dangerous animals
would be called by their attributes or with a flattering term. Kirghiz women
would call sheep "the bleating ones." Dogs in Madagascar were "barker" or
"driver away." The fox in Sweden was "blue foot." A tribe in Sumatra would
call a tiger "grandfather," "he with the striped coat," and "the roaring trap."

Among the Proto-Indo-Europeans a cow was called *kwom*, which is
thought to imitate the sound of lowing. This is not simply onomatopoeic; it
described an attribute of the cow. The word for fox derived from "the creature with a bushy tail," the word for horse derived from "the creature that
runs or leaps," pig from "the creature that digs," bear from "the brown one."
In Ireland the bear was called "the good calf," in Wales "the honey pig," in
Sweden "twelve men's strength" and "golden feet," in Finland "apple of the
wood" and "beautiful honey paw," in Lithuania "the licker," and in Russia
"the honey-eater." But the animals' true names remained hidden; they were
taboo. This is also true of the word "wolf," which appears in all the Western languages and derives from the Proto-Indo-European. But it has no clear
meaning. It is a word intended to obscure itself. The original Greek meaning
of "euphemism" referred to the taboo system. It meant the use of a favorable
word in place of an inauspicious one. For instance, the Erinyes, or Furies, the
avenging deities sent to punish criminals, were called the Eumenides, meaning
"the kindly ones." One of the names of Hades, the Greek god of the under-
world, was *Plouton*, "the wealth-giver"; the Roman form was Pluto.

Gordis wrote that such epithets could be used to avoid many ordinary
words. For Highland fishermen on a fishing trip, the word "rock" was replaced with the word "hard," a "knife" became "the sharp one" and a seal the
"bald beast." Gordis concluded, "It must be kept in mind that these epithets
are not voluntary variations in speech for the sake of novelty or vividness

but obligatory usages, the infraction of which, it is believed will expose the speaker and his fellows to grave danger and loss."[58]

In these societies there had to be a source for these verbal displacements and epithets. The word would have no power if it were invented by just anyone. So in most instances it was created by the poet or shaman. This was another reason for the poet's value. He or she kept the tribe safe by creating language to deflect the many taboos. But the poet didn't simply invent the word; he or she believed that it suddenly appeared in the mind, having arrived from another source such as a muse or god.

As for the Proto-Indo-Europeans a certain amount of information can be inferred about them from their language. The absence of words for ocean or sea and the various words for meadow and field, along with words for beech tree, salmon, river, and snow, suggest the Pontic Steppe. Their society was divided into a clerical class, warrior class, and peasant class. The warrior class identified themselves with wolves or dogs. They had cattle, and a man's wealth might be determined by how many cows he had. The English word "fee" derives from the Proto-Indo-European word for cattle, while in Latin we can see the similarity between *pecu* meaning sheep or flocks and *pecunia* meaning money and property, from which derives the English words "pecuniary" and "impecunious."

Most Proto-Indo-European words derived from metaphor. As noted in an earlier chapter, the word "word" goes back to an expression for breaking off or biting off something. The Proto-Indo-Europeans believed that we have a steady stream of preexisting sound and we bite off chunks to make the words we speak. The word "speak" derives from a word for strew, sprinkle, scatter, which have the same root. To speak, then, is to bite off pieces of sound from a stream of sound and scatter them in front of others.

Words for emotions give further metaphors. "Anger" comes from an Indo-European base—*angh*—for "constricted, narrow, a strangling." "Angina" has the same source. Hate meant to have a bad temper. Lust meant to be eager. Terror meant to tremble. The word "fear" comes from a word meaning ambush or snare, a sudden attack. The word "threat" comes from an Old English word for a group of men, a "throng," both of which go back to the Indo-European base word—*trenk*, meaning to shove or press hard. "Thrust" has the same root. With the word "threat" the Old English speaker was describing Scandinavian raiders that attacked outlying farms, plundered, and took slaves.

The Proto-Indo-European base for "right" means straight, stretched out, put in order. "Wrong" means twisted, curved, bendable. The word "worm" has the same root—to turn, bend. But the base word for "right" is also the base word for "rich," "reckon," "rule," and "rex" or king—arising from the earlier meanings of unbending, straight, ordered.

The verb "hide" meant to "cover" or "conceal," but the noun meant "the thing with which one conceals oneself," for example, a cow hide. To "mourn" came from the word "remember." The word "bury" came from "to protect" or "preserve," which again gives a sense of grave rituals and the denial of death. The two-word phrase *kred-dhε,* meaning "to put to the heart," became the Latin verb *credere,* "to trust," "to believe," from which derives the English word "creed." A "companion" is a person with whom one shares bread or "pan." "Wife" derives from the Proto-Indo-European base—*weip*—meaning to twist, turn, or wrap in the sense of "the hidden or veiled person," which gives us an idea of the social customs of these people.

The words of many primitive groups were based on metaphors drawn from the world around them, a world that, in Cassirer's phrase, "is not a dead and mute thing." The metaphors upon which their language was based expressed their solidarity with life. And their first metaphors, it is thought, derived from the body—the trunk of a tree, the arm of a river, the face of a cliff, the foot of a hill, the eye of a storm.

Most words that derive from metaphors we use with no visual image. They have become signs or abstractions. Many have became what is known as faded metaphors; that is, the metaphor took the place of the word it was meant to exemplify. "A running brook," "a rumor runs through town," "a fence runs around a field"—the word "run" was originally a metaphorical description or a simile; a brook runs as a man runs. Now it is a faded metaphor, and we use the verb in these instances without any thought of legs.

In *Philosophy in a New Key,* Susanne Langer wrote: "Every new experience, or new idea about things, evokes first of all some metaphorical expression. As the idea becomes familiar, this expression 'fades' to a new literal use of the once metaphorical predicate, a more general use than it had before."[59] It is here that we see the beginnings of abstraction, which is the point of comparison between one thing and another. "The fact that poverty of language, need of emphasis, or need of circumlocution for any reason whatsoever, leads us at once to seize upon a metaphorical word, shows how natural the perception of common form is, and how easily one and the same concept is conveyed through words that represent a wide variety of conceptions. . . . [Metaphor] is the power whereby language, even with a small vocabulary, manages to embrace a multimillion things; whereby new words and merely analogical meanings become stereotyped into literal definitions."[60] As noted before, English has more synonyms than any other Western language. There are 700,000 words in English, and the Western language with the second-highest number of words is German with 400,000. At times one hears non-English speakers who are learning English say that spoken English uses fewer metaphors than their native language, that it often has the exact synonym that their native language may lack. And to return briefly to the metaphor that began this essay, it was through metaphor that Adam and Eve attempted to transcend the limitations of language.

In the evolution of language there came a time when people realized their trust in the magic word, or Mythos, had been in vain. Nature didn't understand their language. "All hope of subduing nature by the magic word had been frustrated," Cassirer wrote. "But as a result man began to see the relation between language and reality in a different light. The magic function of the word was eclipsed and replaced by its semantic function. . . . Physically the word may be declared impotent, but logically it is elevated to a higher, indeed the highest rank. The *Logos* becomes the principle of the universe and the first principle of human knowledge."[61]

Cassirer described this process in Greece among the pre-Socratic philosophers as the word stopped being valued for its magical power and began to be valued for its semantic and symbolic functions, permitting early Greek thought to pass "from a philosophy of nature to a philosophy of language."[62]

A similar process happened with mathematics. In the Middle Ages, numbers were still being valued for their magical or esoteric qualities by numerologists, astrologists, magicians, alchemists, and so on. There is a story attributed to Thomas Aquinas about a young man who decides to summon up a demon to help him with his studies. To protect himself, he drew a circle on the floor and a pentagram within it. He then stepped into the center, secure in the belief that the demon couldn't cross this barrier. When the demon arrived, the young man said, "I need your help with my studies, especially mathematics." "So I see," said the demon, stepping into the pentagram and dragging the student away.

In discussing the fifteenth-century Italian philosopher Giovanni Pico della Mirandola, Frances Yates wrote, "Pico in his Mathematical Conclusions had stated that 'By number a way may be had for the investigation and understanding of everything possible to be known.' In his mind the Mathematical Conclusions supported the Cabalist Conclusions. The letters of the Hebrew alphabet have numerical values; the names of God and the names of angels can be expressed numerically. In its way, Cabala encouraged a numerological approach to the world (for the Hebrew alphabet was believed to contain the world being the creative word by which the world was made)."[63]

But beginning in the late Middle Ages, belief in the magical qualities of numbers began to fade, and at Oxford and Cambridge universities, those who had thought that numbers could reveal the secrets of the universe turned their attention to what became mathematics, as we know it today.

In another chapter in *An Essay on Man,* Cassirer discussed Immanuel Kant's hunt for "a general criterion by which we may describe the fundamental structure of the human intellect and distinguish this structure from all other possible modes of knowing."[64] The answer, Kant concluded, was that human beings are the only creatures capable "of making a sharp distinction between the reality and possibility of things."[65] He then attempted to distinguish between "discursive" understanding, which derives from the human intellect, and "intuitive understanding," or what Langer calls "nondiscursive understanding." Kant wrote, "Concepts without intuitions are empty; intuitions without concepts are blind."[66] This dualism, according to Cassirer, "lies at the bottom of our distinction between possibility and actuality. . . . We cannot think without images, and we cannot intuit without concepts."

As evidence, Cassirer described a patient suffering from hemiplegia (paralysis of one side of the body) and an inability to write with his right hand who found it impossible to say, "I can write with my right hand," but could easily say, "I can write with my left hand." Cassirer then quoted the psychopathologist conducting the tests as saying that the patient had "a lack of capacity for approaching a 'possible' situation." The cause was the patient's "inability to grasp what was abstract. . . . He can only live and act in a concrete sphere."[67]

Studies of the human brain have advanced considerably since 1940, and what the psychopathologist was describing were differences between the left and right sides of the brain. It was once thought that the left brain was the dominant half because it was larger and because much of the right brain could be removed and a person could still speak and more or less function. Now that is seen as incorrect.

The left side of the brain is the side that tells the truth; the right side is the side that lies. Or one could say, the left side is the side that describes what exists; the right side can describe what doesn't exist. Or, more exactly, the right side has the ability to imagine, to hypothesize possibility; the left side doesn't.

For me it is interesting to compare the two sides of the brain because of what it says about metaphor. The ability to appreciate humor, for instance, is mostly located in the right side of the brain, although the left has a liking for slapstick. In experiments patients with damaged right brains or whose right brains were put to sleep with sodium amobarbital were unable to understand jokes or cartoons. They were unable to grasp the surprise aspect of the joke, and the implausibility. For example: A horse walks into a bar; the bartender asks, "Why the long face?" The patient says, "They don't let horses into bars." A joke surprises our anticipation by suddenly shifting in an unexpected direction. It should be said that such patients would be equally unable to understand metaphor; the phrase "a man locks his barn door after the horse has been stolen" wouldn't make sense to them.

With a damaged right hemisphere, a patient can talk but cannot sing; with a damaged left hemisphere a patient can sing but cannot talk. When reading poetry with various formal elements, the rhyme, meter, line breaks, alliteration, and so on are processed by the right brain; the sentences by the left brain. The left brain takes in and processes speech; the right brain processes facial expressions, hand gestures, and body language. The right brain invents words; the left brain controls syntax. Cassirer quoted John Stuart Mill as asserting "that grammar is the most elementary part of logic because it is the beginning of the analysis of the thinking process . . . the principles and rules of grammar are the means by which the forms of language are made to correspond with the universal forms of thought."[68]

Recent studies in neuroplasticity have shown that the left brain and right brain differences are not as clear-cut as was once thought, that if one part of the brain is damaged it is often possible for that function to be taken over by another part through the formation of new neural pathways. But the basic, normal, undamaged brain of right-handed people works pretty much as I have described.

As might be supposed, the right brain is the source of metaphor, simile, symbol, and so on. All are forms of hypothesis. Most brain researchers believe that the ability to dream is situated in the right brain. And hallucinations originate in the right brain. Studies have shown an unusual number of cases where one sibling is an artist and another is schizophrenic. This is a difference between controlled and uncontrolled creation. In *The Origin of Consciousness in the Breakdown of the Bicameral Mind,* Julian Jaynes argued that "the speech of the gods [of ancient Greece, for example] was directly organized in what corresponds to Wernicke's area on the right hemisphere and 'spoken' or 'heard' over the anterior commissures to or by the auditory areas of the left temporal lobe."[69] Whether one accepts Jaynes's assertion or not, it might be said that one's conscience speaks through the right brain, since one's conscience hypothesizes the consequences of particular actions. The left brain turns them into rules. And Jaynes wrote that the Greek muse of poetry, as described in Plato's *Ion,* spoke directly to the right hemisphere. After all, one doesn't logically deduce a metaphor. It suddenly appears—out of the right brain—and then the left brain works out the logic. Finally, one's sense of spatial relationships derives from the right brain. When it is damaged, a person can't even find his or her way around the house. And one can see that something like spatial relationships plays a part in metaphors, similes, and so on. The equation "A is to B as C is to D" is, in part, a comparison describing a kind of spatial relationship. A sense of spatial relationship is also necessary to process facial expressions and gestures.

The left brain thinks discursively and linearly, moving logically, step by step in a sequence. The right brain thinks nondiscursively with images—intuitive understanding, in Kant's definition. It is also called "presentational." A metaphor is an example of nondiscursive thought, and its meaning comes not sequentially but strikes us all at once. Consequently a nondiscursive or presentational symbol is spatial, while a discursive sign is temporal; we work it out through a linear progression.

For early primitive groups, dreams came from the outside, as did hallucinations. Similarly, for the early poet or bard, metaphors also came from the outside. How else to explain their sudden appearance when a moment before there was nothing? The early poet's ability to coin a word was not a sign of his or her own cleverness; it was a sign that some higher power was speaking through the poet, a sign that the higher power demanded that such and such a sound have a particular meaning. The Vedic hymns were thought to be created by a god and then passed through the mind of a rishi or composer.

It was the right brain's ability to hypothesize, to conceive the difference between the possible and actual, and to imagine the consequences of present actions that let primitive man survive in a hostile environment. At the center of those qualities was the ability to think metaphorically, the ability to compare one thing to another thing, whether actual, possible, or impossible, and form abstractions based on that comparison. This, for instance, is one purpose of the dozens of similes found in the *Iliad*. They describe a world off the battlefield and enable us to form hypotheses about life in ancient Greece.

It would not be implausible to suggest that the Neanderthal lacked a right brain or at best had a very small or undeveloped one. Without art and ornamentation they were doomed literalists. They could see the function of a stone axe, but not a bow and arrow, which requires a degree of hypothesis. The Neanderthal had a diminished sense of consequence and so was banished to prehistory.

Metaphor and the right brain is the source of language. Without them we could signify, as a chimpanzee is able to signify, but we couldn't converse. The job of a poet or a fiction writer is to create metaphor. The work itself is a metaphor and it contains metaphors within it.

In her book *Feeling and Form,* Susanne Langer wrote, "The poet uses discourse to create an illusion, a pure appearance, which is a non-discursive symbolic form. The feeling expressed by this form is neither his, nor his hero's, nor ours. It is the meaning of the symbol. It may take us some time to perceive it, but the symbol expresses it at all times, and in this sense the poem 'exists' objectively whenever it is presented to us."[70]

We can see this very simply in Bashō's death poem, which is a haiku:

Sick on my journey
across withered fields
dreams continue to wander

Although over three hundred years old and a pale shadow of the original Japanese, the haiku "exists" objectively whenever it is presented to us. "Journey" of course is a common metaphor for life, but we also see that "withered fields" refers to his present condition, his imagination and memory in old age.

Bashō is sick and is trying to recall his past, or perhaps he is the victim of his dreams, though such a paraphrase greatly diminishes the poem.

One's preoccupation and occupation as a writer is to pursue and increase one's ability to construct metaphor. It is obvious that to be a writer one must also be a reader, but it is less obvious, though equally true, that a writer must expand his or her sense of consequence. Yet a writer has evident gifts with which to do this. To imagine is to hypothesize. One must educate the ability to hypothesize, to imagine consequence, which is not only the job of the right brain, but one of the functions of art. It is through the process of transforming a possibility to an actuality that material is moved from the right brain to the left, and so educates our sense of cause and effect. In such an instance an effect becomes subject to the rules of logic. This fulfills one of the needs of the writer, which is simply to increase the tools at his or her disposal.

M. L. West states it as an axiom that "all people of all times have had poetry and song."[71] But in the nineteenth century there was a change in poetry, caused partly by Romanticism and partly by the nature of the Industrial Revolution, and the lyric replaced drama and heroic narrative as the preeminent form. As Graham Hough has written, the grandiose was replaced by the exquisitely restricted form; the public utterance by intimate communication. But the lyric, too, had changed. Formerly, the lyric poet chose one of a few recognized roles: lover, courtier, patriot, sage, or religious contemplative. "But," as Hough writes, "Baudelaire . . . cannot be assigned to any of these roles, and when he claims kinship with his readers, which he does by means of a calculated insult, . . . it is through the shadow side of their lives . . . , [through] all that is unacknowledged or rejected by their social selves, that he professes to be at one with them. . . . Baudelaire . . . is the first to accept the declassed, disestablished position of the poet who is no longer the celebrant of the culture to which he belongs, the first to accept the squalor and baseness of the modern urban scene."[72]

But if Baudelaire is the first proto-modernist, then Rimbaud is the first modernist. His poems written between 1870 and 1873 contain the roots of not only modernist subject matter, but also method. This is not the place to discuss the history of modernism, but by rejecting "a single cultural stream,"[73] poetry entered a period of tremendous diversity and changed from being national to become international. The poet had been cut free of all his or her traditional roles. Hough writes, "The tide making for technical progress and the scientific organization of society flows on; but whatever our social and political desires we cannot plausibly pretend that poetry swims with it."[74]

Poetry continues to have an uneasy relationship to the society in which it is written. It seems to have lost its historical function. It has replaced cultural definition with forms of invention and self-definition. Not only is it impossible to say where it is going, but it is impossible to say where it is. It would seem that, now that modernism has gone by, we all could be called postmodernist, but that term has been co-opted by another group, which rejects metanarratives, theories, and belief systems that seek to explain history and the course of knowledge; which rejects the possibility of universals and objective truth; which values pastiche, chance methods, and the absurd, and harbors a distrust of language and a hyperconsciousness that polices intellectual backsliding and the embrace of "traditional" values.

But surely Rimbaud wasn't the first writer to reject the possibility of absolute truth; rather, absolute truths have been changed over time to contingent truths, but perhaps that is too extreme; perhaps they only became well-argued possibilities. After all, it was Hume who denied that rational faculties existed and that ethics was a field of subjective beliefs. But many poets after Baudelaire and some before him have rejected the objective for the expressive and subjective. We learn more from human differences than from human similarities. Instead of truth, we see degrees of truth, if we're lucky.

What one sees in much postmodernist poetry is expressivity and often a sensitivity to the absurd without any need or desire to communicate. In fact, communication becomes a doubtful commodity, and if ten different readers come up with ten different readings, that's just fine.

But poetry is a form of communication between human beings with different experiences and different views of the world. This communication may be rudimentary and incomplete, but it still exists and metaphor functions as one of communication's necessary tools. Through poetry I can see my life more clearly, which is very different from seeing my life clearly. Hough concludes his essay on modernism by saying, "The fact that poetry is not of the slightest economic or political importance, that it has no attachment to any of the powers that control the modern world, may set it free to do the only thing that in this age it can do—to keep some neglected parts of the human experience alive until the weather changes; as in some unforeseeable way it may do."[75]

How different this is from the poets of the Vedas who century after century continued on their straight path perfectly secure in their belief of their place in the world. For thousands of years poetry was at the center of society, but then it began to change. Perhaps that began, as Cassirer suggests, when Mythos was replaced by Logos. And then Romanticism changed it completely, while Freud and a variety of psychiatrists tried to map the unconscious and made the subjective self seem quantifiable. As has been said, Freud and Marx created the two great religions of the twentieth century. They, too, offered metanarratives. But with Baudelaire and the Symbolists, metaphors changed from being mostly modifiers and exemplars to functioning as primary carriers of information about human complexity and the poet's particular subjectivity. They became the tools with which poets explored and expressed their inner selves as they tried to bear witness to the world and articulate in their separate ways the question of how does one live. As Hough suggests, as long as poetry remains at the periphery of society, this will have to be enough.

glossary

accent	The degree of stress placed on a syllable primarily in metrical verse, but may also be used in nonmetrical verse.
accentual meter	A meter in which only stressed syllables are counted.
accentual-syllabic meter	A meter in which both syllables and stresses are counted, such as iambic pentameter.
acephalous	A foot with a missing syllable at the beginning of a line; also called a headless line.
alliteration	The repetition of initial consonantal sounds within one or two lines: "The knight that had knotted the nets of deceit."
anapest	From the Greek meaning "beaten back" (a reversed dactyl). A metrical foot made up of two unstressed syllables, followed by a stressed syllable, as in the line of a limerick beginning with an iamb: There WAS a young LAdy named SMITH.
assonance	The rhyming of internal vowel sounds.
caesura	A pause in a line often marked by a piece of punctuation.
catalectic foot	A foot with a missing syllable at the end of a line.
conceit	A complex metaphor extending past a single line.
consonance	Similar or identical consonants with differing vowels rhyming with one another.

dactyl	From the Greek for a finger with one long and two short joints. A stressed syllable followed by two unstressed syllables: Peterson, beautiful.
dimeter	A line made up of two feet.
end stopped	A line ending with a definite pause, usually marked by punctuation.
enjambment	A line that runs over to the next so that the line break creates a degree of emphasis.
foot	Basic unit in a line of metrical verse.
hexameter	A line made up of six feet.
iamb	From the Greek, "to limp," a metrical foot made up of one unstressed and one stressed syllable: a line, at risk.
meter	The breaking up of the rhythm of the language into formal units.
octave	An eight-line stanza.
near-rhyme	The blanket term for different varieties of inexact rhyme.
pentameter	A line made up of five feet.
pyrrhic	From the Greek, "used in the war dance." A foot made up of two unstressed syllables: of the.
quantitative meter	A meter in which only the duration of syllables is counted.
quatrain	A four-line stanza.
relative stress	Meter, if unapplied, is an abstraction. When applied, the different feet are influenced by their aural environment, so a pyrrhic or spondee might become an iamb or a trochee.
sestet	A six-line stanza.
spondee	From the Greek, "used at a libation." A foot made up of two stressed syllables: fencepost, dogtrot.
syllabics	A meter in which only the syllables are counted.
tercet	A three-line stanza.
tetrameter	A line made up of four feet.
trimeter	A line made up of three feet.
trochee	From the Greek, "running." A metrical foot made up of a stressed and unstressed syllable: stanza, single.

permissions

notes

introduction

1. Nadezhda Mandelstam, *Hope Abandoned,* trans. Max Hayward (New York: Atheneum, 1981), p. 96.
2. Ibid., p. 47.
3. Walter Jackson Bate, *The Burden of the Past and the English Poet* (New York: W. W. Norton, 1972), p. 5.

chapter 1: approaching subject matter

1. William Butler Yeats, *The Collected Poems* (London: Macmillan, 1963), p. 88.
2. William Wordsworth, "The Preface to the *Lyrical Ballads,*" in Walter Jackson Bate, ed., *Criticism: The Major Texts* (New York: Harcourt, Brace, 1952), p. 342.
3. Susanne K. Langer, *Problems of Art: Ten Philosophical Lectures* (New York: Charles Scribner's Sons, 1957), p. 67.
4. Ibid., p. 24.
5. William Blake, *The Complete Poetry and Selected Prose of John Donne and The Complete Poetry of William Blake in one volume* (New York: Modern Library, 1941), p. 558.
6. Walt Whitman, *Leaves of Grass* (New York: W. W. Norton, 1973), p. 14.
7. Sylvia Plath, *Collected Poems* (New York: HarperPerennial, 2008), p. 222.
8. Susanne K. Langer, *Feeling and Form* (New York: Charles Scribner's Sons, 1953), pp. 214–215.
9. Lawrence Ferlinghetti, *These Are My Rivers: New & Selected Poems, 1955–1993* (New York: New Directions, 1994), p. 113.
10. Ibid., p. 115.

chapter 2: joining form and content

1. George Saintsbury, *A History of English Prosody: From the Twelfth Century to the Present Day,* 2nd ed. (New York: Russell & Russell, 1961), vol. 1, p. 305.
2. Yannis Ritsos, *Subterranean Horses,* trans. Minas Savvas (Athens, OH: Ohio University Press, 1980), p. 16.
3. John Berryman, *The Dream Songs* (New York: Farrar, Straus and Giroux, 1969), p. 6.
4. Susanne K. Langer, *Feeling and Form* (New York: Charles Scribner's Sons, 1953), p. 241.
5. Susanne K. Langer, *Problems of Art: Ten Philosophical Lectures* (New York: Charles Scribner's Sons, 1957), p. 91.
6. John Berryman, "The Art of Poetry No. 16," an interview conducted by Peter Stitt, *The Paris Review* (New York, 1972), Winter 1972, no. 53, pp. 1–33.

7. Nadezhda Mandelstam, *Hope Abandoned,* trans. Max Hayward (New York: Atheneum, 1981), p. 41.
8. Ibid., pp. 41–42.
9. Ibid., p. 42.
10. Ibid., p. 45.
11. Louise Glück, "Ersatz Thought," *The Threepenny Review,* Winter 1999.
12. Ibid.
13. Ibid.
14. Walter Jackson Bate, *The Burden of the Past and the English Poet* (Cambridge, MA: Belknap Press, 1970), p. 5.
15. Ibid., p. 7.
16. Ibid., p. 5.
17. Ibid., p. 10.

chapter 3: reconciling paradox

1. *Stories of Anton Chekhov,* trans. Richard Pevear and Larissa Volokhonsky (New York: Bantam, 2000), p. 116.
2. *Anton Chekhov's Life and Thought,* trans. Michael Henry Heim in collaboration with Simon Karlinsky (Berkeley: University of California Press, 1975), p. 279.
3. Franz Kafka, *The Castle,* trans. Willa and Edwin Muir (New York: Alfred A. Knopf, 1954), p. 54.
4. Ibid., p. 60.
5. Rainer Maria Rilke, *Letters on Cézanne,* ed. Clara Rilke, trans. Joel Agee (New York: Farrar, Straus and Giroux, 1985), p. 67.
6. François Rabelais, *Gargantua and Pantagruel,* trans. Burton Raffel (New York: W. W. Norton, 1990), p. 407.
7. Ibid., pp. 407–408.
8. Ibid., p. 408.
9. Milan Kundera, *Testaments Betrayed,* trans. Linda Asher (New York: HarperCollins, 1995), p. 7.
10. Rabelais, *Gargantua and Pantagruel,* p. 185.
11. Kundera, *Testaments Betrayed,* p. 5.
12. Ibid., p. 6.
13. Bill Knott, "First Sight," in *Plaza de Loco: New Poems 1998* (Boston: privately published, 1998), p. 2.
14. John Berryman, *The Dream Songs* (New York: Farrar, Straus and Giroux, 1969), p. 206.
15. Kundera, *Testaments Betrayed,* pp. 32–33.
16. Ibid., p. 7.
17. Charles Baudelaire, *The Painter of Modern Life and Other Essays,* trans. and ed. Jonathan Mayne (London: Phaidon, 1964), p. 148.
18. Ibid., p. 149.
19. Ibid., pp. 149–150.
20. Ibid., p. 151.
21. Ibid., p. 152.
22. Ibid., pp. 152–153.
23. Ibid., p. 153.
24. Ibid., pp. 153–154.
25. Bill Knott, *Ear Quire: A Selection of Rhymed Quatorzains* (Boston: privately published, 2004), unnumbered.
26. Baudelaire, *The Painter of Modern Life and Other Essays,* pp. 107–108.
27. John Gardner, *On Moral Fiction* (New York: Basic Books, 1978), p. 107.
28. Ibid., p. 108.
29. Ellen Bryant Voigt, "Cow," *The New Yorker,* December 6, 2010, p. 40.

30. Yannis Ritsos, *Selected Poems: 1938–1988* (Brockport, NY: BOA Editions, 1989), p. 131.

chapter 4: aspects of the syllable

1. Paul Valéry, "The Poet's Rights over Language" in *The Art of Poetry*, in Vol. 7 of *The Collected Works of Paul Valéry* (Princeton, NJ: Princeton University Press, 1989), pp. 170–171.
2. *The New Princeton Encyclopedia of Poetry and Poetics,* ed. Alex Preminger and T. V. F. Brogan (Princeton, NJ: Princeton University Press, 1993), pp. 1249–1250.
3. William Barnes, "The Hill-Shade," in "A Symposium on the Dead," Christopher Ricks et al., in *The Threepenny Review,* Winter 2004.
4. *The New Princeton Encyclopedia of Poetry and Poetics,* pp. 1019–1029.
5. Philip Larkin, "Aubade," in *Collected Poems* (New York: Farrar, Straus and Giroux, 1989), p. 208.
6. Donald Justice, "The Poet at Seven," in *Collected Poems* (New York, 2004), p. 7.
7. Philip Larkin, "The Explosion," in *Collected Poems,* p. 175.
8. Sir Thomas Wyatt, *The Essential Wyatt,* ed. W. S. Merwin (New York: Ecco, 1989), p. 33.
9. Janet Lewis, *The Selected Poems of Janet Lewis,* ed. R. L. Barth (Athens, OH: Swallow Press/Ohio University Press, 2000), p. 21.
10. W. B. Yeats, *The Collected Poems of W. B. Yeats* (London: Macmillan, 1963), p 211.
11. John Frederick Nims, *Western Wind,* 2nd ed. (New York: McGraw-Hill, 1973), pp. 161–171.
12. John Keats, *The Essential Keats,* ed. Philip Levine (New York: Ecco, 1987), p. 20.
13. Robert Lowell, *Collected Poems,* ed. Frank Bidart and David Gewanter (New York: Farrar, Straus and Giroux, 2003), p. 14.

chapter 5: line breaks

1. T. S. Eliot, *Collected Poems, 1909–1962* (Orlando, FL: Harcourt Brace Jovanovich, 1991), p. 3.
2. William Shakespeare, *The Pelican Shakespeare: The Sonnets* (New York: Penguin Books, 1977), p. 84.
3. Edward Lear, *The Complete Verse and Other Nonsense* (New York: Penguin Books, 2002), p. 428.
4. James Wright, *Above the River: The Complete Poems* (New York: Farrar, Straus and Giroux, 1990), p. 162.
5. Thomas Lux, *New and Selected Poems: 1975–1995* (New York: Houghton Mifflin, 1997), p. 127.
6. Louise Glück, *The First Four Books of Poems* (New York: Ecco, 1995), p. 144.

chapter 6: context and causality

1. John Berryman, *The Dream Songs* (New York: Farrar, Straus and Giroux, 1969), p. 20.
2. W. B. Yeats, *The Collected Poems of W. B. Yeats* (London: Macmillan, 1963), p. 241.
3. Ibid., p. 211.
4. R. F. Foster, *W. B. Yeats: A Life Volume II: The Arch-Poet 1915–1939* (Oxford: Oxford University Press, 2003), p. 496 ff.
5. Three dots indicate a stanza break.
6. H.D. (Hilda Doolittle), *Hymen* (London: Egoist Press, 1921), p. 23.
7. Anna Akhmatova, *Poems,* trans. Lyn Coffin, intro. Joseph Brodsky (New York: W. W. Norton, 1983), p. 5.

chapter 7: a sense of space

1. Henry James, *Complete Stories, 1892–1898* (New York: Library of America, 1996), p. 335.
2. Ibid., p. 354.

3. W. B. Yeats, *Collected Poems* (London: Macmillan, 1963), pp. 168–169.
4. A. Norman Jeffares, *A Commentary on the Collected Poems of W. B. Yeats* (Stanford, CA: Stanford University Press, 1968), pp. 181–182.
5. Ibid., p. 1.
6. Ibid., p. 1.
7. Ibid., p. 1.
8. Ibid., p. 1.
9. John Unterecker, *A Reader's Guide to William Butler Yeats* (New York: Noonday Press, 1959), p. 141.
10. W. B. Yeats, *The Autobiography of William Butler Yeats* (New York: Macmillan, 1963), p. 353.
11. Ibid., p. 379.
12. Jon Stallworthy, *Between the Lines: Yeats's Poetry in the Making* (Oxford: Clarendon Press, 1963), p. 9.
13. Yeats, *Collected Poems*, p. 142.
14. James Longenbach, *Stone Cottage: Pound, Yeats and Modernism* (Oxford: Oxford University Press, 1988), p. 149.
15. Ibid., p. 148.
16. Ibid., p. 148.
17. Yeats, *The Autobiography of William Butler Yeats*, pp. 380–381.
18. Ibid., p. 374.
19. Richard Ellmann, *The Identity of Yeats*, 2nd ed. (New York: Oxford University Press, 1964), p. 135.
20. Unterecker, *A Reader's Guide to William Butler Yeats*, p. 141.

chapter 8: closure

1. Billy Collins, *Sailing Alone Around the Room: New and Selected Poems* (New York: Random House, 2001), p. 33.
2. W. S. Merwin, *The Shadow of Sirius* (Port Townsend, WA: Copper Canyon Press, 2008), p. 58.
3. Jane Kenyon, *Collected Poems* (St. Paul, MN: Graywolf Press, 2005), p. 127.
4. Eyjólfur Kjalar Emilsson, *Plotinus on Intellect* (Oxford: Oxford University Press, 2007), pp. 195, 198.
5. Kenneth Rosen, *The Origins of Tragedy & Other Poems* (Fort Lee, NJ: CavanKerry Press, 2003), p. 37.
6. William Shakespeare, *Shakespeare's Sonnets* (Arden Shakespeare: Third Series), ed. Katherine Duncan-Jones (London: Arden Shakespeare, 2007), p. 169.
7. Tomas Transtromer, *The Great Enigma: New Collected Poems*, trans. Robin Fulton (New York: New Directions, 2006), p. 85.
8. Phillip Nast, Unpublished poem, 2010.
9. Bill Knott, published as "Obsolescent," in *Becos* (New York: Vintage, 1983), p. 31.
10. Kay Ryan, *Say Uncle* (New York: Grove Press, 2000), p. 35.
11. Charles Simic, *Night Picnic* (New York: Houghton Mifflin Harcourt, 2001), p. 25.

chapter 9: revision

1. Kenneth Rosen, *No Snake, No Paradise* (Portland, ME: Ascensius Press, 1996), p. 9.

chapter 10: moral inquiry

1. Isaiah Berlin, *The Crooked Timber of Humanity*, ed. Henry Hardy (Princeton, NJ: Princeton University Press, 1998), p. 1.
2. Charles Baudelaire, "The Painter of Modern Life," *Selected Writings on Art and Artists*, trans. P. E. Charvet (Cambridge, UK: Cambridge University Press, 1981), p. 392.
3. Isaiah Berlin, *The Crooked Timber of Humanity*, pp. 8–9.

4. Peter Gay, *Modernism: The Lure of Heresy: From Baudelaire to Beckett and Beyond* (New York: W. W. Norton, 2008), p. 280.

5. Marcel Proust, "Sainte-Beuve and Baudelaire," *On Art and Literature, 1896–1919,* trans. Sylvia Townsend Warner (New York: Meridian Books, 1958), p. 123.

6. Ibid., p. 223.

7. Ibid., p. 124.

8. Ibid., p. 121.

9. Walter Benjamin, "The Paris of the Second Empire in Baudelaire," in *The Writer of Modern Life: Essays on Charles Baudelaire,* ed. Michael W. Jennings (Cambridge, MA: Harvard University Press, 2006), p. 48.

10. Ibid., p. 48.

11. Ibid., p. 136.

12. Ibid., p. 184.

13. Ibid., p. 142.

14. Walt Whitman, *The Essential Whitman,* ed. Galway Kinnell (New York: BBS Publishing, 1987), pp. 105–109.

15. Three dots indicate a stanza break.

16. Robert Wilcocks, "Towards a Re-Examination of L'Héautontimorouménos," *The French Review,* vol. 48, no. 3 (Feb. 1975), pp. 566–579.

17. Charles Robert Maturin, *Melmoth the Wanderer* (London: R. Bentley, 1892), p. 321.

18. Charles Baudelaire, "Of the Essence of Laughter," *Selected Writings on Art & Artists,* p. 145.

19. Marcel Proust, "Sainte-Beuve and Baudelaire," *On Art and Literature, 1896–1919,* p. 129.

20. Alexander Herzen, *My Past and Thoughts,* trans. Constance Garnett, rev. Humphrey Higgens (New York: Alfred A. Knopf, 1968), p. 750.

21. Gay, *Modernism,* pp. 3–4.

chapter 11: bearing witness

1. William Wordsworth, *Selected Poems* (New York: Penguin Books, 2004), p. 171.

2. Mark Sullivan, *Our Times,* vol. 2, *America Finding Herself* (New York: Charles Scribner's Sons, 1927), p. 63.

3. Ibid., p. 63.

4. Robert Lowell, "Mother Marie Therese," *Collected Poems,* ed. Frank Bidart and David Gewanter (New York: Farrar, Straus and Giroux, 2003), p. 96.

5. Lowell, "Skunk Hour," *Collected Poems,* p. 191.

6. *The New Princeton Encyclopedia of Poetry and Poetics,* ed. Alex Preminger and T. V. F. Brogan (Princeton, NJ: Princeton University Press, 1993), pp. 920–921.

7. John Stuart Mill, "What Is Poetry," *Monthly Repository,* n.s. VII (London, Jan. 1833), pp. 60–70.

8. Werner Jaeger, *Paideia: The Ideals of Greek Culture,* vol. 1: *Archaic Greece: The Mind of Athens,* trans. Gilbert Highet (Oxford: Oxford University Press, 1965), p. 22.

9. Homer, *The Odyssey,* Book 22, trans. Alexander Pope (New York: A.L. Burt Company, Publishers, 189), pp. 346–347.

10. Homer, *The Odyssey,* Book 8, trans. Richmond Lattimore (New York: HarperPerennial, 1991), pp. 122–123.

11. Homer, *The Odyssey,* Book 8, trans. Alexander Pope, p. 128.

12. Ibid., pp. 128–129.

13. Primo Levi, "On Obscure Writing," in *Other People's Trades,* trans. Raymond Rosenthal (New York: Summit Books, 1989), pp. 173–174.

14. Homer, *The Odyssey,* trans. Alexander Pope, p. 347.

chapter 12: counterpoint

1. William Shakespeare, "Sonnet 76," *The Sonnets* (New York: Penguin Books 1977), p. 96.

2. Flannery O'Connor, *Mystery and Manners: Occasional Prose* (New York: Farrar, Straus and Giroux, 1969), p. 72.

3. Ibid., p. 73.

4. Ibid., p. 76.

5. Ibid., p. 65.

6. Ibid., p. 101.

7. Ibid., p. 98.

8. Ibid., p. 100.

9. Ibid., p. 82.

10. Ibid., p. 70.

11. Ibid., p. 70.

12. Anton Chekhov, *Short Stories,* ed. Ralph Matlaw (New York: W. W. Norton, 1979), p. 171.

13. T. S. Eliot, "Hamlet and His Problems," in *The Sacred Wood: Essays on Poetry and Criticism* (London: Methuen, 1920), p. 58.

14. Yuri Trifonov, "The Exchange," in *The Exchange and Other Stories,* trans. Ellendea Proffer et al. (Evanston, IL: Northwestern University Press, 2002), pp. 23–24.

15. Isaiah Berlin, *The Roots of Romanticism* (Princeton, NJ: Princeton University Press, 1999), pp. 137–138.

16. Zbigniew Herbert, "Mother," in *Selected Poems,* trans. John and Bogdana Carpenter (Oxford, UK: Oxford University Press, 1977), p. 6.

chapter 13: the nature of metaphor

1. Neil Forsyth, *The Old Enemy: Satan and the Combat Myth* (Princeton: Princeton University Press, 1987), p. 425.

2. Ibid., p. 425.

3. Holy Bible, Book of Genesis, 11:5–10.

4. J. P. Mallory, *In Search of the Indo-Europeans: Language, Archaeology and Myth* (New York: Thames and Hudson, 1991), p. 12.

5. Andrew Robinson, *The Last Man Who Knew Everything: Thomas Young, the Anonymous Polymath Who Proved Newton Wrong, Explained How We See, Cured the Sick, and Deciphered the Rosetta Stone, Among Other Feats of Genius* (New York: Pi Press, 2006).

6. David W. Anthony, *The Horse, the Wheel, and Language: How Bronze-Age Riders from the Eurasian Steppes Shaped the Modern World* (Princeton, NJ: Princeton University Press, 2007), p. 98.

7. Vincent Macaulay et al., "Single, Rapid Coastal Settlement of Asia Revealed by Analysis of Complete Mitochondrial Genomes," *Science,* May 13, 2005, vol. 308, no. 5724, pp. 1034–1036.

8. Stephen Oppenheimer, *The Real Eve: Modern Man's Journey Out of Africa* (New York: Basic Books, 2003), p. 45.

9. Macaulay et al., "Single, Rapid Coastal Settlement."

10. Ibid., p. 1035.

11. Oppenheimer, *The Real Eve,* p. 29.

12. Antonio Rosas et al., "Paleobiology and comparative morphology of a late Neandertal sample from El Sidrón, Asturias, Spain," *Proceedings of the National Academy of Sciences,* December 19, 2006, vol. 103, no. 51, p. 19269.

13. Ernst Cassirer, *An Essay on Man: An Introduction to a Philosophy of Human Culture* (New Haven: Yale University Press, 1944), p. 116.

14. Susanne K. Langer, *Philosophy in a New Key: A Study in the Symbolism of Reason, Rite, and Art* (New York: New American Library, 1951), pp. 97–98.

15. "Noam Chomsky" on Wikipedia.

16. Cassirer, *An Essay on Man,* p. 109.

17. Ernst Cassirer, *Language and Myth,* trans. Susanne K. Langer (New York: Harper & Brothers, 1946), p. 84.

18. Ibid., p. 88.

19. Cassirer, *An Essay on Man,* p. 110.

20. Ibid., p. 87.

21. Ibid., p. 82.
22. Ibid., pp. 83–84.
23. Ibid., p. 86.
24. Ibid., p. 104.
25. Ibid., p. 104.
26. Ibid., p. 105.
27. Ibid., p. 105.
28. Ibid., p. 106.
29. Ibid., p. 107.
30. R. H. Codrington, *The Melanesians: Studies in Their Anthropology and Folklore* (Oxford: Clarendon Press, 1891), pp. 118–120.
31. Cassirer, *An Essay on Man,* p. 95.
32. Cassirer, *Language and Myth,* p. 64.
33. Cassirer, *An Essay on Man,* p. 75.
34. Cassirer, *Language and Myth,* p. 98.
35. Ibid., p. 98.
36. Diodorus Siculus, *The Library of History,* Book V, vol. IV (Bury St. Edmonds, Suffolk, UK: The Loeb Classical Library, 1939), pp. 179–181.
37. 213 Strabo, *The Geography,* Book IV, Chap. IV, vol. II (Bury St. Edmonds, Suffolk, UK, The Loeb Classical Library, 1923), p. 245.
38. Diodorus, *The Library of History,* p. 181.
39. M. L. West, *Indo-European Poetry and Myth* (Oxford: Oxford University Press, 2007), p. 27.
40. Ibid., p. 29.
41. Ibid., p. 30.
42. Ibid., p. 30.
43. Ibid., p. 30.
44. Ibid., p. 43.
45. Ibid., p. 46.
46. Ibid., p. 50.
47. Ibid., p. 56.
48. Diodorus, *The Library of History,* p. 179.
49. Genesis 2:19.
50. Robert Gordis, "Some Effects of Primitive Thought on Language," *The American Journal of Semitic Languages and Literature,* vol. 55, no. 3 (Chicago, July 1938), p. 270.
51. Ibid., p. 270.
52. Ibid., p. 274.
53. Ibid., p. 276.
54. Ibid., p. 277.
55. Ibid., p. 277.
56. Ibid., p. 276.
57. Ibid., p. 276.
58. Ibid., pp. 283–284.
59. Langer, *Philosophy in a New Key,* p. 141.
60. Ibid., p. 141.
61. Cassirer, *An Essay on Man,* p. 111.
62. Ibid., p. 111.
63. Frances Yates, *The Occult Philosophy in the Elizabethan Age* (New York: Routledge Classics, 2001), p. 30.
64. Cassirer, *An Essay on Man,* p. 56.
65. Ibid., p. 56.
66. Ibid., p. 56.
67. Ibid., p. 58.
68. Ibid., p. 126.
69. Julian Jaynes, *The Origin of Consciousness in the Breakdown of the Bicameral Mind* (New York: Houghton Mifflin, 1976), p. 105.

70.   Susanne K. Langer, *Feeling and Form* (New York: Charles Scribner's Sons, 1953), p. 211.

71.   West, *Indo-European Poetry and Myth*, p. 26.

72.   Graham Hough, "The Modernist Lyric," in *Selected Essays* (Cambridge: Cambridge University Press, 1978), pp. 238–239.

73.   Ibid., p. 241.

74.   Ibid., p. 242.

75.   Hough, *Selected Essays*, p. 247.

index